Square Dancing
in the Ice Age

Also by Abbie Hoffman

REVOLUTION FOR THE HELL OF IT
WOODSTOCK NATION
STEAL THIS BOOK
VOTE! (co-authored)
TO AMERICA WITH LOVE (co-authored)
SOON TO BE A MAJOR MOTION PICTURE

Square Dancing in the Ice Age

by Abbie Hoffman

South End Press
Boston

Copyright © 1982 by Abbie Hoffman
All rights reserved. This book, or parts thereof, may not be reproduced in any form without permission.

Portions of this book have been previously published in slightly altered form.

Published in Hardcover by G. Putnam's Sons, New York.
Published in Paperback by South End Press, 302 Columbus Ave., Boston MA 02116

Library of Congress Cataloging in Publication Data

Hoffman, Abbie.
    Square Dancing in the Ice Age.

    1. United States—Civilization—1970—Addresses, essays, lectures. 2. United States—Popular Culture—Addresses, essays, lectures. 3. Radicalism—United States—Addresses, essays, lectures. 4. Hoffman, Abbie—Addresses, essays, lectures. I. Title.
E.169.12.H632   1982   973.92   81-19174
ISBN hardcover 0-399-12701-1   AACR2
ISBN paperback O-89608-194-X

Hi, MOM!

Bow to Your Partner:
A Foreword

~~~~~~

THIS BOOK is something of a literary freak. Almost all these articles were written during the years I lived as a fugitive. Aside from one article and some Weatherpeople communiqués, there really is no underground American writing. A few fugitives have written about their experiences after surfacing but even these efforts are more often than not told to ghost writers.

This book is not the complete collection of my fugitive writing. In addition to co-authoring a book of letters (*To america with Love*) and writing an autobiography (*Soon to Be a Major Motion Picture*), there were at least fifteen more articles not included here. Unfortunately the original manuscript was lost along with my luggage by Pan Am Airlines. At some early age I must have gotten the screwy notion that Xerox was a communicable disease because I'm notorious for not making copies. Exhausting search and rescue missions to various warehouses have failed to locate the lost manuscript. Luckily, there is someone who collects my work—Samuel Leff, keeper of the yippie archives—and it is through his patient efforts that any book exists at all. He supplemented his own collection with good detective work and tracked down several pieces thought to have been gone forever. Many, notably "Square Dancing in the Ice Age" and "The Great St. Lawrence River War," were only published before in part. Mr. Leff located the originals. In order not to shortchange the reader, I have included four articles that were written while in prison subsequent to surfacing. The chronology has been changed to provide a better read but I think the flavor of writing on the run has been maintained throughout.

This is a book about survival. It is not the odyssey of my long adventure or a handbook on how to make it underground, but for the most part I earned my living while a fugitive as a writer. Some articles were even written under a nom de plume. For the first three years I worked as an English teacher in Mexico, as a cook in Santa Fe and Amarillo, and briefly as a construction worker in Montreal. In the fall of 1976 I began writing in earnest for any magazine that would risk having me, and for the following four years that is how my running mate and I survived financially.

Obviously a fugitive with headline potential for FBI agents has to go through some complicated twists and turns in dealing with magazine editors who are complete strangers. In fact, the first article I wrote back in 1974 for *Harper's* magazine (called "Steal This Author" and incorporated into my last book) presented me with severe stage fright when the editor proved quite eager to give helpful information to the authorities. It took me a good two and a half years to refine a strategy I felt would not threaten my security. By the time things were worked out, not a single magazine employee could have assisted the FBI, though except for the *Harper's* editor, none chose to cooperate. Besides, I never wrote about a place until we were about to leave.

The real difficulties of being a fugitive author lay in other areas. What is not apparent to the outsider is the immense problem of keeping my public persona hidden from the various networks of new friends we made along the road. On several occasions these friends brought up an article or an "Abbie escapade," not realizing who I was. The article on touring the new FBI building was the subject of conversation at a party we attended in our neighborhood. Had I told anyone there the same story they were reading, even given the same political observations or used "Abbie's language," I would have been found out. Thus the "Great Gourmet Rip-off" piece couldn't even be published until I surfaced because "Barry Samuel's" friends in Paris knew he was posing as a gourmet critic. A lot of stories bit the dust this way. I also took the liberty of changing some details to protect my identity. In the tennis piece for *Sports Illustrated* I mentioned getting cortisone shots for a sore elbow, since my regular tennis partner subscribed to the magazine. In reality I took Butazolidin tablets. Similarly, I "translated" our battle to save the St. Lawrence River to a fight against a proposed nuclear power plant. None of these changes, however, really affected the accuracy.

The ideas for the articles were essentially my own, and I wrote on speculation rather than assignment. This presented more problems because all magazine publishers have strong preconceived opinions of what their audience wants to read and very few articles are accepted on speculation. I would have to second-guess each publisher, then do a slight imitation of each magazine's style and hope I scored on target, which I did in about two-thirds of the cases. Since I had no expense account, I had to find subject matter in my immediate vicinity. When the now defunct *Crawdaddy* made me travel editor, I took it seriously and went out and wrote a batch of tourist pieces. Where face-to-face interviews were required, I often had to use disguises, identification from various media (often the *Wall Street Journal, Playboy*, or CBS-TV, all of whose credentials I had managed to collect) and other bits of deception, such as phony hotel room numbers. When a "hit" had been made, we had to cover our tracks.

Once I had an idea to get inside the Brown's Ferry nuclear plant near Huntsville, Alabama. A photo-essay of a fugitive inside would show how lax security was. We drove several hundred miles out of our way, did extensive research on the plant's near-disaster, and made elaborate arrangements to avoid detection. Just a day before we arrived at our target, President Carter announced plans to beef up security at nuclear plants. When we entered, our rent-a-car plates along with our cover story were carefully checked and we felt that following through with the caper would have been too great a risk.

Communication was complicated by the fact that neither my agent nor any editor ever knew how to reach me, although during one brazen period, I got an answering service in New York City. When the FBI tracked down some of "Howie Samuel's" business cards, the answering service was quickly terminated.

Getting paid was also a major obstacle. I had read with interest how Woodward and Bernstein's "Deep Throat" encouraged them to "follow the money." No matter how many launderings were carried out, each payment eventually reached my hideout and could be trailed. A lot of credit here goes to my agent, Elaine Markson, and her staff; they managed to confuse the Feds enough for money transfers to occur in secret. Agents tried to harass and intimidate Elaine, but she bravely held her ground and I decided to continue my writing career despite the increased surveillance. After I surfaced, the FBI issued a press statement saying I was able to escape them for all those years because, in fact, they had not been searching. Two months later, however, I received my Freedom of Information Act files concerning the underground years. They consist of more than five hundred pages and show an FBI eager, from day one until the final hours, to catch their prey. In addition, their documented search does not include the many pressures put on relatives and friends as they repeatedly made it clear they wanted me very badly indeed.

Fortunately, however, I was underground during the years the FBI was caught in its own morass of exposed illegal activities. As much as I can tell, they played it by the book, unlike previous years where records show burglaries, illegal mail surveillance, wiretaps, forged letters, and a wide array of police-state tactics used against me as an antiwar and civil-rights activist. No less than eight government agencies had me under surveillance before I went underground. The FBI's files alone numbered 26,000 pages. It is probably safe to say the body hunters knew more about me and my friends than any fugitive they ever went after, and my unwillingness to shut up—not only in these writings but in a half-dozen interviews—annoyed them no end. The pressure of being chased and constantly uprooting our lives, as well as the hassles involved in dealing with the publishing world produced an emotional roller coaster existence. The fugitive life is functional schizophrenia: at its best controlled, at its worst wildly out of gear. An early article, called "Cracking Up on the Run," detailed the pain of living with colliding identities in the underground. Since I used most of it to end *Soon to Be a Major Motion Picture*, I did not wish to repeat it here, but it provides an important balance to some of my, as the New York *Post* headlined it, "Laughing at the Law." There was considerably more pain behind what you are about to read than is readily apparent.

There are some things I should point out about magazine writing that are not often realized. No one can make a living free-lancing for magazines. My fees ranged from $3,000 down to $50. In all I managed to earn about $30,000 from four years of work. The popular press myth had me living "high on the hog," and I suppose if I heard of a fugitive bopping from country to country and dining at fancy restaurants, then threw in exotic locales like the Thousand Islands, I might cotton to the mythology.

Truth is, my running mate and I lived very close to the edge financially as well as every other way. When we first met, Johanna was living in a maid's room in Mexico City, I in a lower-middle-class boarding house in Guatalajara. But we were an exceptionally clever act and managed to get by on little money in a style I dubbed "primitive elegance." Lost among the missing Pan Am papers were two articles on how to survive in Europe on very little cash, similar to the one on Mexico you are about to read. In addition to political and artistic objectives, I've always strongly felt the American urge to pass along tips on how to live the good life at discount prices. Nothing aggravates me more than seeing the press refer to me as some type of eccentric millionaire when in fact I own no property, stocks, bonds, or anything of substantial material value. It would not upset me so much were it not so central to what I want to say, namely that we can live very well for much less than we are led to believe and still manage time to battle social or environmental injustices. My vision of a better society was often at odds with a publishing world that currently likes to picture idealism as something of a quaint oddity, an artifact of a bygone era.

This is a tough time for die-hard optimists. The utopian communal town you will read about here fell on hard times two years later and was plagued by a wave of violence, including murder. The piece on the prison writing of Jack Henry Abbott, although offering a muted warning, wants desperately for him, and all ex-cons, to make it. Six weeks after "The Crime of Punishment" was written, he allegedly was involved in a despicable murder. It has hurt the chances for a thousand similar cases and given cannon fodder to reactionaries who wish to throw away the key on all convicts. The fire burns below, while at the top the aimless square dancing of the Carter years has been replaced by the cold-blooded precision of a military drill. The Philistines have elevated their champion Goliath to power. The culture of the Right has called for repealing two decades of social progress. The article on the Christian Broadcasting Network, written four years before we ever heard of any Moral Majority, gave some indication of this trend to come.

The world I returned to was far different from the world I left. The cynicism of the new ice age has been raised beyond healthy skepticism to a glorified mass-cult status. As I reread some of these efforts, I almost want to apologize for unbridled enthusiasm, for not taking middle age seriously enough. There's plenty of revolutionary romanticism here, pages upon pages of heroes, villains, angels, rats, depression, and manic energy. Gunther Wallraff is a good example of one of my heroes. He is David taking on the Philistines, but he is also everything

American journalists are not. No pretty boy bathing in the glow of video terminal objectivity (see "Cold War Language: An Editorial Reply"). Gunther writes with his body and his blood. He wants the bosses run out of power. It was a pleasure to introduce Gunther to an American audience. Philip Agee is also a person worth watching in Europe. The popular press writes about Agee as a traitor. They don't see the awesome power of the CIA being brought to bear on someone fighting for free access to information—a battle that could affect their own freedom should they ever care to exercise its limits.

Then there's the Fugitive, of course, as a character in several articles. I was never sure if it was autobiography or biography when I wrote about myself playing roles outside my daily life. Sometimes I would read back over long sections and notice that I jumped from first to third person unconsciously. To this day, I stumble over saying the name on the cover of this book and often catch myself referring to myself as another person. When I assumed the different identities along the way I really *became* those people. We carried an "Abbie box" all locked up and carefully hidden. When friends and neighbors were not around I'd pull out the box and secretly go to work, then drive a few miles and call members of my assistance network to research some fact or try out an idea. When it was done I'd slip back into my other self. The person named Barry Freed, who emerges in the last article living on the shores of the St. Lawrence River, is the persona with whom I identify even now, a full year after coming out of hiding. We count the days until we can return to the place we consider home. In time I hope to start a school for grass-roots organizing there in the islands. I want to take young people's hands and hold them in the rushing waters. Here is where a community came together to fight for something good and beautiful. Here is where a battle was won.

New York City, 1981

Contents

A Note from the Underground, to Uncle Sam, from Abbie Hoffman, Fugitive

Re: Sec.1900.3 Federal Code
To Deputy Attorney General
Justice Department
Washington, D.C.

Dear Sir:

Well, I'll be darned. What's this stuff about some Freedom of Information Act. As I understand it you guys have to turn over my file or a copy thereof to me upon request. We both realize a rather extensive file does exist now, don't we? Through the years not only I myself but various lawyers and reporters have seen bits and pieces. I think it goes back some years. You started to pick me up about 1964, when with CORE we staged several sit-ins in your offices in Massachusetts.

In 1965 I was a field worker for SNCC and we were picketing the Holiday Inn in McComb, Mississippi. The maids there were earning only forty-nine cents an hour, and we were protesting that fact. While the sheriff's department and members of the Ku Klux Klan were stomping the ———— out of us, one of your agents leaned over my battered body and drawled, "Do you all feel your civil rights have been violated?" I can't recall his name.

I do, however, recall the name of Jack Mahoney of

1

Worcester, Massachusetts. Good ol' Jack and I used to play basketball after school almost every day. He ended up on your team. I ended up on ours. At a New Year's Eve bash in 1972, Jack got a little plastered and told the partygoers that he was engaged in harassing my relatives, old friends, and neighbors of such for some time.

Then there's agent Hunt or Hill. In the final days of September 1969, while preparing strategy with counsel for our Chicago conspiracy trial, something we all understood to be privileged information, we opened the door to our conference room and lo and behold there was a shaky agent Hill. Guess what he had in his God-fearing hands? That's right—an electronic listening device. I believe that's what the *New York Times* called it the next day. You can check the article quite easily to refresh your memory. It was Hill I'm sure. Hunt is another story.

As long as we're on the matter of listening devices, you guys must have a terrific selection of tapes. There were two wiretaps admitted to in the Chicago trial. There were five taps admitted to in a Washington, D.C., incitement to riot and assault on a federal police officer. You remember how I assaulted the officer's club by getting my nose broken in six places. God that was a time, hmm gang? How I escaped from your compound in RFK Stadium and you searched for three days until eighteen of your special agents (I never met an agent that wasn't special) discovered my wife and I entering our apartment.

Of course these 7 wiretaps are chicken feed compared to the 144 taps on me uncovered in the 5,800 hours of tapes you were ordered recently to turn over to a team of defense lawyers by a Washington, D.C., judge, bless his merry soul.

As I understand the law all these taps were illegal. So in case there's a case of invasion of privacy—Tag! You're it. Consider yourself sued.

Wait, there's more. A copy of the report you hired a University of Miami psychologist to prepare on Mr. J. Rubin and myself. And let's not forget recorded copies and notes of each and every speech I gave. Often at universities, officials told me the FBI had requested two

front-row seats to record my lecture. Some you have
already admitted to: for example, University of Maryland
in 1969 and Oklahoma State University and Oklahoma
U. in early 1971. At the University of New Hampshire in
1970 there were more of you guys than students.

And it would be just terrific if you folks have a copy of
my speech to the Harvard Law School. My lawyer really
liked that one and we both knew you had a better
collection than we could ever put together. In fact, for
the Harvard tape we'll trade you two University of Miami
ones. Just in case you missed that one because of the
ensuing riot your paid Cuban provocateur friends caused.

I would greatly appreciate your including a copy of my
address book you confiscated and photographed in May
1971, during an arrest. I subsequently lost the real one
and could use a few of those numbers.

What else? Special agents John Robinson and Daniel
Lucking's surveillance report of September 1968. Special
agent J. D. Anderson's report on me while I was
changing my kid's diapers in the Virgin Islands. His
theory was that I was smuggling fugitives out of the
United States. God, we were so lucky he and his
companions didn't trample the marijuana growing in the
yard.

I can't recall each and every arrest or encounter but
there was one bust in September 1968 for carrying a
concealed weapon aboard an aircraft. A small black
pocketknife.

Now my final request could get sort of sticky but I am
formally requesting all data related to your current
campaign of harassment of friends, relatives, and various
radicals and hippie communalists who I don't even know
in your attempt to apprehend.

I really am anxious to see your report on my father's
funeral, the copy of my father's will in your possession,
interrogation of my mother-in-law, and just exactly what
was in my wife's refrigerator when you opened the door.

Then there's the raid on a Midwest commune and
surveillance of rock singers and movie actresses thought
to be harboring this fugitive. It seems you guys' fantasies
are the same as mine. Wish they were true.

So just send your general plan, photographs, taps, surveillance reports, etcetera from when you started to the present day. Don't forget a list of agent provocateurs you employed under direction of the now famous J. Edgar Hoover memo of May 1968, instructing agents to use such people to "infiltrate and disrupt radical organizations."

And there's one more thing. In October 1968 I was grabbed on my way to a congressional hearing to confess my sins. You folks grabbed me and ripped the shirt off my back. It was my favorite red, white, and blue one. You remember the bust. You guys ripped the shirt up and I was charged with defacing the flag. Right. Well only half the shirt ended up as evidence in the trial. You owe me half a flag shirt.

Well I gotta run now, so send everything to my counsel of record, Gerald Lefcourt, and I'll drop by and pick it up next time I'm in the city.

Thanks for your cooperation and Happy Bicentennial Year,

Abbie

August 1975

I Remember Papa

PAPA DIED one month after I went underground. My friends decided not to tell me for fear I would go to the funeral. They were right. The funeral was swarming with FBI agents—one, incidentally, a guy I used to play basketball with at Newton Square in Worcester.

My father, Johnny, was a leader in the community. He was president of the Probus Club, one of his long-time ambitions. He received many awards.

One of his proudest moments was when he was appointed to the board of athletics for Holy Cross College. He was probably the first and only Jewish person ever to hold that position. He was an avid fan and Holy Cross football games were a Saturday ritual around our house. Section E, row AA, seats 5 to 10—very good seats. Especially when they beat Boston College. After the game it was lobster dinner for all.

The funeral was held in the big temple just a few blocks from his house. Perlman's funeral parlor was just too small for the huge crowds. Judges, politicians, businessmen, old friends, and family crowded the aisles to pay their last respects. It is sad not to be able to go to your own dad's funeral.

He and I had a very complicated relationship. Sometime next year my autobiography will be published. Throughout the writings and rewritings about growing up

5

in Massachusetts, my views on my father kept changing.

In the first draft we fought a lot. I explained how he was not my hero because during my youth in the war years all the heroes were "over there" fighting the Nazis. He stayed home and my hero became my uncle from Clinton. We all sent him presents and admired the pictures of him in his soldier's uniform.

On and on I continued to struggle in the book, just as we had continued to struggle when he was alive and I was not a fugitive. We fought continuously, not without its proper measure of love on both sides but a battle nonetheless.

My father arrived in this country as a Russian immigrant. A border guard gave him the name Hoffman. He was a strong believer in the American way. Strangely, my father was the only person to continue to call me by my formal name, Abbott. Only the U.S. government still uses that name. I secretly suspect that my father, being a druggist, named me after Abbott Laboratories. It would have been good for business and he was a good businessman. I remember him writing to "Abbott" on the eve of our famous Chicago trial. He told me how good America had been to our family and how we should respect the courts and the law. I had hoped that trial might change some of his rock-ribbed faith in the system. It didn't.

My mother was strongly affected by the government's activities. She began to think it was unfair of the FBI agents to jump out of alleys and snap pictures. It seemed unfair of them to pressure my father's clients, harass relatives and neighbors. She knew of IRS harassments that still continue.

My brother Jack, who tries to keep the business going and does quite well at it, wondered a lot about the American way. About three years ago he was to receive a citizen's award for work done with handicapped individuals. He had set up a program teaching them commercially productive skills rather than the usual basket-weaving nonsense. He earned the award honestly.

When the committee discovered Governor Francis Sargent was to present the award, they decided it would look bad for the governor of Massachusetts to be photographed with the brother of . . . The committee withdrew the award. A doctor-friend of the family for over thirty-five years and a member of the committee was elected to tell the bad news to my brother. But my brother knew you don't do good work for awards.

Before I went underground, I wrote Dad a long letter. I explained that I knew what he was going through now that I had kids of my own. "Perhaps you're right, Pa," I wrote. "Kids might be here just to give us heart attacks. So what's the problem? How are you and I different from anyone else?" Jews always end letters with a question mark. Hillel started that practice centuries ago.

During the last year my feelings toward Papa mellowed. I heard how my mother was growing in new ways, a regular women's libber at seventy years. I think about my *bubbe* (Yiddish for grandmother), now nearing one hundred years of age. I think about my children, and how someday soon I'll be a grandfather, a reality which probably will shock most Americans. I realize how much my father taught me and how much I miss him now.

I know he tried his best and I understand it wasn't his fault he died unhappy. His bitterness about life near the end was not any of his own doing. He adopted America's values without question, he supported its wars, its courts, its charities, its police, its government. He had great trust in America's leaders.

Watergate killed my father. He had argued throughout 1972 in support of Nixon and finally events proved Dad wrong even to himself. Unfortunately, he died before Nixon resigned. He passed away a loyal citizen, but with a lingering doubt that maybe his *meshuggener* (crazy) son had some good points to make after all.

You know, I have a silly conspiracy theory. It has to do with my father's chief and only addiction. He was hooked on good cigars. He loved cigars. He used to chew them to shreds playing gin rummy with the boys. He used to leave them lying all over the place: in the car, in the office, at the house, and at the YMCA where he went for a steam bath each day. Everywhere he went he left soggy cigar butts in case he might return and need a quick fix.

His heart problems and general *kvetching* (complaining) about life began in the early sixties, just about the time the government was implementing its economic boycott of Cuba. Now, as everyone in the world knows, there is no cigar like a Cuban cigar. So for the next fifteen years poor Papa had to make do with ground cabbage leaves sprayed with cheap French perfume. I offered to get him cigars from Havana, trying to show the advantages of having a radical son. "Corona Corona," I would mumble teasingly. Dad considered it but decided he'd follow his government's dictate to the end. It was a tough decision. I tried to turn him on to grass. No, he said, he would go down with the *Titanic* even at the cost of a good smoke of anything.

The CIA killed my father, not quick with a bullet but slowly, with a puff of each tasteless cigar. A filter tip Muriel was my father's Mata Hari.

Viva, Papa! I hope heaven recognizes Cuba.

June 1976

On Being Invisible
in the Big Apple

~~~~~~

BIG APPLE Beacon. Candle to all moths sniffing fame flame. "Purdy woman, lemme take your hand, purdy woman."

I hear ya callin', ol' Broadway. I feel the hot breath of the Village, fingernail caress of Bloomingdales (only twenty-two shoplifting days till Christmas), and the gallstones of the Lower East Side.

The sign on the door reads: B & H Luncheonette Closed Due to Bankruptcy. "But breakfast," mumbles the Fugitive, "I need a good breakfast and the place that got me through the sixties is bankrupt!" Quickly he crossed Second Avenue eyeing the possibilities. Ukrainian. Cuban-Chinese. Burger King. Chinese-Cuban. His bladder starts to ache. Where do you pee in New York? Gas station! Walk east. No! No! That's country, you're in the city, he remembers. The Tenth Street Deli! Dash. Phew! Made it. Alibi. Need a good one for using the john. "Give me a half pound of corned beef and six slices of rye," he blurts out. It's 9:30 A.M. Already late in the country. He walks south, along Second Avenue, noshing on the corned beef sandwich breakfast. He laughs, suddenly realizing what his new friends think about New Yorkers. "They can eat and walk at the same time," one had once remarked, making a brilliant anthropological observation.

He checks his watch. Being on time is essential in his life. The Fugitive had come to terms with Time. It was elitist to show up late, and now being underground had confirmed his disgust with tardiness. People could end up in prison or get killed because of it. He was stunned the night before to read that Castro wore two watches. What tricks the media plays. Gossip insisted Castro was absent-minded and tardy. Indeed, was not that cinema gem called *Waiting for Fidel*? Just another mañana spic, huh? *Two watches.* The Fugitive thought Castro did it to teach the importance of being on time—guerrilla theater by a master communicator.

R is sure to be late! Angel has sworn she will never go to an airport with R again. Inhale. Run down the checklist of R's qualities. A good guy. Obviously. One did not survive by picking apart friends. Relax.

The Fugitive searches for new comics at the Lower East Side Book Store. He makes it a point to check in on St. Mark's Place every time he's back in town. A reference. He has circled the multinational benchsitters at Tompkins Square Park, visited his favorite pawnshop, and wandered around the Church, now a gutted shell. Soon to be rebuilt he read on the bulletin board in front. A street leaflet hot off the offset announced the Hope Poetess was still in business. A good ol' fast-talkin' gal she was.

The book store itself recalled memories. Author's pride tempted him to see which section now held his books. A year ago a very strange thing happened to him here. He was having a conversation with the clerk when a woman burst in, stared him in the face and proceeded to talk to the clerk. "Rude! *My god it's E!*" He watched the animated conversation, admiring her ability to manipulate Clerkman. He backed up a step, fading into the emptiness of the store. His heart fluttered with pulsating wows. Could it be? he thought. They had been together a few weeks . . . adventuring . . . wolfpacking at the Miami Convention. Could it be? Either he was now invisible or . . . Ha! Maybe he was just a boring lay. How soon they forget!

He scratched his crotch and the yellow cab pulled to the curb. The Fugitive had a travel strategy. When to go slow, when fast. Plane = horizontal elevator. Horse = boat. When to hitchhike, when to go first class. The breathing exercises of scuba diving had taught him how to relax when walking. Swami Muktananda was a time traveler. The subway was not yet a safe means of transportation. He thought of Emmett Grogan's dead body racing to Coney Island on the subway. He had another paranoia of subways: Sitting with banks of people staring at you was hard on fidgety fugitives. Maybe in two days he could use the subway. Besides, being underground being underground was redundant.

Taxicabs, on the other hand, created their own anxieties. He often suffered claustrophobia with the new-style security seatbacks and heavy metal grilles. There was a sneaking suspicion that all such taxis wanted to take him downtown to jail. *Luck!* A car-cab and not a meat wagon. He can talk to the driver. Eyes scan the dash for clues. Ouch! A pair of handcuffs dangle from the dashboard. The thin bearded blond could be no more than five feet huddled there behind the wheel. "Hey, what's with the handcuffs?" he says, choosing the dialect of Greenwich Village. Wrong. The French accent is right off the charter flight. "For zee bad men." A vision flashes of two huge muggers with guns drawn and Frenchy trying to get the cuffs on. "Are you sure it'll work?" he inquires. "If zee don't work, I got zee mace," he says, holding a blue and white cylinder. "If zis no good, I have zees!" he beams triumphantly, displaying a camping hatchet as his final solution.

Lord, lord, he thinks, winking eyebrows. Welcome to the Free World of Opportunity.

Destination is now the World Trade Center for a secret rendezvous with the Stranger. At exactly 9:00 A.M. the Stranger had been searched by J using the detectors to make sure he was not packing a weapon or transmitter. Subject was then taken on the evasion voyage and then passed to R. The three continue moving through the city, finally jumping off the subway train just before the door closes. Now the subject is clean enough to rendezvous.

Meanwhile the Fugitive waits on the north side of the tower, staring at the city below, conversing with the Acquaintance-Tourist he just met during the fastest elevator ride in the world. His cowboy costume carefully thought out. Neo-Amarillo. Midway between *High Noon* and the *Midnight Cowboy*. The special heels of his boots, elevated and sculptured forward, change his gait. The wide-brimmed hat, although attention attracting, draws the gaze away from the eyes. Eye contact is the secret to recognition. The great Russian scientist Luria proved this twenty years ago. The Fugitive is well aware that as he moves through the city his ability to control reflexive eye movements is what differentiates him from the swarming mass of people. To forget what your body is doing, is to forget you are a hunted animal.

Coincidentally the Acquaintance is a nuclear scientist from England. Blond hair, blue eyes, bureaucrat type.

Lucky catch! thinks the Fugitive, a chance to pick the brain of a fascist. "See that black building over there on the left with the grayish border around, the one with no windows?" he says, adjusting his cowboy hat and voice to appear richer. "Yes, I see it," nods the Scientist. "That's supposed to be the only building in Manhattan capable of withstanding a nuclear attack." The Scientist laughs. "It'll cook like a hot dog, if the bomb were to hit anywhere we can see," says the Scientist. "What's in it?" "The telephone company," answers the Fugitive. "But of course!" laughs the Scientist.

They argue nuclear energy for a half hour while the Fugitive plays tour guide, constantly checking his watch. "Delay, delay, that's all you people are causing," exasperates the Scientist. "That's the point; we're not in any rush on this," answers the Fugitive. "We have to hire ten public relations experts for every nuclear plant project to counteract your effort," mentions the Scientist. The conversation continues. "The world now has one person for every thirty square meters," calculates the Scientist. "Yes, *less* people and *less* consumption. We have to deprogram the planet's greed for *more*," says the Fugitive. "You are gazing on the world's greediest consumers. Every time you turn on the TV down there, someone's ordering you to buy something that's either bad for you or unnecessary." "Interesting you mention that," continues the Scientist. "India's problem is overproduction, decentralized overproduction and underconsumption." The Fugitive is not sure he understands.

"Magnificent view today. I wish we could see clear up the Hudson to the Indian Point Nuclear Facility, that's the closest radiation death plant," he says, changing the subject.

The World Trade Tower is a good place to meet the Stranger. The technique is simple. The Stranger is directed to one of the window seats. The Fugitive quickly sits and identifies himself. The subject is directed to look toward the ground while they converse. The vertigo sensation unlocks the mind's defenses and the Fugitive can see if the Stranger lies. What surprises him this time is the music he hears, a new and exciting song. The Stranger vanishes and the two become brothers. The ex-Stranger will now help with a huge favor. Less than a handful of people will ever know.

Meeting accomplished, the Fugitive-showman cannot help put-on the bewildered Scientist. "Oh, we're just exchanging some plutonium. You know how hard it is to get the stuff. It's our last resort. Building our own bomb." The Scientist smiles nervously. Always leave 'em laughing, he remembers from his vaudeville lessons.

The rest of the afternoon is taken up with movies. He sees four features, rushing out at moments to phone contacts. The Fugitive is considering peddling the movie rights to his book to a certain Texan. He is going to see *The Best Little Whorehouse in Texas* to confirm the positive reports his spies have sent.

The Fugitive's date, so to speak, is a sailor who's in town and has never seen a play before. Buddy will be a quick readout of how any movie will play Heartland. He does not want them to make a cult film. The last thing the world needs is another cult anything.

They eat at Molfetas on West Forty-seventh. "Melina

Mercouri took me here, Buddy," tells the Fugitive. "These people opposed Greece's military junta; she wanted me to know which restaurants were cool." He was glad to see only the prices had changed. After the meal, on to the theater.

He was not that familiar with stage plays so he would concentrate extra hard. Halfway through, the Fugitive became convinced the movie would work. After the show they wangle their way backstage with a bouquet of roses for the star. He has already been favorably impressed with her interest in the ecology movement. A photographer takes pictures of the historic meeting. Buddy requests the roll to develop.

The Texan who is the leading lady's husband, also the co-writer and co-director, arrives. The party moves to Joe Allen's. The play-hosts are nervous about people recognizing their new "Responsibility." Some tricks have been learned. *Anyone wishing to be invisible must practice being a nobody.* "Pete, just introduce *Buddy* as *your* friend and I'm his friend, see. 'This is my friend Buddy and his friend.' Let your voice trail off."

While they drink tequilla and conspire, Actors Studio people keep buzzing the table. The Fugitive studies everyone. Life is a casting call. What makes a good actor? He is looking for trust. Confidence. Psychological health. Click! Click! Click! After an hour, he's convinced they can pull off the movie heist of the century. He arranges to give the manuscript of his book to the Director tomorrow. Warm embraces for new good friends. "Adios, amigos." "Who was that masked man, Carlin darlin'?"

On to the next stop. The climax of our adventure story.

We're headed to the Late Night Party. New York is party town. The Fugitive must use all his power to stay invisible. Many, many people at this party have known him ten years or more. He could easily be recognized, but if things got out of control the party would quickly be flooded with the Blue Meanies. He never wanted to be a party pooper. Most certainly not at one honoring that great liberator, Mister William Burroughs. A drop of good cheer was needed. It was a gloomy week.

Tom Forcade, the founder of *High Times,* had just blown his head off. The Fugitive and Tom had made their peace two years ago, after a period of bickering. He felt relieved their conflict had been settled in time. How, he thought, could you ever pay money back to a dead man? He was saddened by Tom's death. Down in Guyana poor souls by the hundreds were trying to keep up with the Joneses, and in San Francisco post-Vietnam White insanity had cut down the mayor and a courageous freedom fighter, Harvey Milk. Horrible Horror. The Fugitive shivered. A good party was in order. One could not afford the luxury of extended unhappiness.

He met his guide under the arch in Washington Square. Each showed up two minutes early. They agreed the costume was correct: *Anyone who wants to be invisible must learn to dress for the occasion.* Dress. Manners. Voice tone. Breathing. Eye movements. Above all, the eyes. We follow our eyes. If they don't know where to go we get lost. When we are lost we panic. The Fugitive, by the way, has in his suitcase contact lenses with another eye color and more eyeglasses than Elton John and Gloria Steinem combined. In the beginning he had bought prescription glasses with a slightly different vision than his own to deliberately *force* a new vision. Sunglasses are too suspect. Polaroids are perfect since they leave two large black circles on any photograph. He inhaled deeply, realizing the strenuous discipline had become second nature after five years. How his eyes used to swell and tear during his apprenticeship. But it worked. Till now, anyway.

They crossed the street. Catty-corner. One University Place. Crowded door. *Mickey! Oh gods! It's Mickey Ruskin's floating water hole!* There were many surprises in store. "We're friends of Patsy." "Okay," he says. No recognition. The Fugitive lowered his eyes and smiled, knowing he was probably the only one at the party who had never borrowed money from Mickey. Expertly, gently, they pushed their way through the crowded bar, heading for the back room. Faces lit up. People he had not seen in six or seven years. Many he loved. Many he admired. Indeed, a good hunk of his closest friends were now in this very room. Just a few days before he had celebrated Abbie's Birthday, and except for Paul Krassner via national television no one had wished him happy b-d. It mattered not that much because among other things the Fugitive was now an Aquarius born in February.

Steve Ben-Israel. Larry Rivers. Ann Waldman. Jim Fouratt. Lola Cohen. The faces stream by. No one recognizes him, of course. He flashes on the Pieman without really having ever met him. "That person is not to know I'm here, watch him," he tells the guide. "Yes, that's him," he confirms. The guide and he interact well under crowd conditions.

We are headed for the Ginzo. Allen will decide if it's okay to stay. Ginsberg and I first met in 1959. We both talk simultaneously. It's a tough conversation to record. Hence there are no FBI tapes of our telephone calls. "If he is nervous every single person including me will freak when I say hello," reasons the Fugitive. Paranoia is remarkably contagious. Given electronic media it is now possible to spook the planet in minutes. Observe reaction to Jonestown.

We talk of ecology action and movies. "I was arrested in Rocky Flats," reports the Poet. "We're doing this movie and need you to play the rabbi in the two wedding scenes," manipulates the Fugitive-producer. "I'm not a rabbi!" says Allen, spitting at labels. "That's just one opinion, Allen; it's a *movie*." "Are you meditating?" he asks. "Doing those sitting exercises?" "Yeh," fibs the Fugitive-student politely. "You don't want me to show you here, do you?" Half smile. The Fugitive has still not found his center but the therapy is working. They are moving in the right direction. The conversation shifts to religion. He wants to avoid the People's Temple business. Too soon to learn anything yet. The people had more choice than the soldiers who went to Vietnam and it's going to ruin the Kool-Aid market, thank God!

"What about God, Allen?" he asks. "Yes, yes, an all-pervasive force . . ." The Student translates the Poet's language. Gestalt. Holism. The Great Spirit. Check! Check! "I'm a pantheist now," he interrupts. "The ecology movement convinces me there are many gods. Trees. Birds. Mountains. Rivers. Humans. Definitely humans. Aren't humans gods, Allen?" he answers questions. "It allows anarcho-commie politics while maintaining spirituality and . . ." The rabbi intercepts, "but it ends up a hierarchy. . . . Like the Greeks and Romans who . . ." "Always a macho Zeus?" interrupts the *yeshiva bucher.* Allen lists several current pantheists. The Fugitive asks about Swami Muktananda. The Poet has doubts. Carl Solomon is introduced. "Carl, this is Mark. Mark, Carl." The past leaps out at the Fugitive. He is glad Carl Solomon is alive and well living in the body of an uptown psychiatrist. "Oh wow, the Howl Solomon!"

Cameras close in and Allen instinctively fends them off. It dawns on the Fugitive that he might be the only person in the room who is so camera shy. During the conversation he said hello to two people he's certain are not gossipers (the woman P and the man S). Much gossip has hurt him and given him extra work. Fear and anxiety accumulate in his head and a good part of his mental energy involves sorting one from the other. He asks Allen to take him to Tim Leary.

He wants to see Tim face to face. He's upset by only one important item, but he wants to get over all bad blood. The Fugitive believes one of the aspects differentiating the sixties from the fifties is the fact that no movement people squealed. He wanted to hear from Tim that that historical achievement was still intact. By exposing himself, the Fugitive was saying he would give the benefit of the doubt. There had been a few years of misunderstanding brought on by KK, an evil nerd.

The Fugitive positions himself to the side and slightly to the rear of the Pied Piper of the sixties. A voice change, a touch. "Timmy, don't believe all you read on bathroom walls," he says, apologizing for words not his own. "Yes, yes," the ex-con/pitchman exclaims, recognizing him. He squeezes the Fugitive's waist, fraternally.

Three seconds have passed. We've *almost* made our
peace. Tim's nervous about being in the room. One
thought sticks in the Fugitive's mind as he walks away:
four years of prison show in the man's eyes. He shudders
for the Daring Doctor's ordeal and fears for his own ass.

Later, much later, he is to hear the Pieman has
targeted Leary with a cheesecake.

By now he's made up his list, not unlike a debutante at
the junior prom. Naturally there's only one Angel in the
place but he must try to avoid her tonight. She knows
he's here. After four years of sneaking around, they can
communicate without even making eye contact. The
Fugitive has long realized she is a witch with extraordinary powers. He does not understand everything about her
but he's well aware of her abilities. He has let her know
he's present by raising his arm above the pushy crowd
and using a finger signal. She would recognize the signal
as well as the cuff of his jacket. Every once in a while he
peeks her way and is glad to see her having a good time,
since she's been down in the dumps lately. He's deathly
afraid of losing her and would choose her even over
Freedom itself. Each night he prays she will never have to
return to heaven.

He decides to thank everyone who helped make the
"Bring Abbie Home" rally last summer a success. Terry
Southern. Carol Relini. Joe Lo Guidice. John Giorno.
He proceeds methodically yet quickly, considering the
crush of people. Ann Waldman and he talk about St.
Mark's Church. "I tried to help your Paris act, Annie,"
he said. She's very smooth, indeed; no one at the table is
aware we are conversing. "You're a conceptual artist,"
she tells him, complimentary. She had understood what
he was up to very early in the game but he did not know
exactly what the word *conceptual* meant. He had no label
for her. Slum Goddess of the Lower East Side? No, she
was too much a lady. Virgin of Saint Mark's? No, she was
The Poetess. But of course, he thought, in the Renaissance it was hard to label artists. "Aren't you Michel-
angelo, the interior decorator?" Ann introduced him to
her mother and they kibbitzed. "Mrs. Waldman, you
have a lovely daughter."

Next he calls on Larry Rivers. Larry had taught him things about Death. Accepting its inevitability. Larry looked like someone who had tried everything once, even Death. He admired Larry's acting ability, especially his performance on *$64,000 Question*. Tonight he looks like he's tried everything twice. And nervous. He is not sure I'm invisible. How can I convince him? "But Larry, I was sitting right there directly across from you just a moment ago." Larry the Skeptic says nothing. The Fugitive rattles off foreign languages and voice changes. Still no reaction. "Hey, see Bob Williams over there? Call him over." Larry does it. They talk. "Bob, meet my friend Moe from California." We talk. Bob leaves. "Now, Larry, Bob and I hung out in Zihuatenejo. Are you convinced?" Larry is half convinced. Larry wants to introduce him to son Steve. "Sorry, later."

Howard Smith is searching for the Fugitive and vice versa. The guide has found them both. Howard is going to do for him what he did for Plato's Retreat. (See to it that they both don't get busted.) "Amazing! Amazing!" Howard exclaims. While they talk, propped against the post, Howard says the word *amazing* twenty-seven times. Even tall and slim with a bushy mustache, he reminds the Fugitive of Santa Claus.

It's getting hot now. The Fugitive has an alarm system to let him know when he's becoming visible again. Before he leaves he must pay his respects to the bereaved widow of *High Times*. "Sadness will pass, Gaby. Soon you should get on to the next movie." She's strong, he thinks, a student from the streets. "Yes, the next movie," she concurred. He is very pleased Tom gave half the magazine money to marijuana's future legalization. An honorable will. We are all getting more mature.

Close to the door, he edges next to Steve Ben-Israel, so anxious he drops all his poems on the floor and the two of them bend down to gather them up. The Street Poet sells him one for free. "Suicide Mass . . . what is common to us all . . ." it begins. The Fugitive scans it quickly. He will study it on the subway.

On the way out, he whispers his name in Mickey's ear, thanking him for a good party. "No! don't look," he commands, touching Mickey on the nose to turn his head slightly. Mickey looks at him but does not see his face. Fifteen minutes later he confirms this by trying to reenter the party. Mickey refuses him entrance. He can easily get in using one of many entry tricks. But he feels the relief of being a nobody again and accepts the rejection. It's time to go "home" anyway. Country mornings. City nights. Exhausting. I'm not getting any younger, he figures.

Nice party. Can't do this every year. Never repeat. Remember, never repeat, he warns himself.

The Fugitive's gait speeds up now, he adjusts the brim of his hat, and with a few quick motions changes his costume. He moves swiftly around the corner. I can take the subway back, it's hard getting a cab late anyway, he reasons, glad to know the New York turf is again becoming familiar. On the subway wall he scrawls *Happy Malcolm X-mas. See Ya Next Year.*

December 1978

Bye-Bye Sixties,
Hollywood-Style

"AMUSING." People said I would find it amusing. They were right. Neither here nor there. Good nor bad. Just amusing. In fact, people who get emotionally involved with this movie, in particular its nostalgic attitude, revealed so tellingly as Moses Wine (Richard Dreyfuss) watches old clips of the sixties, express their own psychological hang-ups. Nostalgia is a form of depression both for a society and an individual.

The *Big Fix* must be viewed as psychological drama. A case study of a nervous breakdown. It's not a detective story. It's not a comedy. And it's not a morality play. Indeed, what we are presented with is a clash between psychic stances. The sixties cast against the seventies. Optimistic idealism versus disillusionment turned cynical. My former jail-cell buddy Tom Hayden expressed it in his senatorial campaign: "Yesterday's radicalism is today's common sense." Tom and loads of others have gone that route, shedding tears with Moses as they watch the spark of their youth flicker by. But it's not my trip. And if we take the time to read an exhaustive survey called the *Woodstock Census*, we'll have some serious doubts about the way the media wants us to view that transition. This study of more than one thousand "Woodstock veterans" shows that although those who only adopted the language and dress of the counterculture returned to the mainstream, the activists have for the most part stuck to their radical beliefs.

Back to the *Big Fix* and behind-the-scenes gossip. Len Weinglass, our attorney in the Chicago Eight (not the Seven but the Eight!) trial was offered the part of the lawyer for the "California Four." He turned it down, saying the script was a cop-out. Word reached me that I could play, if possible (all is possible), the role of the fugitive. I never saw a script but also said *nyet*, partly out of courtesy to Len's opinion. This has not been the only movie part I've been offered. Richard Dreyfuss, who was interested in playing another "character-based-on" in a far more revolutionary script, had to forgo his own concept of the sixties-turned-seventies when that movie project could not get funded. Even despite the presence of two more "bankables"—Julie Christie and Jon Voight—who accepted major parts. My closest friend in Hollywood says it's myopic of me to expect a revolutionary movie to ever come out of Tinseland. A view my myopic soul can never accept as absolute. Granted it'll be a cold day in Havana before anything like the Cuban movies shown in a recent New York film festival comes down the freeway, but American revolutionary cinema can only be *influenced* by that style, it cannot mimic it.

Everything must be defined within the given context of American culture, itself not a static entity. Even with this in mind, however, Hollywood has not produced its *Memorías de Desarollo* or even its *Battle of Algiers*. I don't find this so discouraging that we have to go through intellectual contortions to give a Marxist interpretation to *A Day At the Races* or *Grease*. Even Castro went a bit overboard when he interpreted socialism in *Jaws* because it pictured the capitalist motives of the folks who ran the beach-resort as the enemy of the masses. I really doubt the producers of that chew-'em-up sat down with the intention of destroying capitalism, or put in a less shrill tone, replacing it with a better idea.

You cannot make a truly radical movie without having that intention somewhere up your sleeve, and I don't mean one has to accept the limits that such a movie has to

end up a cult film or, worse, a money-loser. A revolutionary movie might not play the drive-ins but then again . . .

Let's turn to the bright side. There are some movies I
would not be at all shy about recommending. *Coming
Home* and *Who'll Stop the Rain* told honest stories. The
first made several breakthroughs, and its faults, such as
the contrived ocean suicide of the "cuckold" soldier-
returned, were negligible to its important, well-told story.
The same for *Who'll Stop the Rain*. Of the movies seen in
recent months, Terry Malick's *Days of Heaven* not only is
something of an aesthetic masterpiece but its attitude
toward class struggle is excitingly accurate and refreshing.
The notion that there are no villains or heroes, just the
exploitive system with those dangerous threshing machines, hovering but (to the director's credit) never
maiming the workers, is worth pursuing. Anyone who
loves movies can look back and find something good,
politically, to say about several movies: just about all of
Chaplin's, *Burn, Grapes of Wrath, Viva Zapata* to name a
few. But I know what my friend means about Hollywood
never making a radical movie. He means a radical movie
about contemporary Americans.

To add another log to the revolutionary bonfire, I'd
like to offer my candidate for the most radical movie to
date dealing with the era of the *Big Fix*. Strangely enough
it was a made-for-TV flick created by none other than the
chief instigator of the *Big Fix* itself, Jeremy Kagan. It
came out in '75, was called *Katherine*, and this recent
Kagan effort is nowhere close to its brilliance and
accuracy.

Hyped as a "Patricia Hearst" spin-off, it was, if
anything, based on the life of Weatherwoman Diane
Oughton. Its sensitivity to detail, insight as to what
motivates U.S. radicals and plot-evolving-in-modern-
history technique is amazing. Performances by Sissy
Spacek, Art Carney, and the rest of the cast were
exceptional. Jeremy Kagan has a marvelous fix on this
era and *Katherine* is a movie I could easily see again and
again. I saw it in Canada. Chances are very good you
never saw it because it aired in the States on an off-beat

hour and Fred Silverman was furious that ABC ever got connected with something he considered "anti-American." It's doubtful, even though its stars have gone on to greater fame, that it will ever be shown again.

There's one other thing that has to be said about *Katherine*. The male lead (Henry Winkler) plays a curly-haired radical with a sense of humor who worked in the civil rights movement, goes to the Chicago police riots, participated in the "Days of Rage" (a "title" I came up with, incidentally), but chose not to become a Weatherman.

In summing up Katherine's life after it ends in a bank-bombing, he stands in contrast to all other attitudes. "She was right!" he states defiantly. That character played by Winkler was a lot more accurate (thanks, Jeremy) than the elusive fugitive Howie Eppis of the *Big Fix*.

Howie Eppis! Let's talk about Eppis. The name's interesting. . . . A Yiddish word difficult to describe, it means "something," as in "Give him something to eat" or "happening" as in "What's happening?" I've always been fascinated by Yiddish as the language of survival. Half insults, half complaints. Its subtleties, its built-in irony (all Yiddish paragraphs end with a question mark), the historical road it has traveled, have often made me think the person who could tell my story better than anyone was Isaac Bashevis Singer. I also flashed on the name being almost identical with one of the unsung movement organizers who disappeared after a major role at Kent State. Could be? Kagan pays attention to this sort of detail, and bravo for that little extra effort. Essentially when we're discussing the character of Howie Eppis, the long-haired movement activist turned fugitive who wrote *Rip It Off!*, we're talking about how good a guess has the movie made about where I am and what I'm doing. What my life is right now, in a strange way, is what the whole movie is about. To say anything else, I'd have to conjure up some false modesty. If it be ego, in this case it's justifiable ego.

So everybody's wondering what became of Howie and at the precise moment (assuming by now you've seen the movie and I'm not spoiling the plot) we all learn that he's alive and well, living in suburbia with a comfortable job in an ad agency. For could not the inventor of "Don't trust anyone over thirty" (not me) invent jingles for soap and cereal? A very interesting guess. Very plausible. Certainly within my realm of capabilities. But—and this is the Big But to the *Big Fix*—it just isn't so. It's saying a lumberjack is equal to an ax murderer because they both use the same tool.

I suppose I paid more attention to the Eppis scene than anyone in all the movie theaters of America. His history of odd jobs, food stamps, and flight was mine. That happened on a much more excruciating level than Eppis even suggests, but when the moment of choice arose I refused to eat that little piece of shit e. e. cummings once wrote about and a prerequisite to renting out your brain to Madison Avenue. Howie has to turn just as cynical and bitter as Moses Wine and all the sixties-turned-seventies stock figures in order to live with himself. There is just no way, not even with all the excuses ("He paid his dues"), a fugitive can go from the Howie of the sixties to the Howie of the seventies and be true to his own self. I rejected that life long ago and I reject it just as emphatically today. I say this not to brag or even to put Howie down. I rejected Howie's solution because the price has always seemed too great. "*No vale la pena*," say the Chicanos. I value happiness even above my own security and I don't see that as particularly heroic. I never understood why people find that so difficult to grasp when to me it's as obvious as the nose on my face. My life is geared to avoidance of unhappiness.

So tell us, boychik, what makes you happy? Fuckin', good food, good friends, fresh air, good news. When the Red Sox caught the Yankees in the pennant race I was ecstatic. When they came so close but blew it on that bitter fall Monday I almost threw up. I have my freedom, and it really warms a body's heart knowing 26,000 Americans have now recognized me and no one's been cynical enough to play Judas. One appreciates little things like that. But what *really* makes me happy is a good fight with a powerful bureaucracy in the wrong. That makes the juices flow!

As to where I am? If I'm to be found in a class, it's the working class. That doesn't mean I'm in a factory. I'm not. But my allegiance is with the proletariat and I believe in class struggle. I have two kids that I worry about on welfare and one on near-welfare. I drive a six-year-old car, own no property, have no bank account, and keep everything I own in two suitcases. I carry another box—called the Abbie bag—and when I've got something to say, best said by him, when I need some quick money, or I think it'll help in getting the charges dropped I unlock the case, get into my Abbie head and costume and fly off like Superschmuck! To answer Bob Dylan's question to me publicly—"No, I don't want to go back," with the qualifier that I don't want to be dragged back in chains either. I'm one of your off-beat rebel types that wants to live to see the movie.

Okay, that's Abbie. What about the person *I* am, the identity I live six days a week, the one who lives outside the locked bag? The answer's certainly not to be found in the *Big Fix*.

But before I let you in on the secret, I have to introduce the old Abbie, because to me he was never the "movement prankster," the "media genius," or any of those cliché definitions linked to fame. Back in the early sixties I was a community organizer—in ghettos both white and black, later in the rural South, still later on in the Lower East Side. Eventually the community got to be the whole U.S.A., and I spoke to millions with a single gesture or slogan. Throwing money out at the Stock Exchange was no different actually than any other gesture I used in the seven years of organizing prior to that occasion. And not to interrupt your train of thought, the character who did *that* gesture could not, even ten years later, rush down to the gallery floor and gather up the bills. Not without feeling awfully rotten inside or being terribly dishonest. Money is important to this little analysis. Leaving aside Murray Kempton's favorite Abbie gesture of signing the largest check he ever received (four times the largest) over to a stranger's bail fund, no one launches a radical assault on government and institutions with the notion of becoming rich. It's wise to remember the causes were not popular at the onset, and we had precious little support—contrary to the myth of "our entire generation in the streets." I would not say I had no desire to become famous. But let me hasten to add this interesting supposition. I'm the most famous, relatively poor person in America who hasn't killed a whole bunch of people or assassinated a political candidate. In other words, of all the people who have been on the talk shows, the six o'clock news, in *People* magazine, or made into a poster more than just once—I'm the poorest. Still there are reporters, columnists, critics, and because of what they say, a huge mass of the public who believe I'm not only pulling down the hundred grand a year Howie Eppis takes home but am probably doing him one better. That's a very weird reversal on reality because I'm the only living American I know for whom fame does *not* equal riches. And, what is bound to piss off the capitalist in us all, I don't particularly give a merry fuck!

When I went underground, I had to undergo a huge transformation. An operation, new speech and walk, a new family and friends, indeed, I suspect, a new class, although class in America is a long discussion in itself. I traveled a lot, wrote (with most of the funds going to Abbie's family), had odd jobs, and much of the time lived exceptionally well on little capital. "Primitive elegance" or "hedonistic communism," I call the life-style. After all, I *did* write *Steal This Book* and it's still unpublishable sequel. Think of all the cost-cutting tricks I left out or have picked up on the road. *I* should be telling consumers how to save, not Bess Myerson! Years went by and although I was as confused as my contemporaries I couldn't let unhappiness get the best of me because I was convinced, barring accidents, that that was the only way I could get caught. I never once said or did anything the Abbie of the sixties would have been ashamed of.

Finally, about a year ago, I ended up in a beautiful valley. There was a nuclear plant in the works. The people were untrained in opposing authority. The land I had come to call home was going to be ruined. I'd dreamed of this battle all my life. Of being the inside agitator up against the outside agency intruder. So I've been a community organizer for the past year. I've used every trick in the book. I've been on TV, radio, given speeches in bars, in universities, on the street corner. I've written pamphlets, held meetings, gotten an office together, united people to fight, and even managed to pull off some yippie escapades. I'm better at it than before. Even with my peculiar handicap and having to devise a strategy circumventing civil disobedience, as arrest means those telltale fingerprints. There's less ego involvement because security insists I help others become leaders, and I work on the principle "make no enemies." I put in ten hours a day body-time, and all day mind-time. I don't make a nickel. Vacations are when I unlock the bag and work on Abbie's book and articles, or sneak off to the pay phone to hustle his *shtick*. I'd have to be the blindest schmuck on the block not to see this fantastic movie I'm living.

Okay, that's it. The same ol' Howie Eppis if you will, ten years older, better at what he set out to do, and the question still is, Is Hollywood daring enough to tell it like it is and really was? There's a lot of bidding going on for the new book, big bucks, almost all of which will go to the kids. But while I'm alive they gotta come through me. I saw how Broadway crucified Paul Robeson by pulling out his political guts. I know why Hollywood rebels die at the end of each movie. Why people like James Dean, Marilyn Monroe, and Lenny Bruce are immortalized. The difference between Joe Louis and Muhammad Ali. At this point in time, when odds makers back in '73 gave me six months underground tops, I know a lot of shit. A lot about Hollywood and a lot about America. I'm never going to sit in a movie theater and walk out sick to my stomach after watching the wrong story. Not for all the tea in China, not for a million bucks. It's happened too often in the magazines and newspapers. I'd hate to watch a ninety-minute misquote.

But a good honest shot? The future, including Hollywood, is up for grabs, and I'd certainly throw in with the right collective (movies *are*, after all, a collective art form) willing to take the same honest shot. Anything is possible. And if I guess wrong? Hey, five years ago I got stuck in a hotel room with some undercover cops and a pile of coke, but I'm still here to say I screwed up and who knows what tomorrow brings. So the cynics read this and say, "He's not going to win." Didn't he see *One Flew Over the Cuckoo's Nest*? Doesn't he know what happens to stubborn weirdos like him? They die and some conglomerate does a Paul Robeson on him.

Here's a bit I pulled just before I went underground. I've learned a little law in my day. Studied with the best, of course. A really close friend who doesn't work for money, but who is rich and powerful, accepted my offer. Just before I split we drew up a legal contract giving him movie rights to my entire life for the total sum of one buck. It's legal in every court of the land. Future trespassers beware, no cosmetics or that contract comes out and you'll be in court longer than I ever was.

So that's the story, guys. Kagan's *Big Fix* was not my story; it didn't embarrass me, as Dreyfuss thought it would. I laughed in a few places and even admired certain scenes, such as the prison scene and the police interrogations. The music was wretched. Moses Wine was a likable enough character. The right-wing conspiracy was not that surrealistic and I'm puzzled by folks who had trouble following it. It made sense to me. What I do reject is the underlying theme of this and all the sixties-turned-seventies movies, books, and TV series to come expressing the idea that with age inevitably comes disillusionment, cynicism, and eating that little piece of shit in order to survive. I suspect it happened to the people who made the movie; I thank my lucky stars it hasn't happened to me . . . yet, anyway.

November 1978

Inside the New FBI

A chill sneaked up my spine as I crossed the moat and wandered up and down, looking for the right door. I wondered if I hadn't checked my brains, along with some manuscripts, extraneous identification, and other telltale items, in the station locker. A guard approached me in the middle of a heart-to-heart conversation I was carrying on with my fingerprints.

"Excuse me, I'm looking for the tour."

"Are you with a group?" he asked, as I searched the courtyard.

"Uh, no, I'm alone," I answered, feeling I should raise my hands in the air.

"Oh, that's okay. Generally, folks make appointments through their congressmen or come in tour groups," he said. "Just take the stairs to the left and follow the runway to the waiting room on the right. Can't miss it."

No other country in the world has idolized its secret police the way Americans have. Scotland Yard is more popular here than in England. Sûreté is held in suspicion by most French people and even the Russians regard the KGB with healthy distrust. We have been force-fed on a steady formula of TV shows, movies, books, and children's games until the fabulous Feds have worked their way into our hearts and file cabinets. Public relations was the cornerstone upon which J. Edgar Hoover built the power and glory of the bureau. His efforts were legend-

ary. Once determined to ensure that his ghost-written
Masters of Deceit become a best-seller, he managed to
obtain the secret list of bookstores the *New York Times*
used to determine its weekly list. He then instructed his
field agents to purchase (at taxpayers' expense, no less)
enough retail copies to guarantee the book's success. I
know the story because at one time we shared the same
publisher.

Hoover not only had script approval on the TV series
based on the bureau's activities but also had security-
clearance checks run on all the actors and actresses. For
eight straight years we were treated to an hour a week of
prime-time propaganda. Bank robbers, kidnappers, and
hijackers fell beneath the bureau's sword faster than it
takes an Alka-Seltzer to dissolve. Aside from two disgruntled agents, a few pinko columnists, and bleeding-
heart liberals, the FBI, chiefly through Hoover's manip-
ulation of the media, had established itself as our most
admired federal agency—an institution of integrity. In
1965 a Gallup poll showed that fully 84 percent of all
Americans held an "exceptionally favorable" opinion of
the bureau.

Nowhere else did the Director, as Hoover preferred to
be called, have more control over the public image of the
agency than under his own roof. The famous FBI tour in
Washington was a tourist must, attracting half a million
Americans each year. Most returned to their hometowns
and civic classes like eager apostles, spreading the gospel
of the brave G-men and their tireless, thankless battle
against a horde of criminals prowling our streets, plotting
in dark cellars, and collaborating with foreign enemies.
No one who took the grand tour could forget the
excitement of seeing actual agents blast away at the
shooting gallery ("We never shoot unless we have to"),
the ghostly image of Dillinger's death mask, or the
graphic spider web depicting the intricacies of the Rosenberg spy networks. The FBI Goes to War was my favorite
display. There was a map of the United States with red
lights blinking menacingly off our eastern shores. Here

were the spots where actual Nazi saboteurs had landed bent on wreaking their deadly havoc in the heart of our nation. Wonder Woman herself could not have foiled their plans quicker than did the Feds.

Crime never paid on the tour. The G-men always, but always, got their man. The bureau was above reproach. Mouths agape, we nodded in unison while the heroics of our nation's most dedicated public servants were cataloged. Life-size stills acted out a living comic book. This was the real thing, the honest-to-goodness true "FBI Story." It mattered little that the "story" had more holes than a Liberian tanker. The myth overshadowed reality.

Then in 1972, quite out of character with his infallibility, J. Edgar Hoover died. He was unaware that within the next four years, the myth it had taken him forty-eight years to construct would unravel before a host of congressional hearings and department confessions. Critics who were formerly depicted as guttersnipes were now seen as guardians of the truth. Without the Great Protector, with his American Legion booster clubs, his direct line to the PTA, and those nasty but ever so useful secret files, the bureau was unable to suppress the storm of protest and ridicule. Naked it stood against the chilly winds of exposure. A vendetta against Martin Luther King, spying into the private lives of congressmen, political espionage for presidents, illegal wiretapping of thousands, burglaries in New York, paid provocateurs inciting riots and bombings. Blackmail. Bribes. Black-bag boys. On and on went the charges. A solid decade of dastardly acts. Heavens to Hoover! The FBI was actually out there beefing up its own well-publicized crime statistics. The public could take CIA assassination plots. After all, war, even cold war, was a dirty business. It could take presidents who lied and congressmen on the take. Politicians were by nature not to be trusted. But the FBI, the nemesis of crime, had been sacrosanct. No revelations damaged national confidence more than those of wrongdoing within the bureau. In 1975 a similar Gallup poll revealed that only 37 percent of the citizenry now held the FBI in high esteem.

Of course, our beloved Director was spared all this by tapping out. The myth of perfection accompanied him to that great firing range in the sky. In this he was indeed fortunate. However, if he had managed to hang in there four more years, he would have realized his most cherished dream.

As everyone knows, the FBI operates a branch within the Justice Department. Hoover wanted his own building more than anything else. When he locked up at night, he wanted to rest assured he had the only key. He also longed to leave a physical legacy that would match his own living legend. Rumor has it he even desired entombment in some honored spot on the premises.

There was never any doubt as to the name of the building. Upon completion, the national headquarters would be christened the J. Edgar Hoover Building. It was even called that while under construction, when the old man was still high in the saddle. In 1975, after seven years, at a cost of $126 million, it was finally finished. It is one of the country's largest public (sic) buildings and surely one of its most expensive. No other government building constructed in the previous ten years has gone over $100 million. In fact, with Hoover gone and the newly disclosed background of bureau scandal, liberal congressmen were able to chisel away another twenty or thirty million dollars' worth of extras. A nuclear reactor here, an underground tunnel system there. Testimony to that budget battle can be seen in the thousands of little pockmarks, peppered like bullet holes, along the wall facings. Originally the facings were meant to anchor a granite facade. Alas, that, too, ended up on the cutting-room floor.

The building itself is enormous. It stands across the street from and looks directly down on the Justice Department. A building regulation limits structures along Pennsylvania Avenue to seven stories, but Hoover got around that restriction by setting the main section of the building back off the street. In that way an eleven-story edifice could be erected. It covers a complete city block, is World War II army tan in color, and has a certain hulk that can best be described by the German adjective *zaftig*. It's as if somebody had poured a million tons of concrete into Hoover's head and mounted it. One solid mass of square-jawed tenacity. No frivolity or frills. Wrought-iron fences joined by heavy gates surround the outer courtyard, the type of fencing favored by U.S. embassies in countries somewhat hostile to our presence. Inside the grounds a visitor is impressed by a sense of intimidation. It comes from the thickness of the walls, the difficulty in judging the correct entryway, the water-filled moat one is forced to bridge, and the hanging balconies so ideal for security forces. A courtyard ideally laid out to trap and neutralize an unruly crowd. Hoover and his architects had not forgotten the time 75,000 marched on Justice, protesting the Chicago Seven conspiracy trial. It is very easy to envision tanks drawn up along the walls. Two and a half million square feet of fortified fear. It has already gained a reputation as Washington's most hideous building. That is an honor difficult to come by.

While walking down the corridor, I feel as if I am entering the Orwellian processing center, where misfits learned that two plus two equals five. On rows of low-slung black leather benches sits our group-to-be—about a dozen tourists, mostly middle-aged Middle Americans. Three are teenagers, and one sports a National Rifle Association jacket. Two male guides busy themselves greeting tourists and searching handbags. A guide enters the room and is introduced to our group. Connie is a stout blonde, halfway between youthful exuberance and tired blood. A neatly tailored blue jacket hides a waist stuffed into gray flannel bell bottoms. An emblem adorns the breast pocket. The men wear the same unisex uniforms. Connie gives us a quick introduction, cautions us against taking photos or smoking, and urges us to ask questions as we go along (I was later told there never are any). Our group develops that instant camaraderie Americans forced into close proximity are so good at, and moves out to the exhibit rooms. Large chrome letters humbly solve the mystery of the letters FBI: *Fidelity, Bravery, Integrity*. Exactly the qualities needed for good wire men and midnight burglars. Connie assures us that the 19,000 FBI employees work round-the-clock to provide us with nationwide coverage. She points to a blowup of something I hope never to see again—the credentials of a special agent. We are told to study them carefully (as if there were a lot of people running around flashing counterfeit FBI badges).

Now it's on to the gangster era to meet the folks who made the Feds famous: Al Brady, "Baby Face" Nelson, and Al Capone, to mention a few. Behind every successful chase story lies, of course, the untold pitfalls and abuses. For example, when Hoover's men moved in on a case, they professed cooperation with local authorities but were notorious for keeping information and later ignoring or minimizing the role others played. In chasing the Brady gang, Hoover managed to get an Indiana state police captain fired for objecting to the Feds' modus operandi. In retelling the Lindbergh kidnapping, the FBI persists in overlooking the fact that Treasury agents laid the actual trap. Or that postal inspectors located the notorious Alvin Karpis only to have Hoover rush to New Orleans to grandstand the arrest personally. Even the case of the Nazi saboteurs was cracked by New York City police and handed to the Feds on a silver platter. The FBI never saw fit to share credit but rather sought to portray other law enforcement agencies as a pack of stumblebums who always had to be bailed out by the supersleuths from Washington. "Baby Face" Nelson, "Machine Gun" Kelley, "Pretty Boy" Floyd, and the other dangerous desperadoes of the thirties were in large part creations of FBI press conferences, their escapades built up and their viciousness exaggerated to heighten the drama of that final shoot-out. Dillinger, whose bloody death outside the Biograph Theater is indisputably the crowning moment in FBI history, hardly fit the "mad-dog killer" reputation that earned him the moniker "Public Enemy Number One" and express orders for agents to shoot him on sight. There is plenty of evidence suggesting that Dillinger was far from bloodthirsty. It is true he performed a host of armed robberies and daring prison escapes, but only a single murder charge was ever lodged against him, and it is doubtful that his was actually the finger on the trigger. In fact, the only federal case against him was a stolen car rap. He hardly belonged in the category of a warlord like Al Capone, to whom more than 130 murders were traced, or of a Lucky Luciano, whose Murder, Inc., carried out perhaps a thousand murders at the behest of mobsters throughout the country. Nonetheless the myth of "Mad Dog" Dillinger has been undampened by the facts.

The story of Al Capone is also told, even though it was the IRS that put him away. All the FBI could get the notorious Al Capone on was a perjury charge carrying a six-month sentence. Hoover always was reluctant to move against organized crime. Murder, Inc., Joe Adonis, Frank Costello, Meyer Lansky, Bugsy Segal, and their kind, throughout the thirties and forties, were the names most often identified with big-time interstate crime, exactly the type of activity only a national police force could battle. Curiously, not only did Hoover rarely move against organized crime, but also it wasn't until the early sixties that he even conceded its existence. Instead, he preferred playing sheriff of Nottingham to the Robin Hoods of the depression. The FBI's failure to move against the Mafia enabled organized crime to amass billions, infiltrate the economy, wreck unions, bribe politicians, and effectively cover its tracks.

Throughout the FBI exhibit actual historical photos are juxtaposed with clips from *The FBI Story*. Alas, reality is only black and white, but the photos, like the story, are carefully framed. Next there is a refresher course in disguises and bank robberies, then a zigzag back to the ten-most-wanted list. Connie tells us the list helps focus people's attention on the hunt for fugitives. "Some have even been captured because people on the tour recognized them." We are instructed in what to do should we spot a fugitive. (I'll be damned if I pass on *that* procedure!)

Next stop, the fabled fingerprint exhibit. Somewhere behind these walls are stored 160 million prints. What our group—and yours, if you take the tour—isn't told is that 80 percent of the print records on file are from noncriminal persons. Most people are unaware that every time you give prints, say, for a job, to the armed forces, for insurance, or for license applications, a copy of them is sent to the bureau and stored. In case you ever forget who you are, the Feds might be in a position to help you remember. The telephone is featured in several exhibits. Here we are shown how a call can be traced; later, how a bookie rigs up a "cheese box" so as not to be rudely disturbed during business hours.

Organized crime now rates its own special stop. A chart shows convictions at 281 for 1965 up to 1,417 in 1975. In the land of FBI statistics everything increases. Cops and criminals always get bigger and better. This, of course, justifies the bigger, better budget, in 1975, of a record-breaking half a billion. Here, too, of course, the Feds are never shy about claiming victories for the work of others. The famous Appalachian roundup is discussed but brushed aside, as are the facts that it was the result of a quick-thinking state trooper and that the FBI poohpoohed the raid and for years resisted efforts to establish an organized-crime investigation section.

Espionage—the Silent War That Never Ends—no longer features the Rosenbergs. Other sensitive cases, such as those of Judith Coplon and Alger Hiss, where the FBI was shown to have employed shady methods, have also been dropped. Instead, we're shown the variety of "drop" systems favored, such as the sneaky under-the-counter hand-off. Connie points out the famous hollow nickel Rudolph Abel mistakenly gave to a newsboy, who turned it in to the FBI. Eternal vigilance again foils misdeeds. The tour is big on encouraging junior Federales. We're reminded that if we keep alert, we, too, could break an important case.

John Graham, who blew up a passenger plane just to get at his mother, is immortalized in Crimes Aboard Aircraft. John was electrocuted and later roasted in a Lenny Bruce monologue. No doubt he was a fiend. A replica of the bomb is on view. Bombs, we are lectured, are pretty dangerous, and we shouldn't try to disassemble them ourselves.

Surprisingly few references are made to the old chief. Gone are the life-size stills showing him as a young man blasting away with his favorite chopper. None of his old-fashioned homilies on crime and subversion are quoted. In effect, a posthumous minipurge has taken place. The tour has been de-Hooverized. There is, however, one reminder. Over in a sunny corner we can view his study desk. Here he sat banishing agents to Butte, Montana, reading peek-hole reports of congressional sex-capades, and drawing sketches of the Red Menace. At the end of every working day, a special agent carefully measured all the objects Hoover left on top of this desk, noted their place, removed them, polished the surface, and returned them to their exact position.

We ride the escalator up to the lab. Behind glass picture windows we can see young technicians busy examining blood specimens. Given the plethora of new gadgets, it's a wonder any crime goes unsolved. An electronic fingerprint scanner. Neutron activation analysis, a process that can examine the composition of an object without destroying the evidence. Here are the microbe probers who can solve a case when they are given the barest of clues—a human hair, a chip of paint, a tire mark. In the Document Reference Files are stored samples of typewriting, watermarks, handwriting styles. In one section files contain a million bum checks. Another holds death threats and ransom notes. There are 70,000 file cabinets chock-full of dossiers on people. Everyone arrested, even if no conviction results, has a file. Reporters, politicians, teachers, civil servants, writers, just about anyone who has come to the attention of the bureau in the last fifty years. Hoover began his public career as a file-card indexer at the Library of Congress. Files were always his joy. Under the Freedom of Information Act, you can now write in and request a copy of your file. Thousands do so each day—which, by the way, if there is no file, begins one.

Then we are introduced to the extensive firearms

collection. Hundreds of weapons are on display in show-cases. Rifles, shotguns, revolvers, of all shapes and sizes, a cane gun, "Pretty Boy" Floyd's modified tommy-gun, and other weapons taken during arrests. Their wooden butts and unpolished barrels make them seem quaint in this modern scientific setting. Pity the poor lone bandit who, with one of these peashooters, takes on the computers. Next we pass down a hallway displaying laminated copies of historical documents, such as the Mayflower Compact and the Emancipation Proclamation. Connie tells us her role ends here and informs us we're about to enter the shooting gallery. We quickly enter a glassed-in auditorium, from which we can view the action. An agent dressed in a plain suit enters, dons his ear protectors, removes his snub-nosed .38, squats down, and begins blasting away at a paper target. Pop! Pop! Pop! The paper torso moans: "Ahh, G-men . . . you dirty rats!" It should have anyway. He adjusts the target twenty feet to the rear, working on his point-shoulder position. Some automatic bursts from his Thompson submachine gun turn the torso target into flying confetti. Rat-ta-tat-tat. Everybody cheers each round of fire. The agent joins us in the viewing room and says, "We all try to get down here once a week to keep in shape." Although last year FBI agents were engaged in fewer than twenty-five gun battles, we are on a publicity campaign aimed at blasting away critics of the big budget rather than at shooting down criminals.

Finally, it's over, and we leave the building through the courtyard. It's lunchtime, and personnel are flocking to the street. There are some agents in the garb that has resisted change for thirty years: seersucker suit, striped tie, clean-shaven neck, black shoes. Behind those two-inch cuffs lie the famous white socks, the trademark of authentic federal agents everywhere. Blacks and women can be seen in the courtyard. There's even a chance some of them are agents now that the formerly closed shop has been opened.

I breathe a sigh of relief once outside the gates. At a nearby coffee shop I collect my thoughts. It's really too bad that the *real* FBI has not been captured on this updated tour. The story behind the story deserves more exposure.

Come with us while we reenact the Palmer raids. Hear how we harassed veterans of the Lincoln Brigade. Visit a model of a Japanese internment camp. Sit in a replica of the chair used to fry the Rosenbergs. Here are the burglar tools used to rifle the files of the Socialist Workers Party and some of the chains FBI Ku Klux Klan infiltrators used to beat freedom riders when they got carried away with their assignments. Examine these forged letters sent out to embarrass critics. Listen to 5,500 hours of illegal wiretapping on the Chicago Eight.

If the FBI has gone out of the thought-control business and no longer engages in dirty tricks, why not dramatize the past abuses and junk the worn-out fairy tales? Eighty million dollars are currently budgeted for domestic intelligence, and no legislation has come along to limit programs like COIN-TELPRO, which fostered active disruption and illegal spying on protest groups. But the fabulous Feds keep right on marching along. What's worse, the public assumes sweeping changes have taken place. All's quiet on the tour. The budget and the buildings are bigger than ever. The only curbs are on the sidewalk out in front.

October 1977

Square Dancing
in the Ice Age

~~~~~~

IT WAS a real marrow-searcher: the coldest winter since people had begun keeping score in 1895. There was talk of entering a new ice age. Prophets of doom were saying that we stood at the door of Armageddon; that this was, in fact, nothing less than the end of the world. How would the powers that be handle such a thing? Would the government try to keep a lid on? Who would get the first leak? Would the networks preempt prime-time shows? Who could you believe these days, anyway? Of course, the Fugitive had been suspicious of government long before Watergate and the CIA revelations (the latest of which was that biological weaponry had been used to decimate the pig population of Cuba in 1971), for he had seen many of the dirty tricks up close. Still, he had heeded their word on the impending swine-flu epidemic and had gotten the shot. But there weren't ten thousand dead, nor were policemen hurrying through the streets wearing gauze masks. He should have believed the *National Enquirer* when it said the whole thing was a hoax. Two more hours of 55-mph Top-40 A.M. driving and the Fugitive and the Angel would be in the nation's capital—the world's greatest hoax-hatching center. They were going to watch the government rotate. The forces of power were changing partners. With an allemande left and an allemande right; and swing your corner round and round. Down with Pepsi! Up with Coke! Texaco's out and Exxon's in. And promenade around the hall.

Didn't Ford say as much last night? His final address: "There are no soldiers in the street. The opposition doesn't go underground [it goes to Palm Springs to play Celebrity Golf]. The mantle of power is gracefully and peacefully passed on." The last time a relatively normal transition took place from one party to another was when Eisenhower passed the global ball to Kennedy. Ike had used the occasion to warn the country about the growing power of the military-industrial complex. Quite an honest revelation for a general, but one that went unheeded by the JFK-ing of the New Frontier: Kennedy had campaigned hard on the pledge to close the missile gap. Ford, on the other hand, chose to warn Americans that we had been paying too little attention to our military might, that the Russians had been strengthening their capabilities and we were about to become, if we weren't already, the Avis of the nuclear arms race. Le grand hoax number one. Overkill. If you can exterminate life on the planet eighty-seven times over, you are superior to an opponent who can OD the joint only seventy-two times.

O Washington! O Washington! Great White Phallus of the Potomac rising out of Chocolate City. Seat of Government. Defender of the Constitution. Keeper of the Secret Files. Home of the Button. Where power brokers hidden behind banks of security guards decide whether you should get a swine-flu shot or a sweetheart deal; whether it's recession or inflation; whether maraschino cherries are bad and air bags good. That it is okay to sell wheat to Russia, torture devices to Iran, and Reggie Jackson to the New York Yankees. Buggers' paradise. Where the classified document meets the leak. Where every motel room tells two stories, hers and his— currently in that order. Gossip city. And swing that girlie round and round, then promenade the aisle. The Fugitive would have to be extra-careful here. Already the word was out that he was coming and he feared the whispering machine. Bugs with bionic ears live in these buildings and stalk the wide boulevards.

There were other dangers. Such as the impulse to stop playing mild-mannered reporter for zee French political journal *Oui* and slip into a phone booth, emerging to fuck with the body politic. For Washington was the great staging place for political psychodrama. Indeed, he was one who, in days gone by, had painted the town red. The Pentagon, where he pissed on the walls; the White House gate he had climbed to hang the flag of the Woodstock Nation when Grace Slick and he were kept out of Tricia Nixon's party; the Justice Department, where, with Jerry, he had pounded on the door with boxing gloves, challenging Attorney General Mitchell to come out and fight fair; the Capitol lawn he was dragged across as guards tore the flag shirt from his back; the Washington Monument, where he was once detained waiting for a paddy wagon to cart him across the river and into the barracks. Picketing and marches and long vigils and petitioning of congressmen in less flamboyant days. Getting hepatitis in the D.C. jail. And finally that last demonstration. Where the copper's club had smashed across his face, shattering his nose, and they had trucked him to the internment camp at Robert F. Kennedy Stadium. All for nought, too. Illegal taps. Illegal surveillance. And, besides, he was just one of twelve thousand illegal arrests made that week. "Pick up anyone on the streets," Mitchell had ordered. And they did.

Yes, he would have to control the impulse to gesture. But he wanted to go, to observe the changing of the guard and to mingle with the crowds. An undercover tourist. To overcome the isolation of being long years buried in the heartland and once again to be in touch with history. So he would outline activities, pace himself, finish the job, and get out of town. Even though he had a sackful of credentials and disguises, he would not challenge the eagle-eyed Secret Service; he would keep his scarf high on his face when in the streets, and he would move around sniffing the scent of the newcomers. He had fantasies of a pardon, of falling down on his knees, wailing, "Sets me free, massa Carter, sets me free." And Carter, caught up in the excitement of the moment, might just do it. After all, Carter understood the gesture. A fine craft in an electronic culture. The artist and the pollster coming together as one, creating the consummate politician.

A whole generation of politicians was discovering that mingling with the masses yielded a media bonanza *after* as well as *during* the campaign. Governor Dukakis rides the subway to work each day in Boston. For a week, Jerry Brown slept in a ghetto project. In modern government function follows form. The country has never seen the popular gesture, what used to be called *noblesse oblige,* on such a scale. Carter is designed for easy TV viewing. Gestures fit nicely between commercials. A presidency encouraged by *People* magazine. Visual impact. Maximum visibility with minimal content. Carter was quite the news actor. Anyone who can convince people he's going to run the U.S. government for four years without telling a lie has to be an effective actor. Not that many commentators giggled when he made such an unusual (uncalled for) promise.

So how would this photogenic peanut-butter-and-jelly president fare in a Scotch-and-soda town? Honey bun among the killer bees? Would not such a softy be crushed by tougher politicians? How had he managed to get this far? There was luck, to be sure. If Jackson had organized better in Pennsylvania and if Wallace had been stronger in Florida and if Humphrey had not waited so long and if Teddy—but it was not to be, and who's to say Carter could not have won in any event? That's not a salute to the openness of the democratic process—how outside can a millionaire with a seat on the global power exchange known as the Trilateral Commission be? But an ex-governor of a southern state leapfrogging to the pinnacle of power is not the normal course of events. So Carter exhibited great style and speed in the race, but that was past and now Jimmy was about to enter the Oval Room at the top.

A new president, especially one who prided himself on management, who would run a "cabinet presidency," could now best be judged by those he chose to supply him with information and share in decision making. And in this first task Carter had bitterly disappointed supporters. The Fugitive had always admired Andy Young. They had been together on the voter-registration marches in Americus, just five short miles from the Carter ranch house. But Young had been maneuvered into a job in which he could speak out but not act. He would always be considered the cabinet's black sheep. True, there were two women appointees, Juanita Kreps and Patricia Harris; but, like the ambassador to the UN, they were in positions on the second shelf of the cabinet. Besides, the women were safely tied to big business; Marshall was not that bad at labor; the rest were a sorry bunch.

But perhaps picking trusted bureaucrats, men "in harmony with our business community" and apologists for an evil war, was the way you gathered in the reins of power: Better on the inside doing what I say than on the outside plotting against me. But the Bible teaches that "bad company can ruin even the noblest of men," and Carter had, on this occasion, ignored the warning. The business of America *is* business. Rule one of the ruling class. What's good for General Motors is good for the United States is hoax number two. Aluminum mineworkers in the West had their strike broken when Anaconda tripled operations in Chile; 150,000 migrant workers in Florida were being frozen out of work—work that brought them one-half the minimum wage (average pay sixty-four dollars per week) and zero benefits, anyway. Work exploited by Coca-Cola. Exploitation, incidentally, that was defended by lawyer Califano before he became head of HEW. They were finding frozen bodies in Buffalo while oil companies were reporting record-breaking profits. AT&T, the nation's largest utility, just reported a profit increase of 21 percent for 1976. Very few laborers could boast such an increase in *their* paychecks. And did not the spokesman for natural gas distributors say recently that they were holding back supplies until price ceilings were lifted? And Schlesinger, this ex-Pentagon boss, this champion of the breeder reactor, now energy czar (with all the implications of *that* title), feels the natural-resource and utility companies are not to blame because supply is limited. Limited supply, my gas! Exxon's assets are estimated over 100 billion buckaroos and we're supposed to turn off the heat in the bathroom. The energy shortage is hoax number three. The multinational greed machines would be pampered in this administration as in those past—profits would outrank prophets in priority. When business demanded, Carter would rise above principle. The new version of the Bible reads, "And on the sixth day God created Exxon." So it's hands over, daisy chain. Circle the hall and home again.

Twenty of Carter's top appointments, including Brzezinski, Blumenthal, Brown, and Vance shared seats with him on the Trilateral Commission. Mondale, too. A global blueprint group of bankers, corporation heads, and politicians set up by David Rockefeller to protect corporate investments against rising Third World expectations; to map contingency plans for dealing with guerrilla warfare, oil embargoes, coffee and sugar cartels, and what one too-candid report refers to as "democratic excess on the part of the American people." Fully one-third of the U.S. representation on the commission has moved into the top level of government. IBM, Texas Instruments, Bendix, Chase Manhattan Bank, Coca-Cola, and Exxon were maneuvering for greater power. The corporate empire with its Swiss money, its Liberian tankers, its British overseers, its German technicians, and its American lawyers would be in a position to not only take on its natural enemy—the working class—it would challenge the nation-state itself. Now the question being asked at the top is "Is what's good for the United States, good for General Motors?" General Motors, along with other auto manufacturers will seek government hand-outs, but will it close its sheet metal plant in the Philippines, where it pays workers $1.15 per day? The multinats demanded from the United States global cops, corporate managers, computers, and consumers. "And fuck you to the working class, we can do it cheaper in Bolivia. Good ol' Jimmy's not going to stop us." And the meek shall inherit the leftovers. They echoed what you heard on the streets in Washington: "Jimmy's a good businessman, he'll work things out." And swing your country round and round. McGovern was right when he said any of our past presidents would have been comfortable with this cabinet. After the promised new faces, Carter had turned to the same old dogs, who would, in time, perform the same old tricks. Dirty tricks. Do-si-do and back again. Wiggle your left, but put your right foot in.

The Fugitive's first stop was the Library of Congress to research inaugurations past, so overreported a sequence of events that there's a catalog of books about it three fingers thick. The Fugitive dutifully records that William Henry Harrison rendered a two-hour speech and, as a result of it, caught pneumonia and died a few weeks later; that Grant's guests danced in overcoats and hacked at frozen oysters; and that Andrew Jackson, too, had invited all his chums to share in a people's inauguration. They had torn the drapes in the White House, muddied the furniture, gotten into fisticuffs, and knocked the punch bowl onto the rugs that Lafayette had presented to Martha Washington. Good ol' boys will be good ol' boys, now, won't they? He read through past inaugural speeches and was surprised. True, there were large promises to care for the sick and feed the poor, but a surprising number of presidents felt called upon to rattle sabers. Truman roared on and on about the evils of communism, outlining his vision of the new imperialism, and Kennedy warned our enemies that we were willing to pay any price for liberty. And LBJ urged no nation to doubt our resolve, and Nixon—ha! He couldn't read the empty promise of history's greatest failure without hearing the back-room cackle on those soon-to-be-released tapes. What egomaniacs are the powerful! Nixon collected his barnyard epithets, Louis XIV collected his excrement, and Howard Hughes had his storeroom filled with his precious piss.

So Carter was to change all this. To be ordinary and act decent. Not to weird-out on power, he was going to eat at

McDonald's and carry his own bag. And, with Rosalynn, he would spend Sundays calling folks picked from the phone book just to keep in touch. And Amy would go to public school, and Jimmy would put on his jeans and listen to Dylan. And what more could we ask for but gestures? After Vietnam and Watergate, maybe we could only expect four-year presidents who were competent square dancers. Sweat without struggle. Movement without progress. And smile, smile, smile.

So national health care was being delayed. The past three presidents had promised the same program and failed to deliver. The AMA is better organized than the sick. So the Pentagon budget cuts will now be in *proposed* rather than *actual* dollars. Besides, what's five or ten billion, anyway? A dozen nuclear subs? So we're aiming to reduce unemployment one percent the first year rather than the four percent promised? So two million fewer people will get promised jobs. And we'll get bombers instead of standardized welfare payments. So what's new in square dancing?

The Fugitive grew impatient reading about the economy. He didn't understand the pros and cons of deficit spending. Recession, he thought, was playing in the schoolyard. Stagflation sounded bad, but he wasn't sure if it meant people were slow to spend money for expensive goods or if it were a disease common among reindeer. He did not believe in capitalism, so capitalism's technical language was off the point. Like overhearing ship captains debate navigation in a world they believe is flat. Or, more to the subject, like slaveowners arguing whether kindness or the whip got better results. Nonetheless, he knew firsthand that a job is damned hard to come by unless you are a computer engineer. His own job résumé was seven pauses and three gulps long. He had lost two jobs in the past six months, screwed up his story at the welfare office, and managed to get the food stamps cut off. He now lived among the marginally employed, the welfare recipients, the gypsy proletariat. Down here the solution looked so obvious. Carter had asked for suggestions, so he wrote a letter.

Dear Jimmy:

I can't find a job or a place to live, so why don't you hire me to build a house? I don't like welfare and food stamps. I just got fired unfairly. They canned this Puerto Rican woman for the same reason I was canned, and she cried and said she was going to kill herself. Now, Jimmy, the U.S. is the least unionized country in the world. Eighty percent or more of our labor force is unorganized. Management certainly is. You should support the Humphrey-Hawkins bill, knock out right-to-work laws, allow collective bargaining by public employees and compulsory arbitration, and refuse to invoke the Taft-Hartley Act when vital strikes occur, if they ever do again. Government must become the champion of the worker. An organized labor force doesn't need to be *given* anything. It demands and wins. I know the current labor leaders won't buy this. Everyone knows that the FBI and the Mafia drove out the Communists, the anarchists, and the other idealists long ago. And, with them, the idea of making every working person a union member. But that's what the country needs. It doesn't need any social legislation, it needs national trade unionism so that everyone who produces can . . .

He couldn't finish the thought because it occurred to him that none of this would happen, and he left the library. The corridors were plastered with an exhibit of protest posters. Paper weapons they were called. There the Fugitive was enshrined under glass as one of the Chicago Seven, next to an old poster calling people to MARCH ON WASHINGTON, MARCH ON DEATH. It made him sad to see the poster. True, the movement had, in a decade, ended legal segregation, stopped the world's mightiest imperial war machine, and left a legacy in people's minds that protest worked. But he couldn't help feeling that the movement had failed to deliver. That poster brought one million angry protesters to town. He thought of how they had promised revolution and got sucked into the mainstream or drifted into disillusioned apathy.

The next day he trotted out to Georgetown University. It had always been a fairly conservative school, but six years ago antiwar rallies had emptied the dorms even here. Thousands turned out. Chants of "Bring the war home" rang in his ears, and he could see himself in the courtyard, fist high, exhorting the crowd. The Fugitive picked his way along icy paths toward the cafeteria. Tom Ade, from Morristown, New Jersey, told him things had changed since those days. "The campus went for Ford, you know. We don't really talk much about politics. We just want jobs." Tom was going to head for Atlantic City when he graduated in the spring. "I want to get in on the ground floor when they open the gambling casinos. Right now they're cleaning the blacks out. It's going to be a boom town there." Judy and Pat are more excited that Chevy Chase was just on campus than in anything connected with politics. No one had even heard Kissinger's recent announcement that he would teach there. Notices in the corridor listed lecturers: James Buckley, the minister from the Republic of China, the originator of *Captive Nations Weekly,* and the former ambassador from South Vietnam. Scarcely a broad range. A banner screamed: CELEBRATE NEW YEAR'S AGAIN! JAN. 21ST. CHAMPAGNE! NOISEMAKERS! NO JEANS PLEASE! He blinked and looked at the swarming students again. The students were old, they were junior adults anxious to grow up. Polite, serious, accepting. Solid, C-plus citizens. Long hair was rare and, by golly, they were dressed up. Everyone looked like Dorothy Hamill. Oh, so short and sassy! They flocked to the corporate bandwagon at display tables. "Ford and IBM are recruiting today. They grab up undergraduates and pay for school in exchange for a long-term commitment," Tom explained.

"When I went, parents mostly paid," the Fugitive answered.

"Parents can't afford school. Corporations have taken over the costs. It's not exactly a free marketplace for talent. It's more like the pro-football draft." The students ran off to class. The corporate chill.

The Fugitive made his way back to the hideout to gather in the news. Washington has no fewer than three all-news radio stations, and TV news runs a solid two hours if you switch channels. Besides, all the local stories were about Jerry and Betty and Henry. Political news and gossip were one and the same. The first thing everyone did in the afternoon was read the *Star*'s gossip column, "Ear." Of course, there are two Washingtons—the Big D.C., with office buildings, Georgetown town houses, the malls, the embassies around DuPont Circle, the monuments, and the bedroom suburbs. Washington, N.W. Northwest. The other three-quarters must be where the *other* Washington lives. Some master builder designed the place so that you could spend a whole week sightseeing here and scarcely be aware that you're in a city that is 80 percent a black ghetto. The local news occasionally reminds you of the fact by reporting a murder or a fire or a drug bust, but mostly it's about Jerry or Betty or Henry, and now Jimmy and Miz Lillian and Hamilton Jordan, who folks are betting will be the top draw at coke-tail parties in a month.

Sorenson withdraws nomination to CIA without a whimper from the Georgia peaches. He thought Sorenson would be good in that spot. Maybe ease the lid off a nice little can of worms when the Kennedy assassination committee came asking questions. But Sorenson was out and the assassination committee was proving itself too uppity. They just leaked how Oswald had been seen in the company of CIA agents and Congress was threatening to cut off the mun and shuffle the committee into oblivion.

Next item. Carter's son, it turns out, was booted out of the navy for smoking grass. Peter Bourne, Carter's chief drug advisor, is known to favor decriminalization of pot and it's said he sniffs the white powder and knows all about that hoax. No reason to belittle this as a minor issue. In spite of the liberal trend, over 400,000 drug busts occurred last year. Just like the year before and the year before that. It's nice to know Carter's kid got busted on pot, and he's got a nephew in prison out in California, and his mother ran off to join the Peace Corps in India, and his sister's some wacked-out faith healer in Chicago, and his brother's always hangin' one on and walks around with a T-shirt that says "Red-Neck Power." Norman Lear must be readying a "Jimmy, Jimmy" sit-com.

That night the Fugitive toured the small clubs tucked behind the Capitol. The talk is as stiff as a priest's collar. Social masking for political ambition at a moment when the power relationships all must be reevaluated. Careers could be made or broken tonight over a chocolate moussetake. Everyone's on Valium. Booze flows, but only those who know they're finished pile it on. It's a time for hedging bets. A congressman from Missouri with a gimpy arm hosts a dinner group. Someone ventures yet another dumb peanut joke. Everyone laughs, but there's real tension in the air. A genuine fear of being caught with your hand under the table on the wrong knee. Little do they know Fanne Foxe was a Cuban agent and Elizabeth Ray not only *could* type but was fluent in six languages, one of which was Russian. Nobody talks to Koreans anymore.

After the club scene the Fugitive went to Union Station for the free folk dances. There were two stages. On one you could see Hawaiian hula-hu (remember to keep your eyes on the hands), Indians dancing for sun, and a black jazz group playing "Dixie." Jimmy Connors, whom the Fugitive remembered as a Freedom Singer in the South, was emcee. In the other halls Upper Slavics were teaching about five thousand people a folk dance with a lot of slides, hugs, and good-natured hand-slapping. They were followed by a Bavarian oompah band and the mandatory dancing squares. The rhetoric was integrated, the dances separate but equal.

Wednesday the Fugitive went out early to join the crowds. Soldiers were chopping away the ice on Pennsylvania Avenue and carpenters were putting the finishing touches on the solar-heated viewing box. That was one gesture that stubbornly refused to work, necessitating $6,000 worth of emergency heating units to be rushed into place. Miz Lillian announced that she was wearing "long handles" the whole day anyway.

The wait at the National Gallery was two hours long but well worth it. The glory of ancient Egypt. The treasures of King Tut's tomb. The Fugitive kept trying to focus on their aesthetics, but his mind kept devising capers for lifting a few objects. He was trying to search the people's eyes for other signs of larceny when he was interrupted by the guards scurrying back and forth, calling out "Seven more rooms to see! Seven more rooms to see!" Oops. Then it was on to the Smithsonian for spaceships and antique cars. His favorite had always been this cheery, ultrabright room with an old-fashioned carousel. It had magnificent wooden animals with terrified expressions carved on their faces. Lacquered with a sheen more brilliant than that of fingernail polish. But, alas, the carousel was dissasembled and the horses stacked in a darkened corner under a stairwell. In its place was an exhibit on the inner workings of a telephone relay station. New toys for new kids. He couldn't resist leaving a little three-by-five file card on which he had written the breakdown of the telephone credit-card code for 1977.

He had been given the information only hours before. He had not seen Big Bird in quite some time and when they embraced, Big Bird had whispered into his ear: "L one, D two. Paul's here. V five. Be careful. H seven. Everyone knows you're here. Jolly's a no-show. We all love you. OM."

He nodded and scribbled down the code. "Thanks, good buddy. Send my love to Oli."

"Take care, Ab. Ed Sanders says for you to keep your ka up and your face to the north wind." Gotcha!

Wednesday night he watched the people's gala on one of the people's networks. The highlights included Shirley MacLaine being smashingly smashed, Hank Aaron fouling out on his three lines, Dan Akroyd blunting his sharpest barbs, Edith Bunker coming up from under in a phone booth, Mike Nichols and Elaine May doing a Jewish-mother phone dialog as Jimmy and Mom (Miz Lillian later said Jimmy was no momma's boy but did not deny she was Jewish). Redd Foxx thanked Jimmy Carter for being president; John Wayne thanked God for America; and Louis Jourdan thanked Dodge for zee Mon-a-co. (In all, twenty-six commercials—lucky this was a people's gala.) Freddie Prinze told some disgusting racist jokes about Puerto Rican pickpockets, then turned serious and in a heart-rendering close-up told how happy he was to be here on this joyous occasion. Ten days later he shot himself through the head. He was twenty-two years old. Suicide was the second greatest cause of death among eighteen- to twenty-five-year-olds in America, so this was not a particularly unusual act. A few days later a thirteen-year-old girl in Glendale, California, despondent over the loss of her TV hero, also shot herself. She was, alas, too young for this year's statistics. (The front page of today's newspaper reads: FREDDIE PRINZE DEATH: See Amusements.)

The Fugitive slept through the early-morning rendition of "Amazing Grace" at the Lincoln Memorial. If it had been Willie Nelson's version, he would have made the extra effort. Instead, he got dressed carefully, made sure he had no conflicting ID, checked his disguise in the mirror, and secreted the room key in the parking lot. They parked the car near the parade route and hiked to a spot outside the Russell Senate Building. He shared an icy perch with a young man who looked the way the Fugitive had looked at the age of twenty: Tim Winslow, from Ohio, a Nader Raider by trade. Together they brooded about the cabinet selections.

"Have you noticed the crowd?" Tim asked.

"How do you mean?"

"Very white and very southern."

Tim was right. The black vote had helped to put Carter in the White House, but you wouldn't know it from the crowd. The press of the people was enormous. Soon limousines could be seen coming up Constitution Avenue and turning onto the Capitol grounds. More limousines than a Mafia funeral. Damn it! He couldn't see much.

The ceremonies started. The sound didn't carry in their direction. They crossed the street and moved to the main gate. Just at the entrance he spotted—blink, blink, yes, it was—Paul Krassner, pioneer in radical satire, for years a one-man underground press. They did their mutual winky-blinkies and bumbled through warm greetings, afraid to embrace. Public embracing, they instinctively felt, was suspicious behavior. Paul's not sure how seriously he should relate to the fact that a giant paw could suddenly appear out of the jungle crowd and carry his friend off to a cold cage in distant Atticaland. So they stood trading stories as if they were passing atomic secrets. In the background, a voice with an increasingly familiar clip kept urging them "to learn together and to laugh together." And they quietly chuckled and listened to the words.

Carter was not a great orator, but at least one felt he had written the speech himself. His book *Why Not the Best?*, also self-written, was one of the best in its genre— a genre admittedly somewhat akin to the How-I-Found-God-and-Lost-Thirty-Pounds writing. He delivered the address as a lecture to a 225,523,000-member Bible class. Pledging the country to battle all the traditional Sunday-morning evils: ignorance, poverty, et al. And, furthermore, pledging to work for the elimination of all nuclear weapons and to keep his feet off the sofa in the Blue Room. Amen. Amen. The cannons went boom! boom! boom! and Paul suggested it was the Pentagon's response to the idea of eliminating nuclear weapons. That cracked the ice and relaxed the tension. They followed the crowd back down Constitution Avenue and took up places for the parade. Jerry Rubin spotted them and darted across the street.

"I just shook hands with Billy Carter!" Jerry exclaimed. "You look great. I wouldn't recognize you in a million years."

"Quiet, Jer. That's what he'll get, if someone else does," whispers a helpful voice.

Soon there was a whole group of them standing on the

curb. A regular protesters' reunion, it was. They began mingling and talking to spectators. Luthor and Sandy Bell, insurance salesman and housewife from Portland, Oregon, were upset that Carter was granting amnesty to draft resisters, but then shrugged and said, "It's time, we guess, to heal the wounds." Everyone was getting pretty high on national unity when up popped a group of farmers from that merry little town of Plains—that fact being proclaimed by bright green-and-white ski caps and buttons. Oversized Munchkins from the end of the yellow-brick road. They were all telling their "we knew Jimmy when" stories when the crowd began to get excited. "He's walking! He's walking!" someone cried out. And, glory be, all of a sudden there he was, not more than thirty feet away. Walking home. People cheered and clapped. The Fugitive clapped, too. "Hands higher," he reminded himself. "See, see, Secret Service men: empty hands." Rosalynn's hair is much redder than on TV and Jimmy's hair seems lighter and thinner. They're holding hands and his coat collar is bent upward. It's smiling Jim, all right! He turns and gives a special greeting, probably to the Plains people, but for a moment the Fugitive thought they had made eye contact. Carried away with the excitement, he gulped and cheered. The dissidents and the farmers joined in cheering the president. For a moment the country looked the way his third-grade teacher had described it. Oh say can you sing. . . .

Carter seemed smaller than on TV. Inevitably famous people did. And frailer. The Fugitive felt nothing but goodwill toward the man, and mouthed the words "Good luck, Cracker!" And the parade moved on down the street; Marine bands, a giant Mylar U.S.A. float, an open limousine of waving mondales, trapeze artists, Samoan oarsmen, and a bevy of baton twirlers baring their brave legs to the cold.

"Did you pray for anything special?" Jerry asked.

"Yeah, I asked him not to flush the toilet while we were taking a shower."

The group was away from the parade route now and could embrace, talk freely of days gone by and of tomorrows to come. Ah, tomorrow! Sweet mystery of life's anticipation. Angel and he returned to the room, grabbed a night's sleep, rubbed out the prints, flushed unneeded papers, packed their bags, and sneaked out of town as quietly as they had entered. "Giddap, you gas-guzzling Godzilla. Take us back to the heartland."

The all-news radio station held strong all across Virginia: Carter grants amnesty. Mondale off to Europe. And in the rest of the country: A father in New Jersey shot his kid for smoking grass. A kid in Albany, Georgia, shot his father for not letting him use the car. And in Gadsden, Alabama, police were holding a man on $100,000 bail for running down the street waving a gun, screaming he was on his way to Washington to kill the president. So it's square dancing time in the ice age tonight. Swing a little to the left, swing a little to the right.

Fourteen Semitough Steps Carter Could Take (Any Ten of which Will Guarantee Him a Year's Free Vacation Underground)
1. Keep U.S. troops out of war
2. Reduce military presence completely in Korea and partially in Europe
3. Eliminate arms sales to countries like Iran and Chile
4. Outlaw the production and sale of torture devices
5. End the boycott of Cuba
6. Honor American repatriation commitments made to Vietnam
7. Stop CIA-sponsored covert actions
8. Bring the unemployment rate under four percent by investing $100 billion in inner-city construction
9. Use the army for rural new town construction or similar projects overseas
10. Steer the economy away from defense and space programs into housing and new forms of decentralized energy production
11. Create a consumer protection agency with Nader as head
12. Standardize welfare payments and offer incentives for relocation to rural areas
13. Put into effect a national health program
14. Nationalize the railroads and utility companies

July 1977

Television's God Show

I'M CROSSING America, tuning in on the airwave evangelists. In many parts of this great country, religious broadcasting seems to be about all a car radio can pick up. So as I head on down the highway, I'm getting The Word from my ever-faithful dashboard.

Across the desolate Texas Panhandle, I latch on to a half-hour sermon blasting Darwinism. The preacher concludes by admonishing, "If you want to believe your great aunt was a crocodile, that's your business, but I'd rather think we were created in God's image."

In Oklahoma, I learn that Jesus was "perfectly, psychically, and physically sound." That "He never had a cold in His life but took our suffering when He went up on the cross. He took our headaches, our cancer, our arthritis, our lumbago, just for us. Thank you, Jesus."

In Kansas, I pick up someone called the Cowboy Preacher: "I don't understand all the Bible, but I believe it. You don't understand why a black cow eats green grass and gives milk that churns into yellow butter, but you'd be a fool not to believe it."

In Missouri, one minister works his radio congregation to a climactic plateau with pleas to remember the sick and dying in our local hospitals. Then he boldly plugs a local florist. Sister Hattie has a series of one-minute promos and guarantees "to restore your faith and ease your grief."

On a nice billboard outside of St. Louis: "We Have the Answer—Put Christ Back in Christmas—Buy a Toyota."

Outside of Florence, South Carolina, the tooth-pulling capital of the world, a Sunday morning evangelist does fifteen minutes on venereal disease, ending with a call to close down all the VD clinics. Why? Because easy treatment encourages promiscuity, which is worse than syphilis! Intermixed with all this weirdness are songs about Jesus. Remember when He used to be just a carpenter? Today, He's a railroad man or an astronaut circling the globe. He's a truck driver "hauling souls from Tennessee," and now, with the arrival of spring, "a pitcher throwing curve balls to Satan." He'll always be (till the novelty wears off) "Breaker Number One." If you guessed we're heading somewhere down the Hallelujah Highway, you got it. But first, a pit stop for some fact talk about radio and religion.

I don't care what the Gallup poll says, I'm proud to be a heretic. Evangelists, be they Carters, Colsons, or Cleavers, Pat Boones or Reverend Moons, are all fast-talking peddlers out to cash in on poor folks' sorrows. The morality they preach is so abstract on the one hand (*Let's hear it for those starving Africans!*), so self-centered on the other (*Please, Lord, take away my hemorrhoids!*) that it makes a joke out of any real sense of community. By hiding behind religion, evangelists are free to propagandize for the most reactionary ideas—tax-free. They've managed to corral a huge section of the media, and have, for a few years now, been preparing their followers to move on the political level.

Mark Muska of the National Religious Broadcasters (based in Morristown, New Jersey) assures me there are more than 1,400 radio stations broadcasting eight or more hours per week of religious programs. About half of these run fully 50 percent "religion-inspired" shows. *Time* reports there are 2,000 broadcast preachers reaching 114 million radio listeners. *Christianity Today* states that "one station a week declares for Jesus," a rate that, if allowed to go unchecked, would gobble up all the remaining air space in five years.

Only one effort has been attempted to slow this trend. Three years ago, Lorenzo Milam, who owned a small progressive country and western FM station in Los Gatos, California, and Jeremy Lansman, a broadcast consultant, took up the challenge. In the late forties, the FCC, under Frieda Hennock, made a ruling that frequencies on the limited FM band between 88 and 92 cycles be reserved for use by noncommercial stations who address themselves to the "interests of the public." Milam and Lansman filed a petition, claiming that when a church becomes the licensee, only a narrow section of the public is represented. They point to the Moody Bible Institute out of Chicago as a particular purveyor of one-sided material. Furthermore, local churches in such places as Charleston and Chattanooga, snatching up all free slots on the dial, have virtually imposed a monopoly of thought on FM radio listeners in their areas. Pointing to the high advertising revenues the stations were pulling in, the petition questioned whether or not these stations were strictly "noncommercial" in the sense the FCC meant them to be. The petition was mildly worded, refrained from any direct challenge to any specific licensee, and merely asked that the FCC screen future religious broadcasting applicants more closely to see if they meet Fairness Doctrine requirements.

A fury not seen since the outlawing of school prayer arose from the multitude. I tracked down Jeremy Lansman, now living in Dallas, for his version. "You just couldn't believe what happened. The NRB [National Religious Broadcasters] sounded the alarm. Preachers took to the pulpit. They said Madalyn Murray O'Hair, the devil incarnate for these folks, sponsored the petition and that we were out to get all religious programs off the air. The response was overwhelming. The FCC received more than six million letters. A year after the agency had ruled *against* the petition, letters were still pouring in at the rate of 20,000 per week. It was the largest amount of mail received by the government on any issue—twice the volume pro and con the Vietnam War."

I asked Lansman why they didn't argue on separation-of-church-and-state grounds. "Nobody cares. Once the FCC grants a license, it doesn't monitor a station unless there are a lot of complaints, and nobody but us seemed to be complaining." If it was unconstitutional to have a one-minute prayer in schools, what made federally licensed radio stations, obviously violating the Fairness Doctrine, and in apparent violation of tax-exemption status (by carrying on political lobbying and selling ad space), any different? I called the ACLU to test the validity of the argument. They said I had a good case but, given the makeup of the present Supreme Court, such a legal battle was fruitless.

Back on the Hallelujah Highway, we're traveling west to east along the Bible Belt. We are leaving behind the local Holy Rollers, the tent preachers, the fly-by-night 10,000-watt hackers. We're headed for the big-time gospel. Our destination is Virginia Beach, where the talk is of global networks, $20-million budgets, television satellites, and "conquering the world for Christ."

Satellites? That's right. No longer do missionaries have to fear the dangers of "darkest Africa." God's word is, as of April '77, being beamed by earth satellite 'round the world, straight from little ol' Virginia Beach.

To find out just how such a communication blitzkrieg happened—and how I got interested in it in the first place—we have to go back to the fall of '76, just before the elections. Buried away in some three-channel outpost in the heartland, I was letting my brain simmer on a medium yield of prime-time boob tube. It was getting in shape to take in an hour-long "Pray for America" special produced by the Christian Broadcasting Network. The idea was to raise capital to erect an earth satellite station in Virginia Beach. This was not the first time Virginia Beach had been called upon to bring the word of God to the natives. It was here that the first English settlement was established in 1607, and everyone remembers what success *those* Bible-toters had in saving Indians!

The show was set up much like a star-studded variety funfest, complete with headliners, songs, confessions, prayers, and fund appeals paced and packaged much like any other variety special. The general theme was that we are all getting pulled down by the devil, so let's hear it for God and the Good Guys (us Americans). Johnny Cash sang us a stirring rendition of "The Ragged Old Flag." You remember old Johnny; he does those straight-from-the-heart commercials for STP. Then there was Pat Boone and his vestal virgin daughter, just back from their hard-hitting antiacne crusade (or was it antiabortion?). This time they were profamily. Janet Lynn, Tom Landry, and other "winners" talked about the good Christian life. There were tapes of the two really big campaigners that fall, Jerry and Jimmy, discussing how often they pray and how good it feels. (I had a terrific fantasy of redoing the entire show, substituting another four-letter word for "pray.") Later, I discovered Ford's segment was filmed by a navy communications crew. I mention this to those who still believe we have a church-state division.

To show a little ecumenism, Yitzak Rabin, then prime minister of Israel, was given a guest spot. Unfortunately, Yitzak didn't pray hard enough; a few days later he got embroiled in Israel's biggest political scandal and had to resign. In between it all were the heavy dealers on the Christ circuit, people like Chuck (soon-to-be-a-major-motion-picture) Colson, whom we all know, forgive, and love; Dave Wilkerson, founder of Teen Challenge and inventor of the hip approach to heavenly worship; Billy Graham, who was bouncing back nicely after losing points as Nixon's court bishop, that is, if you overlook $23 million that seems to have vanished from his heavenly hope chest; hard-hitting evangelist Rex Humbard; and Bill Bright, head of Campus Crusade for Christ, a group out to raise a billion dollars in the next four years to saturate the earth with gospel preachers. There wasn't a penny-ante player in the group.

You just had to appreciate the back room arm-twisting and baloney-baiting that went on to get those evangelical all-stars together. Interspersed with the religious mumbo-jumbo, the real heavyweights like Bright and Humbard banged home some of the essentials of their "apolitical" movement. You've heard the litany before: America's in really bad shape. The schools (since no one can pray) are breeding grounds for sin because of the drug and smut peddlers. Everywhere the family is under attack. Television comedies all have to be rewritten. Sex magazines should be outlawed. Day-care centers, termed "warehouses for unwanted children," have to be abolished. Abortion is "legalized murder." Divorce has become too easy and women have been made to feel guilty about being housewives. Israel must be protected at all costs or civilization will crumble. Somehow we have to make our views known to the "Judases" at the *Washington Post* and the *New York Times*. Elections won't change all this (in other words, we're building a political machine that won't be ready for a few years), so let's roll up our sleeves, get down on our knees, and pray.

The whole shootin' match was held together by the founder of the Christian Broadcasting Network, Reverend G. M. (Pat) Robertson, presently the brightest television star in God's heaven.

When the hour ended I was sure I had just witnessed the counterrevolution to the sixties. They, like us, were armed with a cultural-political program and knew how to mix the two effectively. They had mastered television and modern organizing techniques. *Unlike* us, they had millions of dollars behind them. They had bulldozed the presidential candidates into endorsing them, and had wrapped themselves in the tax-free flag of religion. Two hundred and twenty-eight stations carried the CBN special; that's fifty more than carry *Mork and Mindy*. Good saturation.

Pat Robertson is the son of Virginia's late senator, A. Willis Robertson. His life story can be read in the best-seller (it's *de rigueur* to term all Christian books best-sellers) *Shout It from the Housetops*. It's the story of how perseverance and faith in the Lord moved mountains and checkbooks to make CBN a reality. Pretty standard material. One unusual episode in *SIFTH* is the chapter devoted to a rambling account of how Pat was hoodwinked by a woman posing as the illegitimate daughter of H. L. Hunt. She had offered Pat part of her supposed inheritance of $100 million. He spent a great deal of time and effort on her, only to find out she was an imposter. Pat's learned his lesson since: Don't be such an eager beaver; lay back and let the checks roll in.

CBN started in 1959, when Pat came back to Portsmouth, Virginia, and bought a defunct UHF television station, WYAH-TV. Hustling local businessmen (his father's connections made the task much easier than the biography lets on), he grabbed a local radio station and then rounded up licenses and equipment for both. During one TV show a caller, instead of pledging money, asked Pat to pray for him personally. This was a TV first; it caught on like the dickens. It led eventually to *The 700 Club*, Pat's daily one-hour television-radio talk show.

From these humble beginnings grew an empire that today owns four TV and six FM radio stations. In addition, chalk up a few dozen radio stations and transmitters around the world. CBN's Costa Rican transmitter, at a million watts AM, is said to be the most powerful in the Western Hemisphere. (CBN is currently planning an Israeli station.) In addition to CBN's own communications empire, over 130 radio affiliates broadcast *The 700 Club*, and it is currently shown on 200 TV stations throughout the United States. The show can also be seen in 22 foreign countries.

CBN claims that over half a billion people are reached by its proselytizing. This, like many CBN figures, is inflated, misleading, and typical high-pressure sales hype, but it's beyond dispute that CBN is big and getting bigger. To quote humble Pat: "God had told me to claim the world." Most stations he picks up from conglomerates who want to dump a loser for tax benefits, but some he buys outright. Pat acquired the Bogotà station from "a petty bandito with slicked-down hair and a pencil-thin mustache. . . . It was obvious this little Colombian had his eye on the rich American's dollars."

Pat's a pretty open guy who doesn't mask his feelings about foreigners.

The future Israeli station is important because Pat believes the future of CBN is interwoven into the destiny of Israel. He's interviewed several of Israel's big guns (Eban, Peres, and Rabin) on his show, and considers June 5, 1967 the most significant fulfillment of Bible prophecy to occur in this generation. It was on that day that Jerusalem was captured by Israeli forces, as forecasted by Christ in Luke 21:24. Jews are okay in CBN's book, but those Jews who declare for Christ are even better. "Jesus is at the center of Judaism," I was told, which will certainly be news to all of my relatives.

To keep historical continuity going, ground breaking for the high-powered global production center took place nine years to the day after the beginning of the Six-Day War. The 142-acre Virginia Beach site with its satellite control facility was, we are told, the idea of none other than the Big Anchorman Himself. But let Pat tell it: "One day last August in the Grand Hotel across from Disneyland, as I bowed my head to say grace over a lunch of cantaloupe and cottage cheese, the Lord started speaking to me." The Lord's message was, "Buy, baby, buy." Pat did.

Pat often talks to God. God often talks back. In CBN literature and on *The 700 Club*, He's invariably depicted as a super-smart stockbroker always ready to whisper a hot tip in your ear, if only you pray hard enough and don't forget to slip Pat his commission. Image-wise, God's come a long way from the vengeful show-off portrayed in the Old Testament. With CBN handling His media campaign, there can be no question that He is an all-right guy.

We arrive at the studio early. The big multimillion-dollar complex is as yet unoccupied, and the show comes from WYAH-TV headquarters. It's exciting, though; it reminds me of the time my father took me to my first broadcast of the *Kate Smith Hour*. We've ordered tickets just like the other folks, and I've already seen the show so many times, nothing's going to throw me. We're led into the staff chapel for a brief intro and a quickie prayer fix.

Our guide is Tom Wright. Crew-cut, fiftyish, he dresses like Holden Caulfield's dorm master. A little stiff, but again, an all-right guy. "The dome's filled with symbols. See those three flames and the cannons, the 666? That's the Antichrist. God's favorite number is seven; that's why there will be seven pillars on the new building." (Seagram's turned the seven mystery into profit years ago.) "We want you to notice the cross. It's important. You won't see Jesus on any CBN cross. We don't like to think of Him as defeated. To us, He's a winner." (Well, okay, now we're talking about an *American* God.) "A rock of inner strength, tall as a tree, that's our Jesus, a born winner."

Tom shows us studios and control rooms. There are a lot of oohs and aahs from folks who've never been on the sending end of TV. They're right; it *is* all magic. CBN not only produces *The 700 Club*, but a host of other religious shows for its own stations and affiliates. It claims, by the way, to be the fourth largest network in the United States. Aside from running religious programs, CBN stations load up on "wholesome family fare." Ada Fuller, the network's censor, says, "We don't show secular shows with excessive violence or sex, or that talk about gambling, drugs, or the occult." *Bewitched* got rejected because, even though it was humorous, it dealt with the supernatural. Ms. Fuller rejected an old Groucho Marx show because it included a yoga demonstration.

Tom tells us *The 700 Club* got its name from the first seven hundred donors who shelled out the dough to get the show off the ground. Fund-raising occupies a good portion of his rap, and we're given a dozen or so pamphlets on the subject. My favorite is titled *Eleven Things to Remember If You Plan to Remember Us in Your Will*. In the lobby we're shown a mural depicting Christ as king (a winner at last), done in sand and jewelry donated by the faithful. Words simply cannot describe it.

Next we are taken upstairs to see the "heartbeat of this living church." This is the twenty-four-hour-a-day central receiving center for the heal-by-phone program. It's the guts of the CBN ministry. Three dozen cubicles bank the walls. Each has a phone and a healer-in-training. The procedure goes something like this: People call in from around the country and kvetch. They kvetch about everything from losing their faith to losing their dogs. They kvetch about chills and they kvetch about cancer. Bladders, kidneys, dim vision, car payments, Satan's grip . . . you name it. Legionnaires' Disease is suspected in Iowa. There's a high blood pressure case in West Virginia. The aides have manuals to help them quickly find the correct biblical quote to go with the ailment and check pads to code the problem and get the caller's address for the all-important future mail solicitations. Each aide gets a chance to try out his healing rap; the room's abuzz with cries of "Hear me, oh sister" and "Hallelujah." Some prefer the old hellfire and brimstone delivery. Arms wave as aides urge callers to grab the phone with both hands as hard as possible, get down on their knees and cast forth the devil from their bodies. Others prefer soft-spoken encouragement: "Say, together we can lick this thing."

The center of the room looks like the flight deck of *Star Trek*'s *Enterprise*. The senior staff kneels in a circle, holding hands, heads bowed in prayer. In the middle, a railing surrounds the same stylized, Christless CBN cross we saw downstairs. The lighting is very theatrical. "One hour of prayer a day is mandatory," says Tom, "but most people get in two or three." The volume of calls is staggering. In seventy-five telephone counseling centers, nearly seven thousand volunteers answer approximately one million calls a year.

Everyone talks of success, because here in the telephone healing command center is the proof that God is alive and living in Virginia Beach. "Sometimes the power of God is so strong that it would actually knock the people back from the phone." (This is Pat writing in *SIFTH*.) Cancer, arthritis, paralysis, babies with twisted feet all fall by the wind. Sometimes Pat (the master healer, natch) will do a little healing on the show. Once the blind piano player, Harry Van Deventer, asked, "Will you pray for me?" Pat did. Harry opened his eyes and shouted, "I can see!"

"Then," according to Pat, "God gave him a song; he sat down and spontaneously played 'The Miracle Worker!'" Such stuff is standard fare around *The 700 Club*. No one bats an eyelash as accounts of the most miraculous deeds are reeled off like stock market quotes. Faith healing? Probably one out of one hundred, if that many, are unexplained cases. Most are temporary remissions with subsequent relapses. Remember, the scorekeepers are the Lord's and their pencils write nothing but pluses. A magician named The Amazing Randi has for years offered $10,000 for a single case of faith healing that can be independently verified. He's still got his money.

At last our group (about thirty-five) is ushered into *The 700 Club* studio, where we're given instructions and shown how to applaud. The set is modeled after Johnny Carson's *Tonight Show* set. A bandstand lies to the left. Center stage is a modern desk, with easy chairs for guests. To the right, a half-dozen banks of phones are manned by counselors. Pat plays Johnny. Our star is a boyish forty-seven, modeled on the old JFK look. Pat has huge hands and a murderer's thumb. When he orates, he holds his right hand straight out, like he's ready to palm a basketball—or a globe. Ed McMahon is played by a tall, debonair black named Ben Kinchlow. Set decorations show maps diagraming the CBN network, skylines of cities . . . everything pretty low-key. The band strikes up the intro; cameras zoom in on placards; and "Heeeeere's Pat!"

First, a few fan letters. "We're hearing from a guy in Bridgeport, Connecticut. When ninety percent of his buddies got killed on Pork Chop Hill he promised to give his life to Christ." Pat can relate to this; he did time in Korea—also in Connecticut, for that matter, when he was a student at Yale.

When you see Pat at home, a call-in number flashes across the screen, and while the lines heat up he and Ben fill in with happy talk. Today Pat tells Ben the world is freezing, but we don't have to worry because God made it so the water gets lighter when it freezes so the fish can live. Just another one of the great miracles brought to you by the same benefactor who gave us the Great Flood and bone cancer. Thank you, Lord. "God is a person. He's alive! In this room. I can *feel* Him. I can *see* Him!" This really stirs the audience. God's a regular on *The 700 Club*.

Next, there's a little song from opera singer Derek DeCambra, a thin, serious-looking pallbearer type. He baritones, "There's something about that name Jesus." I wonder if we're supposed to applaud hymns? *We are!* Derek finishes and joins Pat for a little chitchat. Everyone has to tell their how-I-found-Jesus-and-was-born-again story. Most are pretty boring, having already been delivered a few hundred times. Derek's is rather good, though. He was performing with Jerome Hines in an opera with a religious theme. "At one point in the drama I had to lift the Holy Chalice, when all of a sudden I was motionless. *I'm not a famous singer*, I thought. In His eyes, I'm a miserable, horrible sinner. I just couldn't drink the Blood of the Lamb." (Try it with a little vodka, Derek.) Derek says he began crying and trembling and spontaneously cried out, "Use me, oh God! *Use me!*" There are lots of "*Praise the Lords!*" and applause from the studio audience.

It's time now to see what calls are coming in. Ben ambles up to the phones and looks for some good ones. "We've got someone from Ohio with a pain in the face that just went away. Over here we have a friend in Alabama with stiff joints. And here a husband in Oregon whose wife left home." Ben's not too excited. He's looking for one of the biggies—maybe a leukemia or an open-heart surgery. Folks who watch the show a lot wait for a suicide call. That's a real showstopper. Better than *General Hospital*. Today's crop is run-of-the-mill, though. No suicides today. No, I'm beating my child and can't stop. Ben senses it and returns to the stage.

It's time for our next guest, who's billed as China's

Singing Ambassador. She does a number with a whole lot of *Sevens* and *Jesuses* in it (hands clasped, near bosom-high), then joins Pat for happy talk. There's some question about her nationality, as she's from the Philippines. *The 700 Club* is really popular in the Far East, she informs us. (Read South Korea, Taiwan, and the Philippines for the Far East. The show probably doesn't play Phnom Penh.) She starts to tell her born-again story. In the middle she relates a fairy tale about a big bad wolf who's out to get someone on her way to grandmother's. She's telling the fable as if it's new to the audience. Everybody's moved by her Oriental naiveté. Anyway, she gets lost giving testimony, lapses back into a heavy accent and says, "My husband, he da boss. God talk through him, he da boss." Everyone thinks this is terrific and she gets the biggest hand.

We're running out of time now. One camera swings around to pan the audience. The band is playing the show's theme song. Ben smiles. Pat waves. The phones go on ringing. I think it's assumed that God has left now, but that He'll be back tomorrow. Same time, same station. That is if His ratings hold.

June 1979

The Town Too High to Die

"WHEN YOU'RE a fugitive the highway's your home,"
sings the cowboy on the radio. Roaming from town to
town, wishing you could settle down. Those dreams are
pretty strong at times. No different from everyone else's
desires, though. a nice out-of-the-way place in the
country, fresh air, no traffic, cheap living, and good
people. Above all, good people. Folks you could trust.
Who wouldn't turn you in no matter how high the price
on your head. I think I know a place. It's way out west,
high in the mountains, where it should be. It's got a wild
past and a wild future ahead. Folks up there have done
some struggling over long hours and the work they've put
in may give us down here in the valley some ideas on the
possibilities of different ways to live a good life. One
thing I know for sure, it's one of the few places I could
say my name and spend as much time as I damn well
please. It warms a hunted man's heart just to know the
place exists.

Up there in the mountains, between Albuquerque and
Santa Fe, there's a new town agrowing. A new vision, if
you please. It's a place they call Madrid.* Central New
Mexico is surrounded by the legends of the Old West.

*Madrid is pronounced with a southern drawl (Maá-drid) rather than
like the city in Spain.

South of Madrid lies Lincoln County, sight of the bloody wars in which Billy the Kid made his name. Pat Garrett rode through these hills tracking the young tough. To the west lay the lands of the Apache, where Chief Nana and Cochise led their braves in the staunchest resistance to the white man's intrusion. To the north, the end of the great Santa Fe Trail and Rayado, founded by the renowned Christopher "Kit" Carson, and Cimarron, home of the Colfax County wars. To the east, Lama Parda, at one time called the "Sodom of the West" so famous were its gambling dens and whorehouses. And Las Vegas, where it was said that in the 1870s a bandit a week was hung from the windmill in the center of town. Through these mountains came the likes of Jigaboo Jones, Pegleg Dick, Scarface George, and Splitnose Mike, brawling, slugging down their Taos Lightning, robbing payroll trains, and outrunning the posse. Sometimes.

These hills were boom country. Treasures of the mountains for those with enough ambition, guts, and good fortune. A thousand and a half years of mining history buried in its rockslides. From pueblo-dwelling Indians scraping the earth for turquoise, to the present, where fancy Cal Tech professors prowl the hills with Geiger counters searching for untapped uranium. It was here, over three hundred years ago, the Spanish, up from Mexico, came in search of El Dorado, their city of gold. They didn't find much, but gold there was all right—and silver and copper and tin and lead and potash and mica and coal. There is no mountain in New Mexico not rich in minerals, and no area is richer than these mountains. By the middle of the nineteenth century the rush was on. Gold was discovered in Golden and Dolores. Silver in Cerrillos. And boomtowns sprung up overnight. Bonanza, Carbonateville, San Padro, and Madrid. Madrid didn't yield much gold. It may still be up there, say the old-timers. "You need tons and tons of water to mine gold and Madrid never had much of that," one explained. What Madrid did have, however, was coal; in fact it was one of the few places in the world where hard and soft coal could be mined simultaneously. And close to the surface too. Easy pickings.

Coal was mined successfully off and on for eighty years in Madrid. By 1928 it was lugging more coal than almost anyplace in the West. Three thousand miners lived in drab, wooden shacks, stacked in neat rows along the slopes of the hills. Mostly they worked the winter so they could melt the snow for drinking water. Work and living conditions were wretched. They got more black lung than money for their pains. When the thirties entered, Wobblies and Communists worked these hill towns trying to organize the miners. Violent battles erupted between workers and hired company guards. The Ludlow Massacre on the Colorado border and the Gallup Coal Strike to the west were just two of the better-known clashes. In Madrid there was constant agitation and fierce resistance. In addition there were fires that would spread rapidly through the dry coal-rich fields, igniting the wooden houses like kindling. Eventually the mine owners closed down most of the production. It wasn't just the strikes and fires. The diesel was replacing the steam engine. Americans were starting to heat their homes with oil, and overnight huge natural gas deposits in the southwest part of the state were discovered, rendering mining towns like Madrid relics of the past. Bustling communities became ghost towns. Except for a brief respite during World War II, when the mine was reactivated to supply the secret city of Los Alamos, Madrid lay dormant. Tumbleweed blew through the deserted houses. Paint peeled from the boards. Porches sagged and roofs collapsed. Old Santa Fe steam engine 874 rusted to its tracks beside a pile of unhauled coal. A few die-hards stayed on, running a beat-up gas pump, a cantina, and a mine museum. The town with all its ghosts, huddled against the windswept mountains, black as the soot on a coal miner's back. Madrid huddled and waited . . . till now.

For most of its active life the town was owned by the Albuquerque and Cerrillos Mining Company, which underwent several changes in name and management through the years. In 1938 Oscar Huber was given supervisory control of the area and ten years later he bought the land outright. After failing at an attempt to reactivate the mine in the early fifties, Oscar died and ownership passed to his son, Joe Huber. Joe tried to sell the whole town, lock, stock and barrel several times. In 1964 Billie Sol Estes tried to buy the place but negotiations floundered when Billie was hauled off to prison. In 1973 Joe announced he had sold it to a big California land broker but in August that deal also fell through. Joe really wanted to sell off the 360 acres in house lots. He was raised in Madrid and wanted to preserve its picturesque character rather than see it turned into some lackluster land development. He wanted to sell to people who would fix up the place but respect its historic roots. The problem was New Mexican law prohibited subdivision in small units. A hustling real estate agent plowed through dusty old land survey charts up in Santa Fe and found that for a brief spell Madrid had been an official town named Kellyville and had, in fact, already been subdivided. The way was opened, and in February 1974, Joe Huber put the 160 lots, each with a sort-of house on it, up for sale.

By then there were already fifty or so hearty souls who had been semirenting, semisquatting on the property. Joe had an affinity for these people. They and he shared the kind of faith that moved mountains, so to speak. He offered them first pick of the lots. Prices were arranged so even the poorest could afford to buy in. Some as low as fifty dollars down and fifty dollars a month. For two thousand dollars paid over two years, former drop-out anarchists who had sought refuge in these rough mountains were turned into bonafide homeowners. The original dwellers, learning of the sale, ran to call kindred spirits in Albuquerque and around the country. In two weeks all the lots were sold. Joe donated the ballfield, the tennis courts, the church, and the waterworks. He kept control of the museum, the Mineshaft Tavern, and mining rights—the last, a common and anxiety-producing aspect of most Southwest land deals.

Many of the lots were snapped up by speculators and

Albuquerque families who wanted a weekend retreat (at three to four times the original two thousand dollars) but the majority were taken by folks who were dedicated to settling the place on a year-round permanent basis. One of the originals, Carol, put it this way: "When the place went up for sale, we ran around like chickens without heads. No one felt we could take on the responsibility. I don't think there were more than three or four of us over twenty-five. The past three years have been tough but almost everyone's stuck it out." The original settlers wanted to establish a new town with values, principles, and structures different from where they had come from. Exactly what and how was not clear . . . but different anyway. "We had all gone through the rat race we hated with a passion—bureaucracies, cops, courts, bosses," said one of the founders. "In fact, no one attending that first meeting even favored making it a town." What they did do was form a landowners association, with automatic membership for all. "That was the condition Mr. Huber laid down to all of us," explained the association's head, Diane Johnson. "Next we drew up a governing document—The Covenants. Mainly it prohibits construction not in character with the place, things like condominiums and other structures. It also spells out some committees, such as water, sewage, and legal. The barest elements of government. Mostly we make decisions at four town-hall meetings held throughout the year."

Bureaucratic control is pictured as the great internal evil. A former government worker now on the water committee put it this way: "If there's one thing everyone has in common it's hatred of power trips. We're probably overparanoid whenever the subject of rules or leaders comes up. Many of us worked for the government in the Peace Corps or poverty program and we saw bureaucracy kill even the most elementary form of initiative." That was in 1973.

Today the town is far from a ghost town. All around you can hear the sound of hammers and saws. Amid the rows of dilapidated shacks, people have restored and

renovated nearly one hundred dwellings. Souls like Fred
Blum, who fled Philadelphia and a high-paying job as a
systems-analysis consultant to pioneer in Madrid. Fred's
sparkling robin's egg blue house, with it's hardwood
floors, new roof and porch and handmade furniture is the
shape of things to come. Fred's away, but a neighbor tells
me Fred did most of the work himself and probably got it
all, house, land, and renovations for five thousand
dollars. It's way more than livable. Some have done it for
much less. George, an ex-school teacher from New York
City, came out here ten months ago and landed a good
deal. "I got a house and fixed it all up for under three
thousand bucks. I only pay twelve dollars a year in taxes.
I won't make two thousand dollars a year teaching at our
school, and even with food stamps that's not a lot of
money." Even so, George insists he'd never go back to
New York. "The survival problems, getting water up to
the house, keeping warm in the winter are tough but it's a
good life, worth a little sacrifice." Come hell or no water,
George echoes the determination of the nearly two
hundred residents to stick it out.

Winter has come to the hills of Madrid. It's six
thousand feet high up here. There's a thin cover of snow
on the ground. Looking out over the hills you can see the
restored houses, their new green or red roofs sparkling in
the bright sun. The morning fires have already been
struck. The sweet smell of piñon burning in the wood
stoves lingers in the crystal-clear air. The sound of a
triangle ringing summons the children to school. Knots of
laughing children are seen everywhere. Tough, bright-
eyed kids with long hair, jeans, and work boots. Just the
type of kids you'd expect of a rough mountain camp
where the average citizen hides the fact that he or she has
a master's degree tucked away in the trunk. The Children's Workshop is located in the old church on the hill.
It has two full-time teachers like George and each parent
works as an aide once a week. In addition they pay
seventeen dollars a month tuition for each of thirty-two
kids attending school. It's accredited, nonprofit, and

takes children up to twelve. Teenagers are bused into Santa Fe and one just began going to the university down in Albuquerque.

Down the valley, on Main Street, we find the nerve center of the town. To the left, a Volkswagen repair shop with a mechanic so good and cheap that almost everyone in town drives an old Volks bus. To the right, behind a clothing store (where the woman announced a private sale because of my friendly face), lies the Madrid Fire Department. The chief's Ed Boniface, who took over from Linda Sneerley. (All positions such as these are filled by volunteers, if more than one person volunteers, votes are taken at the town meetings.) There's a fire truck parked in the garage, donated by the Forest Service. Like many of the town institutions the fire department was formed out of crisis. Explains the chief, "Last spring we had a bad fire. Five or six houses went up like matchsticks. Jack Olsen, the blacksmith, was killed. It was the driest part of the year, the well was pumping less than two or three gallons a minute. We were damn lucky the whole town didn't go up." For that crisis the community needed bailing out by the National Guard. Now they've fixed up the old railroad tank to hold an emergency supply of water. Thanks to that and a series of drills and instructions by a team of rangers, all subsequent fires have been nipped in the bud. The blacksmith's death has been the only one so far in the town's new history. On the other hand, eighteen births have been recorded. A girl named Morning Star, born to the McQuiston family, was the first child to be born in Madrid in more than twenty years. It was an event the whole town celebrated. Children are real important to the town and all around you can see hand-painted flowery signs saying "Drive Slow—We Love Our Children." There's an abundancy of swings and slides and most stores sell penny candy and small toys. Kids pester and often get freebees, reminiscent of those familiar scenes in the Western movies with the kindly storekeeper. Aside from one commune—the Dobie Ducks—a few bachelors, and some women sharing house, almost all the homes are occupied by traditional nuclear families. There're a lot of pregnant women to be seen about. And kids everywhere. Even in the town saloon.

The Mineshaft Tavern, like every store in town, has something of everything. In addition to an Olympic-sized drinking bar catering to the needs of thirsty townfolk and travelers, it features better-than-average New Mexican food, a large fireplace, and the only color TV set in town. There are two pool tables discreetly tucked in a back room and something called the Haunted Mineshaft, a spook house for kids, off to one corner. More than a few of the drinkers in their straggly beards, cowboy boots and hats look like they might have fit in during any period of the town's wild and woolly past. A sign over the bar reminds patrons that possession of firearms in a tavern is a fourth-degree felony. There's a bandstand along the right wall, and four nights a week there's live music and dancing. Charlie, a local drummer, informs me that the town has a disproportionate number of first-rate musicians. Groups like the Ramblers doing country and Night Flyer playing reggae rock make Madrid their base as they bop from gig to gig throughout the Southwest. Last summer there were free jazz concerts given every Sunday down the road in the ball field.

The ball field hosts one of the best-loved institutions, the town softball league, and like everything else in Madrid it has its own personal history. Back in the thirties, the Chicago Black Sox ruled the major leagues with such power that the only financial future the players could envision was to join together with some local gamblers and start fixing the scores of the games. When they were caught, the baseball world exploded in a rage. It was the country's worst sports scandal. A half-dozen or so players changed their names and disappeared into the West. All of a sudden this little-known mining town in the New Mexican mountains was the powerhouse of the formidable Texas League. Most folks put two and two together. No one minded then and no one would today. "We still have our outlaw element," claimed a scruffy-looking gent. "I'm not saying who or what but let's say much of what is illegal out there is legal up here." Later Mel Johnson told me, "We're all fugitives trying to get away from something. Most people have monikers like Bullfrog or Domingo or Rocky Mountain. If you've got a name, it's generally a first name or it's made up. People tend to talk about the future more than the past. We already know everyone's antigovernment. We don't like America's wars, its attitude towards its own land and people and we fled the great money grab."

Farther down Main Street you pass a row of shops catering to the tourist trade. Ceramics, paintings, and antiques. La Modista, which manufactures modern garments with a Southwest desert flavor, ships to more than twenty stores throughout the country. Most residents see this type of enterprise as the future of Madrid. "Our future lies with artists, craftspeople, and writers. People that can make something and sell it someplace else," says one of the shopowners. Tourism, although important to the town, is not that important. In fact, in the past few years, because of the recession and gas shortage, fewer and fewer tourists make their way to Madrid. But tourists come and are treated hospitably. "Things can get out of hand," mentions one townie. "A group of tourists came through town last year and one went into my house (the people are proud they never lock their doors). Next thing I knew she was holding my frying pan in her hand and asking me the price. Can you beat that! They thought the whole town was an antique and everything was for sale."

In the center of town is the entrance to the Mine Museum, where for a dollar Johnny Ochoa, the oldest resident and chief storyteller of Madrid, will guide you around the abandoned mineworks. Farther down there's the general store run by Vickie Van Deusen from Connecticut. It also serves as a post office, town meeting hall, and health clinic. A mobile rural medical team comes by every Thursday. One can't say it's a big profit maker. In fact, today it's closed and Vicky's off in Albuquerque trying to beg up a loan to keep the place going until summer when business picks up. There's a used clothing depot and a place called the Madrid Artists and Craftspersons Co-op. Some goats are tied up in front of another crafts shop. Cats and dogs lie in the street.

"People have tried all sorts of businesses. Independent capitalism, like a carpet store, down to all types of cooperatives you can think of," explain Mel and Diane Johnson, who own La Modista, the town's most commercially successful business. "Naturally we all favor the development of cooperatives, and there's more shared living here than probably anywhere else in America, but some of us wanted to open our own stores. Now we have a policy of trying to support our local shops. It's hard though. . . . We're all living on marginal incomes, probably seventy-five percent are getting some form of assistance. Mostly we find it's cheaper to buy food and gas from the big outlets in Santa Fe. . . . You know, a couple of dollars' difference is important when you're poor."

None of the people living here, not even the merchants, are what you'd call your money-grubbing types. Not for forty years has anyone moved to Madrid to make money. One resident put it this way: "On the one hand there's the temptation to sell out at a good profit because the land values have tripled since we came here, and on the other hand there's the rough life, hauling water and wood. Putting in time digging wells or septic tanks with your neighbor. We're pioneers, all right, but we didn't come out here to strike it rich."

What then keeps the people here? Mostly it's the other people. People with strong ideas on matters like ecology. Almost every family uses recycled water, is experimenting with solar energy, and tries their luck at organic gardening. It's a highly educated group that dreads specialization. Enough so to force themselves to learn carpentry, mechanics, irrigation, and a host of other manual skills. In addition, they've had to educate themselves in the ways of the paper jungle. Learning everything there was to know about water rights, township charters, federal and state assistance programs. They're people content to work in the hotels and restaurants of Santa Fe or start a small pottery business and put a good hunk of their energy into the community and the land.

"We're all scrounging. . . . We know where there's some stolen wood for sale cheap, who's the most sympathetic welfare worker in town, and where there's an apple orchard that needs picking. . . . We scrounge and we share," explained a guy working on a new solar system from a design he just received from the University of California. New Mexico ranks forty-sixth in per capita income. It's the poorest state in the union, with the exception of four Deep-South states, so it comes as no surprise that many of the people here receive federal assistance. That doesn't mean the people lie around. Far from it. Dorsal Woods, who came here five years ago from the East to get his values "realigned," said he worked every day either on his house or a neighbor's. "We're working real hard. We figure we get what we put into the place. No more, no less. There's no place else I'd want to live." Dorsal's a cabinetmaker now. Back then . . . well, all the residents seem to have similar stories. Good educations, urban culture, careers, and dreams of sticking it all in the blender and starting life anew.

Mel Johnson's story is more typical than not. "I was an administrator of the Chicago Art Institute. I wore a beard and drove an old Chevy van with peace and McCarthy stickers on it. Then came the convention in '68. I got three moving violations and had my license suspended in one month. Cops hassled me every day. I started to get more radical. More pissed. When Kent State happened I organized a peaceful march and some right-wing bastard tried to deliberately run me over in the street. Right after that I came out here with a group of people to start an environmental design school up in the hills. The school went down the tubes but Diane and I were determined to stick it out. Some of us moved down here to Madrid and started fixing it up. That was four years ago and we're still here."

Frances and Larry Lee had similar stories. Frances tells them. "Larry came out of Vietnam angry he had been sent to die and kill needlessly. He was a founder of Vietnam Vets Against the War and he also started First Casualty Press, which put out *Free Fire Zone* and other books by soldiers who had fought there. Myself, I worked in Vista and in the Missouri school system. We came here to make a new life and to share it with people we like. We feel good about things because we're at a point where we feel we have a real say about our environment and our community. We all have a real sense that the future is ours. We've changed for sure. When we first got here we were die-hard anarchists. Next thing you know we're homeowners attending meetings about fire insurance and septic tanks. We're still pretty united around the ideals that brought us out here . . . there's strong pressure to build our community our own way." Frances and Larry run the Pack Rat's Nest Gas Station in town and are determined to make a go of it. They've built a greenhouse, and Larry plans to start the press up here again.

So far the community has not taken the easy route. Incorporation as a legal municipality would make federal and state funds available for a good water-waste system, school subsidies, and a host of other benefits. The taxes, small as they are, could go to their own town, rather than to the county or state as they now do. They could gain jurisdiction over a five-mile radius around Madrid. Extremely important, given the horde of land developers grabbing up the hills around the town. To an outsider, it seems like an easy decision. "Not so," say the residents who've examined it more closely. "There's no one really pushing incorporation. . . . In order to get outside help we have to structure ourselves like the outside. We have to set up a government with political leaders, cops, inspectors. . . . It's probably inevitable but right now we're on another trip . . . all of us," says Frances.

Grove Burnett, a Santa Fe attorney who often stands between Madrid and much of the outside world, sees water as the town's biggest headache. "No one knows how much there is or how long it'll last. . . . There are state funds ready to be made available once they establish water rights. The Federal Water Pollution Control Act of 1972 allows federal money to come in on a sixty-forty sharing basis. But they have to get better organized. Lack of water could sink the town. I'm not saying it'll happen.

I'm neither optimistic nor pessimistic. I'm a lawyer."

Tom Andrew, a Santa Fe engineer, has put in some time trying to solve the water problem, and recently a team of environmentalists from the University of New Mexico began working on a comprehensive energy proposal. Mostly however, the people have relied on their own imagination, resources, and willingness to battle a cold, cruel outside world. "I don't want to seem paranoid, but we are surrounded by institutional enemies," said a member of the legal committee. "We've fought Mountain Bell for over a year on just getting one public pay phone [the town has six private phones] in here. We need a public phone for emergencies. The Federal Communications Act of 1934 insures adequate service regardless of economic status or geographical location. They say the phone won't pay for itself but under law they must install it."

I called Sheriff Paul Boca, under whose jurisdiction Madrid falls, but declined a face-to-face interview. Residents say, however, that the county sheriff's office more or less ignores them and they seem to be able to handle law and order problems themselves. Someone recalls a car of toughs shooting at a house once but general opinion has it that this was an isolated individual act. People insist there's no crime such as robbery or assault. Occasionally you'll see guns in a house or mounted in a truck, but violence, everyone claims, is practically nonexistent.

"Our biggest enemies are the land developers and the mining interests," Mel Johnson tells me. "Every day new lots are sold between here and Santa Fe, here and Albuquerque. These lots need wells and wells drain the water shelf. It's like pulling the plug out of the bath tub. One huge nightmare I have is to wake up one morning in a few years, look out from our groovy little town here, and see we've been surrounded by the suburbs."

The mining industry presents an equally big threat. Occidental Petroleum has begun the preliminary steps that soon will lead to extensive copper mining in nearby Cerrillos. "They plan to mine using the largest tonnage of explosives ever detonated in peacetime, anywhere. Those blasts could literally shake down the town," a former engineer from California told me. "Besides that, they'll use one hundred times the water all the people from here to Santa Fe require." Environmentalists and home-owners are holding regular meetings, organizing against the mining operation. It's too early to say who will win out. But the history of New Mexico is a history of corporation plunder. Environmental groups already have their hands full battling efforts to turn one of our most beautiful states into a nuclear waste garbage dump. In addition, there are still 50 million tons of coal beneath the surface of Madrid. President Carter is known to favor reintroducing coal into the nation's energy program for the next few years and folks could wake up to another nightmare someday. To the sound of excavators and earth movers digging up their organic gardens. I asked Mel Johnson how they would handle a crisis like that. "We'd fight. . . . We'd use lawyers and sit-ins and some might use guns. There are people here who've had all that in their backgrounds. Our first line of defense would be to build support of environmental groups and go to court. We're building something. Something worth de-fending."

Evening comes early in these hills. Long eerie shadows reach out from the tall black peaks, crawl across Main Street, and stretch into the houses. On some hilltops are huge wooden scaffolds erected half a century ago to hold "the most spectacular display of Christmas lights in all the West." They stand, unlighted, half fallen, like signal-men with arms outstretched. The sun lays down the richest of sunsets. Vivid pink, purple, and orange clouds extend to the distant snow-capped peaks of the Sangre de Cristo Mountains. The landscape is perfectly still, ma-jestically beautiful.

Leaving Madrid I couldn't help but feel a tinge of sadness. Just passing the New Mexico State Penitentiary on the road out was reminder enough that I probably could not return here again. But who knows? Being there, I felt romance was being reborn by these new pioneers. In these parts a hundred years ago it was the custom to leave a pie on the window sill for the hunted outlaw in the hills. I figure the good people of Madrid might find a way to send up a signal. I'd come back.

November 1976

Pit Stops

WHO CAN pass up *Florence, South Carolina*, just south of South of the Border, South Carolina, itself one of the country's great pit stops. Florence is the tooth-pulling capital of the world. Every day hundreds of dental patients arrive in this small town. You can get all the old ones yanked and a new set of choppers for the budget price of fifty bucks. You can imagine what the motels sound like at night.

Speaking of teeth, if you ever lose your toothbrush, you can pick one up at the legendary Wall Drug Store on I 90 in *Wall, South Dakota*. It's the world's biggest, most advertised pharmacy in a town of less than a thousand. And if you're worried about getting a place at the pump or a place to pee, the *Oasis, Wyoming*, gas stop will promise you space, with its eighty pumps and forty urinals.

If it's quality instead of quantity that tickles your bladder, then pull right on over to the most elaborate public urinal in the country, at the Madonna Motel in *San Luis Obispo, California*. If you pee at the Madonna you will find pastel lights caressing a trough whose bubbling waters cascade down from a model oil derrick.

If you get tired of looking at humans in these wondrous man-made settings, there are always animals to look at for diversion. You can see lions screwing at any one of a host of Safari Lands. Thanks to the popularity of these drive-in jungles, America's lion population is now larger than Africa's. In Las Vegas, you can gamble away a lifetime of savings in the Circus-Circus Casino with a bejeweled elephant as a kibitzer. At the Police Museum Hall of Fame on U.S. 41 just south of *Venice, Florida*, you can sit in an authentic electric chair or try your luck at solving a crime. In Texas, down in *Pasadena*, you can dance with two thousand cowboys and cowgirls at Gilly's, the country's greatest roadside dancehall. And what Texan at heart can fail to stop at the Roy Rogers Museum. There you'll find the real Trigger stuffed and mounted in all his palomino splendor, ready to ride those happy trails eternally when Roy joins him.

Go to *Akron, Ohio*, and watch the kids cheat at the Soap Box Derby. Catch the Little League World Series in *Williamsburg, Virginia*, where you can see yet another team from the Far East carry home the championship. If you liked Altman's *Buffalo Bill and the Indians*, you'll want to see the Wild West Show reenacted at Cody's Ranch just outside *North Platt, Nebraska*. There are frog-jumping contests in *Del Mar, California*. Worm judging in *Sterling, Colorado*. Tobacco spitting in *Raleigh, Mississippi*. Pancake races in *Liberal, Kansas*. And practically anything and everything else a Junior Chamber of Commerce promotion whiz can dream up. So come with us, off the trodden interstate, away from Disneylands and Superbowls. Forget about Niagara Falls and the Grand Canyon. Let's go in search of America's true wonders.

December 1978

Village of the Bomb

HEY, JUST 'CAUSE you're on the run doesn't mean you don't stop and look around. For the past four months, I've been zigzagging my way across the country playing undercover tourist. Taking my assignment as *Crawdaddy's* travel editor seriously, I'll be sending in reports on some of the wackier wonders that make up this gorgeous plastic wonderland called America.

Our first visit is to the birthplace of the nuclear age, a small quiet town they call Los Alamos.

In *Village of the Damned* little brainy kids who all look alike and were born on the same day grow up and take over an isolated town. Los Alamos is the closest we've come to reproducing that celluloid vision. Built as an upper-middle-class suburb to the country's first atomic bomb factory, it is a carefully constructed blueprint for interchangeable modules: mechanical, human, or humanoid. A Safeway is a police station is a Sony TV is a scientist. One builder called it "the most architecturally boring town in America."

You'd be hard pressed to find two different-looking houses on any one street. The nearly twenty thousand residents are organized into more than two hundred civic organizations. The people are young, good-looking and bright. They read *Money* magazine and voted heavily for Ford. Nearly everyone works for the lab, a vast multibillion-dollar marvel, which spreads itself over one hundred square miles of plateauland high in the mountains of northern New Mexico.

Having grown up living farther under the mushroom cloud than most of us, the people of Los Alamos often spend their time thinking about the unthinkable. Early warning radar, an automatic telephone system, and forty-seven underground fallout shelters are ready to alert, hide, and feed the entire town in the event of nuclear attack. According to civil defense experts, it is "the most thoroughly organized town in the free world." The yellow and black fallout shelter symbols, instruction cards ("Don't look at the flash"), and announcements for CD meetings are seen everywhere. It's a paranoid's paradise up here. And why not? This is where the beginning of the end began.

Los Alamos was carved out of an isolated mountain region in 1943 behind the strictest security curtain in U.S. history. Wire mesh fences topped with barbed wire surrounded other fences. The woods were mined. Floodlights lit up the sky. Helicopters and armed patrols circled continuously. The scientists who worked here used aliases and false driver's licenses. Calls and mail were censored. Less than a handful knew what was going on here.

Then, at 5:29:45 A.M., Mountain War Time, on July 16, 1945, two hundred miles south at Alamogordo, the loudest bang in history broke the secret. Three weeks later Hiroshima and Nagasaki were turned into microwave ovens, and Los Alamos—the Atomic City—became a household word.

It was here that the famous Fuchs-to-Greenglass-to-Julius-to-Ethel Rosenberg hand-off of not-so-secret atomic secrets was kicked off. It's here that J. Robert Oppenheimer, founder of the project, was denied security clearance to work on his own inventions. Time, it seems, has restored Oppenheimer to the good graces of the Atomic Energy Commission, which runs the place. At the Bradbury Science Hall you can gaze upon his bust and read through his wartime correspondence: "Here at

Los Alamos, America discovered sin," he once wrote. In March of this year, declassified government papers showed over two hundred incidents of sabotage by scientists opposed to creating the bomb.

But far from burying the deed under a blanket of guilt, the moment has been immortalized. In front of replicas of the bombs dropped on Japan is a plaque dedicated to "One of the greatest scientific achievements of all times." (Please read last sentence again.)

In the museum you can be lectured on the latest in nuclear particle acceleration, hydrogen bubbly chambers, fission reactors, and thermonuclear bomb casings. You can play with mechanical hands, pretending you're working in a hot cell with dangerous radioactive material. Or you can fondle a "Davy Crockett"—an eight-inch atomic bazooka-type rocket-launched subkiloton fission artillery shell. Just the thing to get the grime off the kitchen floor.

It's probably not allowed—and I wouldn't know an eight-beam CO laser module from electronic Ping-Pong—but Angel and I spent hours wandering around the buildings. Some walls had stickers saying, "Smile, You're on Radar." Many of the six thousand employees are glad to discuss the "positive" work going on here—research into geothermal and solar energy, space physics, and cancer cures. "Fifty percent of our work here is for peaceful uses of nuclear power," I was told. Which, of course, is another way of saying that half the work is about finding more efficient grandiose ways of killing people.

Los Alamos is betting nuclear. All you can hear are pluses: "Nuclear Energy is Clean Energy" reads a sign in one of the corridors. The buildings are massive mazes of tanks, cables, lab rooms, and generators with romantic-sounding names, like the Clinton P. Anderson Meson Physics Facility, where primary proton beams interact with suitable targets to produce secondary *pi* and *mu* mesons under linear acceleration. Sounds positively pornographic!

Climb the rugged mountain roads outside the site, where you can gaze down upon this giant erector set spread throughout the juniper forest below. Here you can play Dr. Strangelove and indulge all your Doomsday fantasies. If you want to build your own reactor, look for the Zin Sales Yard, which specializes in used lab equipment. For BombWorld, take 85 North out of Santa Fe to Route 4. Be sure to bring your camera.

July 1977

Did You Hear
the One about
the Guy from Plains?

PLAINS, GEORGIA, sticks in my memory like a piece of unchewed peanut brittle. Having been a civil rights worker in Americus, literally a stone's throw away, I find it hard to swallow all the honey-coated grits being dished out daily by the fawning media. Can we really take four, maybe eight more years of the "good ol' gas station," that "good ol' church," and all those "good ol' boys" swattin' flies and dispensin' homespun philosophy?

Way back then (a dozen years ago), working in Sumter County on one of the toughest voter registration campaigns in the South, we had a slightly different view of all those good ol' boys. Plains was just another one of those small, company-owned towns in southwest Georgia that offered aid and comfort to the White Citizens Council. When someone got word that a group from Plains was coming over it didn't mean Miss Lillian's Relief Brigade. It meant board-up-the-windows-and-duck.

Along about midnight, cars containing your rowdier element would race by, throwing bottles or garbage or letting off a few rounds of ammunition. In general, Plains boys were pretty bad aims. In fact, they often were referred to as the bimbos of the county, although I think we used the term *cracker-heads* then. You know, the type of folk who wake up in the morning, put their shoes on wrong-side-to, and then go to the doctor to get their feet adjusted.

Now that Plains has become so firmly entrenched in the sacred archives of *americanus naturales*, I for one see no harm in taking a little wind out of the town's sails. There would be a healthy effect on our society if we could restore that forgotten image as a boob-town. I'm speaking of an all-out effort to defuse all the southern-fried folksiness by making Plains our own little Bimboville— the butt of every jerk joke we can think of.

This is not without precedent. For centuries there was such a town in Poland (where else?). It was called Chelm. In actuality, Chelm had a pretty rough history, being sacked repeatedly by the cossacks and finally obliterated by Hitler's Nazis. In Jewish folklore, Chelm played an entirely different role: It was strictly Yiddish hicksville, the place where all the country numb-numbs sat around racking their brains, trying to shortcut their way to the big time. Hundreds of tales have been recorded and passed down from generation to generation concerning the schleps from Chelm. In fact, all you have to do to break the ice with some of the old-time Jews on the Lower East Side of New York is to ask them if they know a good story about Chelm. If you do, prepare yourself for some hearty laughs.

Now I propose we join together to make Plains, U.S.A., our Chelm.

Actually, this is going to solve a whole other problem that's bothered me for years. See, I love Polish jokes. I laugh like crazy when I hear a good one. Ten minutes later I start feeling guilty about encouraging derogatory stereotypes of one of our groovier ethnic groups and I forget the joke. I mean, what have the Poles ever done to me? There just doesn't seem to be any redeeming social value in repeating or inventing Polish jokes. I've tried substituting other countries, real and imaginary, and it just doesn't work. The joke is deflated before it even gets off the ground.

So for years this repression has been going on with no solution in sight. Then along comes Plains. Lately I've been able to tell a few Polish jokes in Plains clothes. Or is it Plains jokes in Polish clothes? (Are you getting any of this or am I just communicating with Gerald Ford?) Let me try a few on you and you try them on your friends and see how they work.

Fresh Plains Jokes

1. *"Did you hear they opened a parachute factory in Plains?"*
   "Nope."
   "That's right. Only the parachutes got some unique features."
   "How's that?"
   "Well, for one thing, they open on impact!"

   or:

2. *"Did you know they don't have any ice in Plains?"*
   "I didn't hear."
   "Yup! Seems the lady with the recipe up and died!"

   or:

3. *"Do you know the Plains version of the Galloping Gourmet?"*
   "Nope."
   "Why, that's Billy Carter chasin' a garbage truck!"

   or:

4. *"Did you hear they grow a lot of marijuana over in Plains?"*
   "No kiddin'."
   "Funny thing, though, they use it all to make rope!"

   or:

5. *"It takes a hundred folks to ring that little ol' church bell down in Plains."*
   "Gee, son, why's that?"
   "Well, see, it takes one fella to hold the rope and ninety-nine to shake the church up and down!"

or:

6. *"Do you wanna hear a real funny story about Plains,
Georgia?"*
"Now be careful son, I am from Plains."
"Uh, that's okay. I'll tell it real slow!"

Right. I'm not exactly sure these work when you read
them, but due to circumstances beyond my control I can't
tell them to you in person. But I urge you to try these and
any Polish jokes you've been hiding away, substituting
sweet li'l ol' Plains, of course.

In a more serious vein (if you've got one left)—
southwest Georgia, for the last two dozen years, has been
no laughing matter. It was the scene of some of the most
outrageous oppression of blacks imaginable. During the
fifties and sixties, a virtual reign of terror was instituted
by local police and vigilante nightriders.

Very early in the fifties, instant southern justice was
meted out in Glynn County to eight unarmed inmates
who had escaped from a rural jail. When they were
caught, all were summarily executed.

Many black families have had a relative killed by
whites under strange circumstances. Since Reconstruc-
tion, 324 lynchings have been documented in Georgia.
Black groups in the state insist the count runs to ten times
that number. And most occurred in the southwest corner
of the state. "Uppity niggers" often disappeared, only to
turn up floating facedown in a nearby creek.

In 1958, just an hour's drive from Plains in Dawson,
Georgia, James Brazier was taken out behind the jailhouse and beaten with a blackjack until he died, by a
county sheriff's deputy. The crime was so well-docu-
mented that the Justice Department, in one of the rare
cases of federal intervention, sought to prosecute the
deputy. After only a few minutes of deliberation, a
Macon grand jury saw fit to return no indictment. After
the affair blew over, the deputy was promoted to chief of
police in Dawson. The sheriff, in visiting the dead man's
wife, threatened her with the following statement. It
summed up much of the area's attitude:

*I ought to slap your damn brains out, a nigger like you.
I feel like slappin' them out. You niggers set around here
and look at television and go up North and do like the
niggers do up there. But you ain't gonna do it [here]. I'm
gonna carry the South's orders out like it oughta be done.*

Later, the sheriff told a reporter, "There's nothin' like
fear to keep niggers in line." (For this and other cases,
see the *U.S. Commission on Civil Rights Report*, Volume
5, 1961.)

Laurie Pritchett, sheriff of Albany, Georgia, became
one of the first nationally known villains of the civil rights
movement. "Ain't gonna let Boss Pritchett turn me
'round, turn me 'round," sang the peaceful demonstra-
tors marching in the streets. Boss Pritchett unleashed
specially trained dogs and showed the world a new use for
cattle prods.

In Americus, four civil rights workers passing out
leaflets were arrested in 1964 and charged with "insurrec-
tion against the state of Georgia." The charge carried the
death penalty and, even though the law had been
declared unconstitutional in the thirties, the organizers
were denied bond and kept in jail six months before legal
efforts to release them were successful.

Just five short miles from Jimmy Carter's ranch house,
Clarence and Florence Jordan founded an integrated
study community called Koinonia Farm. Shootings and
bombings were a regular occurrence. Police and county
officials tried every trick in the book to close the place
down. (Koinonia still exists. They carry on several good
community projects in the area, including low-cost housing construction, classes in farming and an integrated free
school for kids. A chief means of support throughout the
years has been a well-organized mail-order business of
fruit cakes, pecans, and peanut products. I strongly
recommend you send for their catalogue. Write:
Koinonia Partners; Route 2; Americus, Ga., 31709.)

I remember well that hot summer of '65; canvassing
door-to-door, church rallies, the black families who took
us in, even if it meant risking loss of a job or other
intimidation. Each day the city council would pass some
new ordinance aimed at thwarting the voter registration

drive. We'd gather in the mornings in one of the black districts to begin the protest march downtown. Rarely did we get more than a block or two into the white section of town before troopers waded in and carted us off to jail. Local people were hit with stiff sentences, some as long as a year in prison, for violating "public nuisance" ordinances or for "parading without a proper permit." Legal efforts to defend people were often interrupted when the judge or city recorder just happened to be "away fishing."

One of the few southern whites who really joined that struggle was attorney Charles Morgan, who roamed the South for the American Civil Liberties Union (ACLU) coordinating much of the legal strategy that did away with the more flagrant forms of segregation. His office in Atlanta was bombed and his home strafed with bullets. Still, Charlie Morgan sweated through that tough struggle in Americus and managed to keep enough of us in the streets to eventually kindle one of the strongest local movements in the South.

And where were the Carters of Plains during this period? Probably at home, sitting on their hands, like almost all the decent white folks of southwest Georgia. Ah, but that was a dozen years ago. Charlie Morgan is now a trusted adviser to the president of these United States. Andy Young, Martin Luther King's chief of staff during the Americus campaign, is now generally considered the most influential black in the new administration, and John Lewis, who was then chairman of SNCC (Student Nonviolent Coordinating Committee) was an early and ardent supporter of Carter. The blacks of Americus turned out in record number for "Brother Jimmy." Even the folks at Koinonia, if they voted (I'm told), went for their neighbor.

Yes, sir, bygones be bygones, times are changing and we certainly are in the Great Transition. Lord knows the country desperately needs the social programs Carter promised.

But Carter or not, it still seems the white folks of southwest Georgia ought to be paying some dues. One characteristic about the fabled good ol' boy is that, along with chawin' Red Man tobacco and sluggin' Dr. Pepper, he likes a good belly laugh. Hee-Haw! Let's see how they take to our Plains Roasting Jamboree. One way or another, we should be able to recapture the Polish vote.

Since we're talking about jokes and Jews and the civil rights movement in the South, I'd like to mention the funniest, most dedicated, outside-agitatin', nigger-lovin' kike ever to cross into Dixieland. His name was Mendy Sampstein. Mendy and I went to school together at Brandeis in the late fifties. He loved to pull off a good joke, like cementing up the entrances to the girls' dorm or dyeing the pond bright green on St. Patrick's Day (remember, Brandeis is *the* Jewish school).

One day when our gang was over at Mendy's off-campus apartment watching *Maverick*, he burst into a frenzy of excitement and announced he was going to start a humor magazine called *BUJAH*—the Brandeis University Journal of Applied Humor. Within minutes, he had organized us all in the project. Let's see, there was Ira, Doreen, Sheila, Manny, Aviva, Louise, and maybe one or two others.

Anyway, a few years went by and we all went our separate ways. Mendy headed south. He, along with Bob and Dottie Zellner, were the first whites in SNCC. He founded the civil rights project in McComb, Mississippi, and was one of the chief architects of participatory democracy, the guiding philosophy of community organizing throughout that period.

One night, I was home in Massachusetts watching a TV news story on a bombing at some civil rights center and there was Mendy crawling out of the rubble. It was then I decided it was time to head south. Almost all of Mendy's friends followed him to Mississippi.

I'm not sure if the humor magazine we all worked on still exists. Our gang turned it over to another group of Brandeis nogoodniks with a ringleader named Marvin Garson. They all got thrown out of school when they reenacted the crucifixion in front of the new science building. My, my, time sure does seem to fly, now, don't it?

March 1977

One for the Money,
Two for the Show

BACK IN THE mid-fifties, when Elvis rose like a Saturn rocket out of the Memphis music world to become the world's most famous singer, there really wasn't a hell of a lot going on. McCarthy had chased the nine Reds out of the government. Edward R. Murrow and the army, in turn, took the broom to ol' Tail Gunner Joe. Going to the moon was still a trip only science fiction writers took and the Pill hadn't made its debut yet. Eisenhower killed off anyone's interest in politics and the Hollywood Code of Ethics produced yawns in the balcony. All the artists fled to Europe. We were a nation hell-bent on conformity, status seekers trapped on a conveyor belt, desperately trying to keep up with the Joneses. No sex, no politics, no art, no dope—a goddamn bore.

Teenagers gazed down a gray flannel tunnel, glimpsed a ranch house at the other end and wondered if the whole trip was worth the energy. They started to argue among themselves, two camps growing up in the land of the teens: the Insies and the Outsies, believers in the Protestant Ethic versus Instant Gratification. Crew cuts versus sideburns, white bucks versus suede shoes. Shetland sweaters and chinos battled leather jackets and peg pants. At roller-skating rinks, bowling alleys, and high-school sock hops, the two camps broke into cliques and stared each other down. There were rumbles.

Nowhere was this cultural battle fought out more intensely than in the world of music. The development of 45-rpm plastic discs, 33⅓ lps and the proliferation of low-cost hi-fi equipment was creating a huge market to which the nation's teenagers avidly flocked. The mainstream, claimed by the squares, featured God-fearing, decent men like Perry Como, Eddie Fisher, Frankie Laine, and Tony Bennett, and sugar-sweet virgins in layers of crinoline—Teresa Brewer, Rosemary Clooney, Patti Page, and Doris Day. They sang waltzes and foxtrots, ballads dedicated to their fathers, quasi-hymns, and raised important social questions like "How Much Is That Doggie in the Window?"

The hoods listened to all this pablum, turned thumbs down, and fumbled with radio dials trying to get obscure stations only audible during the midnight hours. Antennas pulled in Moondog out of New York and the great Symphony Sid from Boston. The music was called rhythm and blues, although it quickly became known as rock 'n' roll. It was all grab-ass and sexy, filled with grunting guitars, pounding drums, wailing saxophones, and lyrics that promised a lot more than candy and cake. A lot more, indeed. Joe Turner, in "Honey Hush," slipped in the line "You big cocksucker, don't want no talkin' back," slurring it too fast for untrained adult ears, and the Midnighters' "Workin' with Annie till meat fell off their bones" (boners).

Rock 'n' roll was mean, it made you want to spit on the sidewalk. Rock 'n' roll was sexy, it made you want to cop bare tit in the back seat of a car. And above all, rock 'n' roll was *black*. It lured young, impressionable white kids into smoke-filled ghetto nightclubs where we flashed our phony IDs, winked, and chug-a-lugged our whiskey sours.

Since the greaser subculture was growing by leaps and bounds, and since black rock 'n' roll was banned from most radio stations, it seemed only inevitable that the record world would launch a massive talent hunt for that necessary hybrid, "a black voice inside a white body." The search ended in Memphis, in 1955, when RCA signed Elvis Presley to one of the most lucrative record deals in history. What followed was the great American legend of our time. Rags to riches! Read all about it! Poor boy from Tupelo, Mississippi, walks in off the street, makes his own record, and becomes a star! Colonel Tom Parker, the sly brains behind Those Swiveling Hips. The one love of his life: "I owe it all to Ma." See him race his motorcycle. Feel him shake, rattle, and roll. Touch him—Golden Boy. A million teenyboppers crawling up his pants. A hundred reporters to quiz him. "Tell us, Elvis, what's your favorite color?"

"Blue, ma'am. I like blue a lot."

"Heartbreak Hotel," "Hound Dog," "Blue Suede Shoes"—rock 'n' roll's brightest hour. How Ed Sullivan, guardian of the golden gate to stardom, announced he was a flash in the pan, unworthy to be on his shewww with all those plate twirlers and dancing seals. But the fans won out and old foulpuss ate humble pie. Half a pie, anyway. Half a pie for half of Elvis. *Half of Elvis?!* My God, they sliced the wiggle. All we saw was belly button up. Can you believe that shit?

Those first few years, '55 to '58, saw Elvis at his best. Certainly no great musician—he never wrote a song, never even learned to read music; and as far as guitar playing, well, a half-dozen chords got him through a show. But he had a natural ear for music. He could sing well in two octaves, with an unsurpassed sense of rhythm and timing. He had stage presence only later matched by Mick Jagger and Bruce Springsteen and sex appeal equal to that of Brando and Dean. Even his movies in those years—*Love Me Tender, King Creole*, and *Jailhouse Rock*—showed he had the potential to become a good actor. Perhaps even more, a champion of the people—a working-class hero, like the characters he played on the silver screen.

But it's hard to stay a rebel once you've sucked at the golden cow, harder still for a poor boy from Mississippi. On March 24, 1958, the most famous haircut since Delilah clipped Samson took place when Elvis swapped his "duck's ass" for a regulation army brush cut. In 1960, when Elvis came home from the service he was not the same person. Folks said it was because his mom died, but who's to say that haircut didn't take its toll? There's a case to be made for hair in history.

So home goes the hero, home to warm himself up in that southern-fried San Simeon called Graceland. Home to Memphis. Home to his bodyguards, his cronies, and, of course, the Colonel. The country had changed in those two years. If Elvis himself didn't kill Eisenhower, then certainly the good-looking Catholic underdog, Kennedy, from Boston did. And besides, the songs of the hour were now echoing from lunch counters and jail cells as thousands of young blacks demanded that we look hard at the reality of America, that we change or perish. Freedom songs born of social struggle.

Elvis was not made for the sixties. He was a die-hard red-neck who had no use for Catholics or Jews. He grew up in a segregated world and felt no need to change the pattern of southern life. He detested talk of being influenced by black singers such as Chuck Berry, Little Richard, and fellow Mississippian Bo Diddley. George Wallace was and remained his political idol. Beyond this, he had a deep-founded respect for authority. He was proud that he made army sergeant, and loved to be photographed in uniform. He enjoyed the praise that police departments heaped on him and, every chance he could, showed off his collection of police badges, his favorite being an official Federal Narcotics badge given to him by Nixon.

No, the sixties weren't made for Elvis. And the Colonel, who never made a mistake, shielded him from the storm of change spreading across the land. He churned out boiler-maker movies by the dozen. There was Elvis in Hawaii, Elvis in Acapulco, Elvis back in Hawaii. A real Kewpie-doll ham. He gave up trying to be an actor and walked through the parts. (In *Roustabout*, you can see him reading from the cue cards.) He always looked like he wandered onto the set, got blinded by the lights, and was forced to improvise. "Ah shucks, ma'am, it shouldn't oughta be that way."

Every meaty role offered him—*Thunder Road, Midnight Cowboy, A Star is Born*—he turned down. Or, to be more accurate, he went along with the Colonel's decision to say no. After all, the singing beach boy and the singing cowboy formula was pulling in the box office bucks. And wasn't that what life was all about? "One for the money, and two for the show . . . ?"

So Elvis's world became the no-talent Hollywood, the Graceland plantation, police testimonials and, of course, Las Vegas, where the golden cow nurtured the dry desert and lit up the sky with hundred-foot neon signs screaming *"Money!"* Working-class hero turned matinee idol. A beautiful bird in a gold lamé cage-suit. There was even a clause in his Las Vegas contract that confined him to his room; his presence distracted the suckers at the tables and cost the house too much. So he'd sit there, locked in his penthouse, eating whole cheesecakes, followed by a handful of uppers, followed by Ann-Margret, followed by a handful of downers, then nameless teenyboppers. And bodyguards would read him fan mail into the night and assure him that no one could get through to kill him. Oh, what a lonely boy.

When the sixties were finally over, the Colonel decided to take the wraps off. Elvis did a TV special on NBC and announced plans to go on tour. Live concerts, wow! Amidst the nostalgia boom, hungry for the lost innocence of the fifties, Elvis opened at New York's Madison Square Garden during the fall of '72. I caught the act.

It's the barest stage imaginable, not even a backdrop. The opening act features the worst comedian ever to appear at the Garden. After five minutes, half the audience is on its feet, booing; the other half is out in the lobby getting drunk. It's as if the Colonel is saying, "If you want more than Elvis, you pay more. No free rides."

The fans are his old faithfuls who have managed to get a sitter for the night and drive in from Queens or Jersey. Finally the lights go out and, after an ego-blasting intro as The World's Greatest Living Entertainer, etc., the spotlight comes on and there's Elvis.

He's not more than twenty feet away, bigger than life. A face worthy of Adonis, with that innocent lock of raven hair hanging over his forehead and those bedroom blue eyes. (He's got a top-flight plastic surgeon back in Memphis, I'm told.) He's wearing that silly-ass Liberace white Superman suit that makes him look like he just flew in through the kitchen window on a white tornado. And the middle-class suburbanites are screaming their lungs out as he twists and turns, his white cape billowing behind him.

Minutes later, the lights dim again. Elvis eases himself down on one knee and then the other (a keen eye can see the girdle ridges beneath the shiny white satin) and throbs . . . *"Treat me like a fool, treat me mean and cruel, but love me."*

The audience is deathly still, as if Pagliacci, high priest in the white Superman suit up there, was praying "a collective prayer for all the shattered rebels of bygone eras." I think I see tears in his eyes, but can't tell for sure, seeing as how I am crying myself.

So now the King is dead. They stuffed him into his skintight girdle one last time before filing him away in some hermetically sealed, lead-lined Cadillac of a coffin. He's down there tonight in that Memphis mausoleum surrounded by flowers and guards and groupies trying to scale the cemetery walls, and supporters and promoters trying to carve up the royalties, and hustlers trying to dream up another crazy spinoff.

Death is as unreal as life for Elvis. They say he died of a heart attack but the coroner's report is Top Secret. It was really a case of too much pills and too many pies. But those are just symptoms of a broken heart, so maybe the official reports are true, in a way. He wasn't a real sinner and he sure as hell wasn't a saint. Elvis didn't die for our sins, he left us here to do it on our own.

November 1977

Mexico:
Less Money,* More Fun

LET'S START at the border. Car crossings are easiest and, besides, the best way to see Mexico is by car. Don't bring a big, shiny American car. If the dirt and potholes don't get it, the mirror bandits will pick it clean, the sludge from the gas pumps will eat out its insides and, in the end, you'll regret the hassle. Think compact, and if there's a choice think Volkswagen. Mexico has a huge Volks assembly plant in Puebla, and every mechanic knows how to fix them.

One word of caution: Mexican Volkses don't have fuel injection, so don't be surprised when mechanics start hunting for the carburetor. You're better off with an older model. The ideal vehicle would be a five-year-old Volks van with some dents already in it.

Before you begin, invest some greenbacks. I say invest because you can pack the van with valuable equipment that you can easily unload for three or four times your investment price, and if you're hustling you can cover nearly all your expenses. Say you customize the interior—bed, refrigerator, tables, sink. You can load it up

*All prices are pre-1978 and from what I hear inflation has been rampant the past few years. The generalities, if not the specifics, remain true.

106

or just do essentials. Say you put in $800 worth of interior stuff. When you're ready to leave, you can easily sell it all for $1,500 to a Mexican with an empty van, who, if he *could* get anything locally, would pay double that. Throw on the best tires you can purchase. These too can be traded for double the price when you leave, plus you get the buyer's old tires.

At the border when you fill out the car papers, write "van" (not "camper") in the blank. Under Mexican customs law you're allowed to bring in a portable TV, AM/FM tape deck, car stereo (CB is actually illegal; the theft problem makes CB a bad idea anyway), and anything else for personal use. Camping equipment, scuba gear, and photography equipment can be sold quickly or bartered for room and board. None of these have to (or should) be new. I sold a used nineteen-inch portable color TV that I paid $90 for, for $400. (And I was doing the guy a favor since he was saving four or five hundred dollars.) Color TVs are the easiest items to sell, but car stereos are also in hot demand.

There's another item that not only is really profitable but is great at establishing rapport. Music tapes cost about ten dollars in Mexico and good ones are hard to come by. Before we head down, we get ninety-minute cheapo cassettes, head for the best stereo system in sight, and spend a week making recordings. Disco music is the most popular. Hard rock also has a lot of fans. You can sell a tape with music for five dollars, or trade it for a night's lodging or a good meal. I've traded twenty tapes for a kilo of grass. It wasn't *prima mota* but for seven bucks a key, who's complaining.

Don't be shy about loading up with a few TVs or car stereos. I once figured I could get one hundred car stereo units tucked away in a van without anything looking suspicious. It's important to remember that if you have trouble at the border, you can return to the States, drive a hundred miles and cross at another point. And remember, every border guard and every cop in Mexico is corrupt. Actually "corrupt" isn't the right term since the *mordidas* (bites) someone in uniform can pull down are considered part of his salary.

Say you had a few thousand dollars' worth of questionable items and the guard gave you a hassle. A fair bribe would be one hundred pesos or one of the items, like a car stereo. Giving too much is worse than too little. They think they have a sucker and will try for the whole load. Dress clean. Arrive at lunchtime (2:00 to 4:00 P.M.) and have two "clean" suitcases easy to reach. Be confident.

The reason I'm putting a lot of emphasis on this is to get you into Mexico with the proper attitude. Trading, haggling over prices, offering the correct bribe, and so on are intricate parts of the Mexican social fabric. It is not impolite, exploitative, or dangerous—to the contrary, acting otherwise is considered antisocial.

I've read all the same scare stories as everyone else, but my own experience is that with the right attitude and the correct bribe you can walk away from the tightest jam. Most drug busts of Americans are made because someone cut into someone else's business, or the people busted had no respect for local sensitivities, which frown on flagrant behavior in public. A man and a woman traveling together should say that they're married; you shouldn't smoke dope in public or bathe in the nude.

Even if you fly down for a week or two, bring a portable color TV, a stereo and tapes; just make sure they're not in the cartons. You can sell all this stuff or trade it as you go along. If you're in the city for any length of time, you can put an ad in the paper. Without too much worry and bother you can easily unload the stuff.

Where to go depends on your time limits and how much you want to see. The west coast is more beautiful to look at, but the east coast has better swimming and diving. The south is the most beautiful, has more isolated Indian villages, mushrooms and rough, winding roads. The north has great deserts, ranch lands, Don Juan and peyote. Mexico City has a superb museum, great international restaurants, the best Diego Rivera (in the lobby of the Del Prado Hotel on the Avenida Juárez), the Zona Rosa, and, if you're an aficionado, the best bullfighter (but not the best bulls) in all the world. Guadalajara has the best climate in the world (after Nairobi, Kenya), as well as terrific language schools.

You'd be wise to sign up for Spanish courses as soon as you arrive. Being a student makes for a more rewarding experience than simply seeing the country as a tourist. Beware, though, of bourgeois, racist teachers who do nothing but try and butter up Americans.

If you want to see ruins, the best are in Palenque, about three hundred miles southeast of Veracruz. Palenque is semijungle, which means lots of rain, which means mushrooms. Even though they grow in cowshit, they are the caviar of hallucinogens, and should be picked and eaten fresh. Get to the cowshit early in the morning as dopers are out in droves. Of course there's more rain in the rainy season (July to September), but in Chiapas and Oaxaca it manages to rain just about year-round and the mushrooms sprout like crazy. If you go to Palenque, drive an extra hour or two down the dirt road to the waterfalls called Agua Azul.

Veracruz, by the way, is a truly exciting seaport. It has the best fiesta in Mexico at Carnival (Mardi Gras), about the second week in February. It's wild and very crowded. It also has the best seafood in the country. Which, given its proximity to the Atlantic, the Pacific, and the Gulf of Mexico, might make it the best seafood in the world. The best I've tasted was at the Boca del Rio about six miles outside of Veracruz heading east. Pompano is highly recommended and you can get a full dinner here for three bucks. *Huachinango a la Veracruzana* is red snapper in a semispicy red sauce. Finger-lickin' good!

Mexican cooking is more varied than you might think. It's the oldest cuisine in the world, older, although in all honesty not better, than Chinese. The problem about finding good Mexican cooking is that there is no real Mexican school; the art is handed down and the United States has a strong negative influence. For example, tortillas are considered to be just for poor people, so if you want to put on social airs you eat white bread *(pan bimbo.)* Too bad, since tortillas are more nutritious, great teeth cleaners and a cultural mainstay.

Probably the best food center is in Puebla. *Chiles en*

nogada, which is a mild chile stuffed with meats and pineapple, then covered with a white walnut sauce and red pomegranate seeds, is probably the most complicated (twenty-eight ingredients) and most prized of Mexican dishes, and it's best in Puebla during the fall. *Huitlacoches* (pronounced wheat-la-coach-ays) is a black mushroom that grows on corn and is considered Mexico's finest. Look for La Fonda de Santa Clara which, for the price—or any price—may be the best restaurant in the country. Also you'll have to try *mole poblano con pollo* or chicken in chocolate sauce, which is infinitely better than it sounds.

I've never really had great Mexican food in Mexico City but I've eaten the best tacos there—La Caminera on Rio Lerma just behind the U.S. embassy makes them. I'll take that back about Mexico City—you'll have to try goat *(cabrito),* a super Mexican delicacy. The Charleston on calle Queretaro gets the most stars. La Hacienda de las Morales is a real swanko joint with flaming torches, tuxedoed doormen, and fountains, and where they have bull's balls in a nice green sauce (they are politely referred to as Rocky Mountain Oysters) and a strong contender for the best *flan* in all of Mexico. The San Angel Inn also has excellent Mexican cuisine in the grand style. These last two places cost a pretty peso and are real snobby.

Most Americans think they're playing it safe if they only eat at Sanborn's, a Denny's or the Hilton Hotel. In general this is really an ass-backward way of looking at things. The best places are those where the average Mexican businessmen eat their afternoon meal. Restaurants must serve them good food at good prices or they'd go out of business. A tourist restaurant knows the tourist won't be back for a few years, the cook's more prone to spit in the soup, and anyway, who the hell goes to Mexico to eat hamburgers and apple pie?

Don't drink tap water but don't get paranoid about it. Drink water where healthy Mexicans drink. Talk of "different stomachs" is racist hooey. Speaking of drinking, you'll want to try their beer, which is better than ours. Bohemia with 6 percent alcohol is the best of the brews. Better than what's imported here. Tequila is, along with grass, tomatoes, and about two hundred other original indigenous foods, truly heaven-sent. Tequila is a type of mescal that comes from the town of Tequila just outside Guadalajara. There are two types, white and *anejo* (gold), which is slightly sweeter. The absolute best tequila in the world is *hierradura* (horseshoe) gold and it's just that—liquid gold. Bing Crosby got soused on it, liked it better than Minute Maid, and bought the U.S. rights; it's now available here.

Another drink made from that fantastic *maguey* (magay) plant is called *pulque*. It tastes like it's made from equal parts piss and Gatorade, and it takes about eight liters to get you buzzing, but the atmosphere in a *pulquería* is the closest thing to an Old West saloon. No women allowed here. There are many unusual soft drinks, of which *manzana* (apple) and a knockout pineapple cider called *tepache* are the best.

For hotels in Mexico City, try the Maria Christina or the slightly cheaper Maria Angelo just down the block on Rio Lerma. Downtown there's Hotel Isabella on Isabel la Catolica and Uruguay, and, if you want a real social scene with loads of young Americans, the Genova in the Zona Rosa is a fair deal. If you're vanning it and just got into town, head for the rich section (believe me, in Mexico you'll know rich from poor), find a nice tree-lined street and park for the night. No one will bother you and it's safe; many streets even have security guards.

In the northwest you'd be wise to take the train ride from Chihuahua to Los Mochis (or the other way). It's a strong contender for the best train ride in the world. You'll see waterfalls, mountains, and villages where the Indians still ride with rifles and *bandarillos* slung across their shoulders. It passes the Barranca de Cobre (Copper Canyon), which they say is deeper than the Grand Canyon. There's only one track so the trains go on alternate days; the fifteen-hour trip boasts some of the most incredible scenery you'll ever see. In Chihuahua, you can talk to Pancho Villa's widow, who runs a small museum featuring the car in which her husband was assassinated. You can put your fingers in the bullet holes. (For some reason, it's a Mexican custom to put fingers in bullet holes. In Zihuatanejo there was a shooting, and the only thing people could comment on was how big the bullet holes were. Even kids made a point of fingering the holes in the still warm corpses.) Los Mochis has the biggest and best shrimp in Mexico and is just a few miles north of the opium fields.

For sunny surf it depends again on how lost you want to get. Puerto Angel below Acapulco is gorgeous; Zihuatanejo farther up the coast is getting pretty well-known. It's got character, though, and great clams. Clams that jump when you touch their bellies. San Blas, farther up, is nice, as is Barra de Navidad, which is not that popular, hence cheap-cheap. On the east coast you can camp right on the beach all along the Yucatán. As you drive south from Cancun, turn off on any of the dirt roads to the left. Isla de las Mujeres is cheaper than the island of Cozumel. If you dive, try and get a guide to take you to the Cave of the Sleeping Sharks. The reefs south of Cozumel have brilliant black coral.

Mérida is Maya Central—lots of ruins around, and you can haggle for a hammock. You want the biggest size, which is called *matrimonio* or "marriage." You'll be bargaining for this and other items in the marketplace. There's a good trick to successful bargaining. Bargain for something you *don't* want. You'll see how low the price drops. Then you'll have an index when you haggle for the item you want. Various towns in Mexico feature various goods. Taxco—silver. Puebla—onyx. Oaxaca—blankets, black pottery. San Miguel de Allende and Guanajuato have the best wool sweaters. They make them in the prisons and you get the best prices right at the jailhouse door. There are distribution marketing towns, like Toluca and Mérida, which sell huge amounts of goods. Don't forget about trading here. If you like marketplaces, El Merced in Mexico City is an incredible display. You could spend a week in this market absorbed in the ambience. Things are cheap (wholesale really, although there's no real wholesale/retail in Mexico), but you have to buy by the kilo.

Nearby is El Mercado de las Brujas (the witches' market) with two hundred different kinds of tea and all sorts of talismans, such as bat's wings and brown Kleenex (which for some reason has been incorporated into Mexican sorcery along with Coca-Cola). If you're searching for Don Juan or Mexico's famous healing bruja, Dona Patchita,* you'd be wise to begin here. The biggest, most authentic Indian market scene (open Sundays only) is in Quetzatlan, an absolute must town. Difficult to reach on a long, winding dead-end road (it's only fifty miles northeast of Mexico City but a six-hour drive), it's well worth the effort. The Indians there are so isolated they have a single word for airplane, car, truck, and train.

In the state of Morelos, just south of Cuautla (Coo-wow-tla), you can tour the ruins of the great sugar plantations, against which Zapata began his "land and liberty" revolution. It was here the guerrilla leader was born, fought, and eventually was betrayed. It's still possible to find people who rode these mountain trails with the legendary hero. The adobe hut in which Zapata was born has been preserved as a national monument, where each Mexican president must pay homage. Unfortunately for the Mexican people it has, since Cardenas, been mostly lip service.

Fiestas are an important part of Mexican life. One of the best is the Fiesta de San Miguel in San Miguel de Allende, a jewel of a town three hours' drive north of the capital. The bulls run through the streets and they have the prettiest bullring in North America. There are, of course, dancers, floats, drunks, music and fireworks. Fireworks are probably the most inventive Mexican art form. At fiestas, they are a measure of a town's economic condition and religious zeal for the year.

Outside San Miguel look for Tlateloco, an eerie pilgrim sanctuary where people whip themselves and press thorns

---

*Unfortunately she has passed away.

into their scalps. Guanajuato also has to be seen. They have terrific fiestas here, street players, a great theater, and Las Mumias de Guanajuato. It seems the town cemetery has some chemical or curse that doesn't let bodies decay, so after five years they dig up the dead and either burn them or stick them in the museum. It's one of the strangest museums you'll ever stumble upon. They sell candy mummies outside and kids love sucking on the skulls.

Death fascinates Mexicans, ever since Aztec times, when the life expectancy was only about twenty-eight years and blood flowed from tribal warfare and cannibalism. It was believed a man was judged by how he died, not by how he lived. November 2, the Day of the Dead, is celebrated nationally; in Pátzcuaro in the state of Michoacan people stay up all night and picnic with the dead by candlelight. It's way beyond Halloween.

There is literally a fiesta every day somewhere in Mexico. October 4 is Fiesta de San Francisco, and for some reason it's the Indian day to gather by the thousands and take peyote. I know two places where this is done; you should put in some effort and find these on your own. Also remind yourself that the fiestas all have religious significance—the alcoholic *machos* bobbing around the plaza are not what's happening. Indian is just about synonymous with poor, so intermixed are the cultures and bloods, but farther south you'll find Indian tribes where they still speak Nahuatl or other tongues and dress in traditional clothing. Drive far enough south and you'll be in Guatemala, where the real adventures just begin.

So don't let the scare stories keep you away. But if you'd like to see Mexico maintain its own culture, its wilderness, and not fall under the plow of land developers turning it into one big Holiday Inn, when you come back be sure and tell about those bandits with the gold teeth and how your cousin died from dysentery, and did you hear about the shark who managed to get into the pool at the Acapulco Princess? I did—I let him in.

Guide Books

Mexico is without question the best travel deal around. It's cheap, it's close, and it's spectacular. You can play it close to the vest or free and loose. Two can live an exotic life for a few thousand a year. The trick is to pay attention to reality and not get sucked down the rumor tube.

Before you go south of the border, there are loads of good books to read. The best travel book is the *South American Handbook.* It's updated annually, and even though it has a high price and covers all Latin America, it's way ahead of *Mexico on $5 and $10,* Fielding, or Terry's guide. The *People's Guide to Mexico* is written by good people who speak not with forked tongue. It's best for people who just want to set up a lean-to on the coast and suck on a coconut for six months. It's also an excellent companion to the *Underground Gourmet's Guide to Mexico,* which not only has the best info on restaurants but also has side comments worth noting. There are two other books worth a plug. Octavio Paz's *Labyrinth of Solitude,* although written thirty-five years ago, is still the most insightful contemporary view of the Mexican mind. Jerry Kamstra's *Weed* not only is accurate in its description of the marijuana trade but leads one to believe he has street smarts on how to get by with little scratch below the border. Mexiphiles anxiously await his next book on the guerrilla movement.

November 1977

The Great Gourmet Rip-Off

~~~~~~

OF ALL the adventures during my seven-year underground safari none seems to have the universal appeal of the Great Gourmet Rip-Off. Over a six-month tour of Europe, my running mate, Johanna, and I ate sixty-five meals at fifty-four of the best restaurants in the world. We devoured miniature sea lobsters, baby boar, fois gras, caviar, goose, sole poached in champagne, and enough truffles to make a dozen pigs sneeze. We drank 1928 Lafite-Rothschild, Dom Perignon vintage bubbly and turn-of-the-century Armagnacs the way school kids waste Dr Pepper. We sugared out on such culinary delights as passion fruit soufflé, white chocolate mousse au Grand Marnier, chestnut cake, and sorbets of a dozen exotic flavors. It was the ultimate *grand bouffe,* service money can't buy, and we had it all *sans un sous,* on the house. It would have totaled $10,000 had we not had a magic letter of introduction I had carefully typed one night in a motel six miles outside Amarillo, Texas.

To whom it may concern:

This letter introduces you to Mr. and Mrs. Mark Samuels, who have been assigned by our magazine to do a survey on the new French cuisine. They are a well-known

writer and photographer. Your cooperation
will be greatly appreciated.

Sincerely,

Laurence Gonzalez
Articles Editor
Playboy

For those six months, in the fall of '77 through the
spring of '78, I learned to snap that letter out of my jacket
pocket and pass it under the nose of a master chef with
such a seductive flourish he could virtually sniff the
centerfold. Beginning as a novice to the exalted world of
haute cuisine, I became so good at the bluff that chefs
would eventually confide in me their disdain for other
critics, at times even insisting they had read my work.
The ruse was so complete near the end, several ambitious
young risers eager to make a reputation were actively
seeking my favor so as not to be left out of the inevitable
top ten list. If not Laurence Gonzalez, then the master
chefs themselves had crowned me *le grand critic de
Playboy*.

This article then brings the escapade full-circle, doing
justice at last to a quest that produced such joy that at
some dinings my companion and I were literally moved to
tears. I came to appreciate the expertise of these master
chefs. The ultimate pop artists who carve and cook with
total commitment, creating a work of exuberance only to
be instantly consumed by strangers. Men, and in one
case, a woman, who manage to work an eighteen-hour
day, at times under the most intense pressure, yet still
maintain the urge to continually experiment. The motions are that of a steel riveter pivoting on the high
girder, the thought that of a movie director holding the
great epic in the mind's eye. So while I began the tour
with my tongue-in-cheek, I soon developed an apprecia-
tion, which eventually grew to obsession. I could, for the
first time, comprehend gluttony as a passion. Finally,
when it was over, we left Europe with a wad of menus six

inches thick, a box full of secret recipes, thirty-two hours of taped interviews and about twenty more pounds between us. We had passed through our first food affair and could not in our lifetime come this route again.

Since we lived most of that fugitive season in Paris, half the restaurants were within the city limits or close by. The rest were spread from Reims to Nice, throughout the French countryside. There were also excursions to the Netherlands, Belgium, and Switzerland. We concentrated on the style of cooking known as *nouvelle cuisine*. Partly truth, partly fiction. The French seem to label everything "nouvelle." The "new" fashions, the "new" philosophy, the "new" wave. Good cooking is good cooking and nouvelle cuisine is just that—an extension of a grand tradition. With the exception of Michel Girard in the Pyrenees, nouvelle cuisine is not as calorie-conscious as rumored. Butter and cream are still plentiful. The amount of booze used to wash down a ten-course meal would in itself negate any dream of holding your weight. But there is a departure from the trail pioneered by Grand Master Escoffier. The combinations are more inventive. The sauces accent rather than smother. Reduction thickens, not flour. Things are cooked faster and in less time, thanks to all the modern gadgetry. With the foreign influence, especially American and Japanese, indeed nouvelle cuisine may be the cutting edge of a true universal style. Besides, a "new" school of anything is hungry for publicity and without the *Playboy* scam our finances allowed for little more than hard-boiled eggs and coffee at the stand-up bars.

For our first restaurant we selected one we had just read about in *Le Monde*, Le Bistro d'Hubert. It seemed to be pretty typical of those we visited. Chef-owned, capacity forty-five, bright as a TV studio-set (better to see the food), waiters often members of the family. A table setting of the best china, a dozen or more sterling silver pieces and five or six sparkling wine goblets. If there is a single word to describe these restaurants, it would be *serious*. You don't drop in on an impulse. These are not places you bring a date, nor a place you hold your college reunion, nor rubber-neck for celebrities. These are places

solely for savoring the best food and wine there is. No
more, no less. Monsieur Hubert is somewhat on the rise
and a good review in *Playboy* could help his reputation,
seeing how Americans are fast determining the style and
pace of haute cuisine. For as the supermarkets replace
the outdoor food stalls and the French turn to things
"Americaine," the Americans are in turn becoming
serious gourmands. You can appreciate this exchange
standing in a gourmet boutique, where amidst the ter-
rines and baba au rhums you can discover a long row of
Kellogg's Corn Flakes, considered by the French an
extremely exotic delicacy. So it's no wonder that a good
half of the patrons, who all seem to arrive for dinner
promptly at 8:00 p.m., are American. Hubert and I share
a round of kir (champagne with a shot of cassis) as
Johanna plays both photographer and translator. Then
we proceeded to the prepared table with the waiters
standing attention in review. Commence! The ten-course
meal that followed was like none we had experienced.
Quite notable were a raw veal liver marinated in fresh
tarragon, which caressed the tongue, and a mixed salad
of lobster and artichoke, which turned that caress to
excited foreplay. Our chief waiter was M. Hubert's
teenaged daughter, and like all French waiters she could
discuss each course with patient authority. When I
complimented the chef for using sweet vinegar in a boss
combination of sole and cucumbers (julienne), she gently
informed me that the slightly acid taste in the sauce came
from utilizing the dark skin of the cucumber. After that
miscue I kept my opinions to myself though when anyone
glanced our way I was sure to pat my stomach or nod
approvingly. I had seen James Beard do that on TV once.
Near the end, as was customary, Hubert appeared
steering a wondrous cheese cart in our direction. Quite
possibly he knows more about cheese than anyone in
Paris, and we gorged ourselves on a dozen suggested
varieties. The check for two, had there been one, would
have cleared $150. Instead we just donned our coats,
kept up the stomach patting and steered ourselves
backward to the street. Feeling like the alley cats who
had just devoured the priceless canary, we walked for

blocks before we broke out in a burst of laughter. We had struck a gold mine and if we played our letter of introduction right we would follow the vein to glory—the best food in the world.

Up to then, the closest I ever got to great French cooking was the time I once stood in line behind Julia Child in a Cambridge meat market. So, to overcome my minimum knowledge I set up an interview with M. Millau, who, along with M. Gault, is generally given credit as the popularizer of nouvelle cuisine. A three-hour session at the office of the team's guidebook gave me a facile tongue in discussing the virtues or limitations of a particular meal. It also gave me a valuable reference if anyone questioned my credentials. But not only did this never happen, after a few more restaurants, my manner became so professionally arrogant that no chef even pretended to read the letter. Instead, they employed a typically Gallic gesture—pushing the closed envelope back to me with the left hand, they would flash their nose toward the north star exclaiming, *"Ce n'est pas néces-saire, Monsieur de Playboy."*

A dozen more restaurants on a par with Hubert's were next on our list. Some we tried two or three times to be sure. We found we could, at the most, handle but three of these feasts a week and that we appreciated it more if we starved ourselves the day before. Also eating in the afternoon left time to work off that "bullets in the stomach" feeling. Myself, I've got a low-tolerance thresh-old for alcohol so I regularly lined my stomach with milk before consuming the three or four bottles of different wines that are *de rigueur.* Another effort we made was to stop by the hit restaurant the day before and secure a menu. Armed with a pocket-sized *Menu-Master* dictionary we prepared for each encounter as if we were raiding the Louvre. All this focused the concentration, and much to my own surprise I developed a judgment near the end I would have risked matching with most any critic on the circuit. I would sneer at the Horn and Hardart of nouvelle cuisine, Dodin Bouffaut. An over-praised restaurant that has carried the idea of undercook-ing "pink" to a vulgar blue extreme (a woodcock I had there still peeps at night).

Also a disappointment was Tour d'Argent, a three-star bastion that made us feel we were eating in a museum, the food itself lying dead on the plate. (Our tour branched well beyond nouvelle cuisine.) Eventually we began, as everyone does, making a list for comparison. Four of the final ten best were to be found in Paris, but since almost half our dining took place there our sample is surely biased. In Paris, our four most unique dining experiences were at L'Archestrate, Le Duc, Olympe and Les Semailles.

Any critic would find it hard to keep Alain Senderens off a list of the best. His bold experimentation alone merits points. Few others would attempt combinations like duck filets and corn, cooked oysters and leeks, or sweetbreads and wild mushrooms. His sautéed kidneys ringed by cooked whole shallots was one of the best single courses we had in Paris. The inside of each shallot was done to creamy perfection and the manner of eating them unique yet obvious. You just suck the insides out of the skins. We also had one of our best desserts here, a perfect whole peach flambéed in strawberry liqueur. Yum! Yum! After the meal we toured the kitchen and spoke with the assistants. Surprisingly, we learned most high-class restaurants pay the help ridiculously low wages (try $50 a week), as the line is long to apprentice with a recognized master. A good restaurant is also the best cooking school. This brings up an important point: If the head chef is absent, the quality of the food can drop by as much as 50 percent. After L'Archestrate you'd be wise to visit the nearby Rodin Museum, where the great sculptor has immortalized "Bunnies" of the past century.

Le Duc, in the Montparnasse section, would not generally earn a spot on a critic's list because Paul Minchelli has turned away from demonstrating his ability at the full range of cooking to specialize in fish and seafood. But what a catch of watery treasures! Oysters from Isle de Rey (only one out of three opened is served). Salmon from Scotland. Pickerel from Norway. Pike from Ireland. Lobster and stone crabs from Brittany. All are purchased daily at the huge Rungis Market now on the outskirts of Paris. What isn't used is thrown away each night. If you go, begin with the sea bass and scallop tartare. Cold, raw, and brisk. This is a long haul from gefilte fish. An equal alternative is the coquilles Saint Jacques (scallops) sliced paper thin (oil and pepper the knife to manage this). To compliment these appetizers have a chilled Bandol wine, following the theory that red makes the raw fish more digestible than white. Then move on to *langoustines en folie,* which are miniature lobsters similar to crayfish but found in the ocean. I've only seen this crustacean state-side in New Orleans. The creatures are boiled no more than thirty seconds in a court bouillon spiced with orange peels, fresh ginger, and mint. The grilled sea bass is as good a whole fish as you can ever eat. For a more unusual experience try the red mullet from the Mediterranean. The house specialty at Le Duc is a mountain of "sea fruits" piled high and served with great fanfare. One order will manage for two as a main course. It boasts at least a half-dozen seafood delights. The desserts, all cooked to order, do not disappoint. Try the stewed whole pear in cinnamon or the surprising lemon meringue. Minchelli has an excellent cookbook if you read French. It features simplified recipes for all his mainstays. His cooking may be simple and limited to seafood but it's the kind that produces dreams long after you've left the table. One sure-fire test of a great meal.

The final two restaurants in Paris to make the list had a great deal in common. Both catered to a theater crowd of mostly young people. We saw Johnnie and Sylvia (a French soap-opera version of Sonny and Cher) at both these places. The chefs are both under thirty and very much the eager beavers. Their style of cooking is fresh and daring. I had a better overall meal at the traditional L'Ami Louis but both Les Semailles and Olympe showed not only class but great promise of things to come. Jean-Jacques Jouteux at Les Semailles is a first-class yippie who presents each meal as a theatrical event. You open the door and stand center-stage. Chopin is playing. The other diners are casually dressed (I never saw evening clothes or expensive jewelry at these places). On cue, the waiters move out to the tables. Jean, in his tall white toque, darts out of the kitchen to answer a difficult query or to tell a joke. Enormous fresh flower arrangements adorn the bar and the fireplace mantel. Without reservation (as we say in the critic bizz) try the *oeuf de salmon* ("salmon egg" doesn't sound quite right in English) covered with fresh chives, the veal steamed in cider, the wild mushroom purée and the highly creative *boudin de langouste* ("lobster sausage" doesn't sound right either). Also here you can get a sampler of five desserts for five bucks, which might be the greatest bargain on your dining tour. Jean's bound to remember us, we ate there four times, cooking in the kitchen once. He worked so hard at pleasing, I just didn't have the heart to forget. His soulmate can be found just a few blocks from La Cupoule (the best hang-out restaurant in the world) and Regine's discoteque. Her name is Dominique Nahmais at Olympe. That's right, *her* name, for while 99 percent of all French cooking is done by women, centuries of discrimination have kept *les dames* out of the best kitchens. It's *le* chef not *la* and the only way women generally get the top kitchen spot is to marry the head chef, then poison him. Dominique, who stands no higher than Napoleon, even in her high-heeled cooking shoes, just might be the one to change all that. With the possible exception of Christiane Massia, she very well could be the number-one female chef in the whole damn *monde*. She cooks ten-course meals to order for forty people in a kitchen the size of a prison cell. Here four workers chop, clean dishes, and whip desserts, while Dominique pretzels her athletic body between the stove and the counters. *"Voila!"* she gestures to me proudly, "everyone is eating and my stove is clean." It is like watching a brain surgeon function—total concentration. Artist. Administrator. Acrobat. Grand Chef. If you go to one of these places by all means try and catch the backstage show. At Olympe taste the vegetable terrine, the kind of thing a lesser chef would display for *Family Circle* but in Dominique's hands it becomes an exciting blend of high Paris and low-down Mediterranean accents. The *gigot d'agneau* was tender and delicious. That's lamb thigh fillet. *Gigot* is a cut not found in the United States, the most tender on any beast. The sauce is sheer satin thickened with lamb's blood. (If you want to try this, buy beef's liver and squeeze it for the blood you will add right at the end of your sauce, off flame.) The house specialty is *écrevisse* (crayfish) and Dominique can cook them a dozen great ways. Olympe is one of the few restaurants of this caliber open late at night, but you should reserve a week in advance as it's very popular.

Before we leave Paris for the most serious of the serious places, I must mention our side adventure at Fauchons. Fauchons is the most expensive grocery store in the world. Try a thousand bucks for a can of beluga or the same for a bottle of cognac. Try five bucks for a box of those ever lovin' corn flakes. Try a pâté in the shape of a standing pig or a pastry butterfly whose almond sliver wings move up and down to the breeze from a nearby fan. This is the place both Lenny Breshnev and Davy Rockefeller shop when in town. Sick of our traveling feast, I decided to cook in, on *Playboy* so to speak. I flashed the letter at the first official-looking person I saw at Fauchons and zingo, we were instantly launched on a merry munching tour. This is the place that catered *Le Grand Bouffe,* the cinematic ode to gluttony. Soon the publicity man catches up and asks if we'd like to try a few "surprises." The proper response at these moments is, of course, to reply in the soft negative. It has about the same effect it had on my Jewish grandmother. They piled a basket of cornucopian delights that would have fed a hippie commune for a week. Too much to carry, so we arranged to return the following day with our car. That night *Le Figaro*'s headline screamed *"Fauchons Pulver-izé."* You didn't need a lot of French to figure that out! Some idiots had blown up the place as a revolutionary gesture and with it went our mountain of freebies. Son-of-a-French-bitch, *my* Fauchons! All that 150-proof booze, all the butter, the sugar . . . it must have been some wienie roast. We learned our lesson. Don't put off till tomorrow what you can devour on the spot.

It's time to leave Paris. We've eaten like royalty but in truth not even L'Archestrate was better than, say, New

York's Quilted Giraffe, which is very good indeed. (He said, looking for a free invitation.) For the very best you have to leave the city. Eighty miles south of Paris you will find the small town of Les Bézards and there the resort-inn known as Les Templiers. Here Roger Doreau prepares the grandest table of wild game cooking in all France. In the fall the region is hunting turf for the French, and you get the best of the hunt here at Les Templiers. The rabbit in cider vinegar, the wood thrush flamed in Armagnac, or the roasted quail should definitely be sampled here if you've never feasted on wild game. Even more exotic is the baby wild boar, without doubt the most tender pork chops you'll ever eat. You must have the necessary deep red wines here. A choice of over two hundred varieties awaits you, some 1803 labels running for nine hundred dollars, or fifty bucks a swallow. A heavy '72 Pommard did nicely though.

An even better restaurant can be found way north of Paris, in Brussels. Here in a very picturesque, quiet square you will find what once was, and quite possibly still would be, Winston Churchill's favorite—Comme Chez Soi. Try as many dishes as you can here—the mousses are tasty winners—pigeon, salmon, and snipe. Continue to the truffles and lobster salad or the *sole mousseline au Riesling,* then the saddle of lamb. Today the founder's grandson, Pierre Wynants, carries on a tradition of top-notch cooking. M. Wynants was actually sweating out his *Playboy* audition. He rushed upstairs to don his Belgian version of the Paul Bocuse cooking chemise for the photo and he made me promise I would send him a dozen copies of this issue. "But Pierre, the customs in Belgium will not allow *Playboy* to enter," I alibied. No go. "My dear Monsieur Samuels, the Inspector General dines here, there are ways." M. Wynants, the youngest, had nothing to be nervous about; he could cook the apron off most French chefs.

Double back south again to the capital of French cooking, Lyon. Here there are a half-dozen boss places. And, if you have a limited time in which to try the very best, by all means this is the place. You will, of course, want to try the world's most famous chef, the Lion of

Lyon, Paul Bocuse. Ego seems to have been invented for Bocuse. He is the Muhammad Ali of pots and pans, the only cook who could proclaim "I am France" and no one would argue. The neon Bocuse sign beckons gourmands from miles away. Inside there are no less than three oil paintings of the master on the walls. Everything is imprinted with his name or the ornate *B* he has claimed as his own crest. The matches, the plates, the bowls that house his world-known truffles soup (too weak and pretentious), the napkins, his chemise, even the chocolates are stamped *B*. Bocuse is an industry, shuttling to his Tokyo restaurant, consulting for Air France, signing autographs, designing his line of copper pots, his cooking book. He is the ambassador of French cooking, the tenth generation of a noble kitchen and he is one of the most unforgettable characters you could encounter. "I was at Versailles when your president met mine. Four hundred guests and I the only worker." He actually pounded his chest as he said this but did bring up an interesting point. These giants who night after night serve the richest of the world fiercely hold on to their working-class heritage. Louis Outhier, who we'll meet later, told me in response to a question, that he would have no trouble cooking in a Socialist or even a Communist France. "A good cook is a good cook. It might be hard to get some ingredients but the challenge of making something taste good transcends politics."

If you want to actually *see* some of these dishes in all their majesty, look at the glossy photos at the back of Bocuse's cookbook. (It's sold here but don't buy it; half the recipes are uncookable, through no fault of your own.) For openers, Bocuse's oysters and saffron soup is absolute heaven. Then the bean salad. Strange as it may seem this is probably the dish that will amaze you the most. If one's reputation rests on turning the ordinary into the extraordinary, Bocuse has done it with his beans. Of all the entrées, the very dramatic whole sea bass encased in pastry is unmatchable. Of course we didn't try everything—the menu has an enormous selection—but two bites and I just knew this to be the case. It's the kind of dining experience that makes you exclaim, "That's it!"

Bocuse has a grand ballroom for weddings and bar mitzvahs down the road. Supposedly it has one of the most formidable organs in all France. He insisted we visit. Inside about forty actors and technicians were filming a TV special, which was promptly halted when "the expert from *Playboy*" arrived. Then, as we all stood at attention, the organ, including a huge brightly colored wall of popping, painted heads and dancing animals, belted out the "Star-Spangled Banner." What could I say, it was "on the house."

Slightly to the north of Bocuse, you will find Alain Chapel in Mionnay. Chapel had just returned from a much-publicized tour of China, and his opening crispy duck's tongue and hearts salad reflected that odyssey. Moving from the whimsical, you will not cheat yourself if you order the sea bream. A very delicate fish, a cross between a flounder and a pompano. Light but not too light. (Always wanted to say that!) For something unusual try the calf's ear. It's slightly oily but when's the last time you had a baby cow's ear cooked really well? The pièce de résistance, as they say, however, is Chapel's *poulette de bresse en vessie*. Chapel does for chicken what Bocuse does for beans. If this isn't the *best* chicken you ever tried send it to me and I'll eat it cold. You take a whole chicken from Bresse (a long way from Kentucky Fried), stuff the cavity with fresh herbs, and slide truffle slices far under the outer skin. Then you sew the bird tightly inside a pig's bladder *(en vessie)* and poach the whole business in boiling bouillon. It's served with great flourish, a whack of the blade and poof! The whiff of perfumed steam will lift you off your seat. The bladder, by the way, serves to lock in the juices and keeps the meat extremely moist. (Don't blame me if your supermarket is out of pig bladders!) After the cheeses, many from the region, came a celebration of desserts. Homemade ice cream, hot caramel apples, lemon mousse, custards. Eat 'em all. Enjoy! Enjoy! Just say Mark Samuels sent you and put it on my account.

Before we leave Lyon and arrive at the two top restaurants, it should be mentioned that the renowned Troisgros Brothers at Roanne were away. There is no question their salmon and sorrel, among other dishes, would have planted them in the top bracket. Also missing were two kitchens too far afield but again certain contenders for the highest honors. L'Auberge de L'Ill in Illhaeusern on the German border and Michel Guerard in the Pyrenees. Both these three-star restaurants represent the extremes of French cuisine. In the first instance, traditional (making something that's been made for years only making it better), and with Guerard something nouvelle (original). Also Lameloise in Chagny and Les Santons upstairs from St. Tropez at Grimaud served food so good they should be listed and two others removed.

But enough. The runner-up envelope please. Without question the best meal we both had in all France was just outside Cannes at Louis Outhier's L'Oasis La Napoule. Now entering L'Oasis a person with revolutionary pretensions such as myself is tempted to suspicion. If Napoleon had conquered New Jersey, Paterson's most expensive restaurant would today look like this. A blend of pink, peach, and rose that would dazzle even Lawrence Welk. But right at course one, the suspicion ceased. Truffle Surprise was just that! Like a rare jewel this shiny black egg of *fois gras* covered with truffles glistened in the spotlight and captured our undivided attention. It lay there in its majestic slumber, surrounded by white port gelatin crystals. A stunning effect and our all-time favorite hors d'oeuvre. Now, most of the restaurants visited cooked one thing so good that you lost track of which was your tongue and which was your brain. The rest was just very good. Outhier hit on every single course—the autumn salad, the casserole of oysters and scallops, the *mille feuilles* of salmon (leaves of thin pastry layered with salmon), the duck and truffles, the caravan of desserts. Halfway through, the tears came and they kept right on coming. Before we left we spent hours in Outhier's enormous kitchen. The stove he works on he designed himself (it is as big as four pool tables) as well as many of his utensils. He's the only chef who refused to part with recipes ("It would spoil the magic"), not that I could cook any of these courses anyway. On parting, he gave us a numbered bottle of cognac from his own vineyard, compliments of the house, naturally. This is *the* restaurant to eat in on the Riviera, and while you're at it make a point to avoid Le Moulin de Mougins, which we both agreed was France's most overrated dining place. It was the only meal we found uneatable. Hey, what can you say about someone who has himself immortalized in a cartoon over the bar showing a dead elephant with proud Chef Roger Verge rushing to the campfire holding a frying pan on which lays the poor beast's cock and balls. Maybe Frank Sinatra can stomach this place but even for nothing I'd pass it by.

And now, Craig Claiborne, the final envelope please. Strange as it may seem, the ultimate eating was not to be found inside the borders of France. But cross the border into Switzerland, head for Lausanne and then to the small suburb Crissier. There you will find Girardet. Fredy Girardet, the man a majority of knowledgeable noshers generally consider to be the top chef in the world. I'm not about to argue. I mean, if you're a great chef in France and have a kid this is where you send him to apprentice. So to this mountainous kingdom, the land noted for inventing clocks, LSD, and money also must go the honor of inventing Girardet.

He looks like the actor who played the assassin in *Day of the Jackal*. Tallish, maybe forty-three, blond, the fingers of a concert pianist, very soft-spoken and extremely modest, to the point of shy—in other words, a real *mench*. His dedication is total. If he leaves his restaurant, which is rarely, he closes it. His father had this place before but he was just an average Swiss cook. Which is to say Average. One spring, as legend has it, the young Girardet went on a tour of France. By chance he happened to eat at Troisgros and from that one meal had visions for weeks. His dishes have since remained, he insists, mystical creations. On long bike rides through the mountains, he "sees" something cooked in a new way. And as anyone who has made the pilgrimage to Crissier will verify, that way is very, very good. We are talking about a true artist. A grand master. Someone with an aura. Perfection. And what was amazing about Girardet, you knew this just from talking with him, *before* even tasting the food. He has an amazing manner, like a mature Bjorn Borg.

Of course, Fredy knows where to get all the best ingredients, and daily planes land at Lausanne Airport with fresh fish from the Atlantic or shrimp from Greece. Trucks arrive with chickens from Bresse or ducks from Vendee. He was unhappy about Swiss breads so he constructed his own bakery and now bakes the best himself. Here's a dish you will always remember—sea scallops sautéed on a bed of cooked endives. The two choice ingredients are tied together by a butter-cream sauce based with a champagne and shallot reduction then accented with a squeak of lemon and ginger, finally topped with thin strings of lime rind. It can be made in just a few minutes and looks deceptively simple. I watched him do it several times. I am a better-than-average cook, yet after a dozen attempts I've never seemed to match his effort. There is a missing ingredient and that is Girardet. You must also try his onion tart. And why not the liver and chives? By now we suggest you give up ordering and take pot luck. Try lobster and fresh pea terrine, or the pigeon, or the basil rabbit. The menu is long, serious, and if Fredy makes a mistake, the tooth fairy will correct it. At the end you must try the passion fruit soufflé, which is guaranteed to melt in your mind for years to come. Fredy is one fuck of a cook. He knows everything there is to know about cooking everything. You have the feeling he's creating the dish just for you. When you go to the kitchen and see the apprentices who come from around the world just to catch his drippings you realize your journey is complete. There is no arguing with Girardet, you just watch, appreciate, and try to absorb some of the mystic. In the end you are convinced this is beyond food, more an exploration inside beauty or truth. A truly great experience. And hey, it's only going to cost the two of you five or six hundred bucks. Of course there are other ways than money. There are even other ways than the letter trick, which now is naturally out of the question (though you could try it with *Popular Mechanics*, they don't have a food critic either). If you are hungry you will eat. If you can hold out long enough you can get to eat the very best.

TOP 10

1. Fredy Girardet, Crissier (Switzerland)
2. L'Oasis La Napoule (Louis Outhier), La Napoule
3. Alain Chapel, Mionnay
4. Paul Bocuse, Lyon
5. Commes Chez Soi (Pierre Wynants), Brussels (Belgium)
6. Le Duc (Paul Minchelli), Paris
7. L'Archestrate (Alain Senderens), Paris
8. Les Templiers (Roger Doreau), Les Bézards
9. Olympe (Dominique Nahmais), Paris
10. Les Semailles (Jean-Jacques Jouteux), Paris

February 1981

The following note appears at the insistence of Playboy *magazine: Anyone out there tempted to follow Abbie Hoffman's lead in impersonating a* Playboy *staff member should know that he does so at his own peril. Says* Playboy: *"We take a very tough stance against people who do this sort of thing, reporting them to the proper authorities for prosecution, conviction, and imprisonment. In this case, the authorities got there first, on another matter. That fact doesn't diminish our resistance to such ruses, despite our residual affection for Abbie Hoffman."*

(Author's last word: Sic, sic, sick!)

Germany's Most Dangerous Man

To my American tin ear, Gunther Wallraff sounded more like a new cocktail than anything else, but when I heard he was doing underground reporting on the Continent I decided to investigate. A quick poll of my European press friends heightened my curiosity. You don't know Gunther Wallraff? Then they'd burst into hysterical laughter punctuated with wild superlatives and still wilder tales of heroic journalism. What arose from the comic strip description was some modern archetype larger than life, like a Rube Goldberg or an Evel Knievel. Gunther the Giant Killer. Robin Hood of the Black Forest. A fearless warrior unsheathing his pen against Germany's dragons of power.

At a More Media Convention a few years ago, Robert Scheer, one of our country's very best investigative reporters, urged his fellow travelers to stop at nothing to unearth embarrassing truths about the Establishment. "Break in, bribe, seduce, and lie," shouted Scheer, "anything to break through that palace guard and get the story." Gunther Wallraff never heard of Robert Scheer but he embraces that motto with a passion. Something unique in Europe because investigative journalism itself is just not that common. There are plenty of paparazzi who'll sneak up on Jacqueline Kennedy or Brigitte Bardot but no one zaps people like General António Spínola or Herr Franz Josef Straus. Nobody but Gunther that is. Those sort of overbloated big shots are typical Gunther fall guys. Barons that own company towns, Nazi war criminals in high positions, reactionary publishing tycoons, and mindless bureaucrats are others. Germany, these days, as in *those* days, seems capable of stocking Gunther's gallery of villains.

The common folk can't get enough of Gunther, and without question he's the most popular reporter in Germany. His last book just completed a four-month stint at the top of the best-seller list. A book, by the way, that underwent no less than five different court-ordered censorings. Any magazine that runs a Wallraff story is bound to increase circulation. Yet none, he claims, will now give him work. Popular appeal is not the only pressure operating in Germany, and powerful forces are determined to shut Gunther up. These days he's in court more than some judges, caught on a treadmill of civil suits and a carefully orchestrated legal attack designed to end his career and put him in jail.

Here's a typical Gunther episode. What has come to be known throughout Europe as the Wallraff-Spínola affair. Two years ago Gunther was in Portugal when he thought up the idea of passing himself off as a right-wing bureaucrat in the Bonn government. First he contacted and proved himself to two aides of General António Spínola. Spínola was a throwback to another era. Schooled on the Russian front under Nazi tutelage, he followed that debacle with two decades of bumbling colonial wars in Africa. Realizing things were going badly, he threw in with the Revolutionary Council and ousted the dictatorship in Lisbon. For a brief period he served as interim president but was quickly retired by the leftist coalition. He attempted two unsuccessful take-overs, fled to Brazil, then Switzerland, where he was, despite public denials, hatching yet another conspiracy. The aides Gunther met wanted arms and money. With a keen nose for bigger game, our reporter brazenly invited Spínola to come to Germany for discussions. Surprisingly, the general accepted. "Of course, he'll want to meet your president," insisted the aides. "Naturally," nodded Gunther.

The scene shifts. Gunther was in a state of panic. For days he'd been unsuccessful at recruiting someone to play the president of Germany. In an hour the Spínola entourage would be landing in Düsseldorf. His costume was a dark suit, patriotic tie, and gold cigarette case. His lawyer had lent a black Mercedes to the charade. The banquet hall in Düsseldorf's most fashionable restaurant had been reserved. Gunther's wired with more electronic gear than R2D2. At the airport, Gunther, with appropriate solemnity, made a speech welcoming the general to German soil. Spínola, his aides and his "traveling niece" stood at attention. Spínola exchanged his sunglasses for a monocle and responded by expressing his happiness to be in Germany, which "has always demonstrated its willingness to bring law and order to the entire continent."

Over venison, the general reminisced about hunting deer at a German baron's castle in his native country. "Alas," mentioned an aide, "the castle's now a collective." Gunther kept slipping away to phone and at the last minute, succeeded in persuading an editor to play the president. "But what do I do?" asked the editor. "Buy a striped tie, an attaché case, and get over here immediately. Just act important," assured Gunther, who returned and informed everyone the president would be there as soon as it got dark. Better to avoid the terrorists.

Once the "president of Germany" arrived, the group got down to business. Spínola admitted past German aid ("the CIA has also been very helpful"); an offer by Bavarian political strongboss Franz Josef Straus to set up camp in Munich if Switzerland proved uncooperative; and details of the plan to crush the "internationalists," thus making Portugal safe for German investments. "With arms?" "With arms," replied the general.

Gunther compromised the general into naming supporters operating inside the Portuguese government along with prominent industrial and church leaders eager to back a coup. Later, in subsequent meetings, we learned how funds had already been channeled through the Konrad Adenauer Foundation and the numbers of secret Swiss bank accounts used by the junta. Very damaging material and *verrry* interesting.

When Gunther's exposé (laced with ample comic dialogue) appeared in the magazine *Stern*, a huge scandal arose. Officials fell over one another with lies and alibis. Straus got egg on his face when he first denied then admitted discussion with Spínola, who, incidentally, has not been heard from publicly since this all happened. When Gunther's book on the affair appeared it was a big success throughout Europe. Readers thought it hysterical that Gunther managed to infiltrate a fascist conspiracy at the highest level and without knowing a word of Portuguese! Well, not everyone thought it was funny. The German courts, for example, summoned Gunther to a hearing for "falsely impersonating a government official" and ordered him to cease his methods. Gunther refused. He was ordered to appear and show cause why he should not be held in contempt and be sent to prison for two years. Like I said, not everyone was laughing.

This was hardly the first time Gunther had been in the docks. In 1968, he had been tried on the same charge in Frankfurt. Acquittal resulted when the court ruled he was ignorant of the law, a verdict he rejected as avoiding the issue. As Gunther sees it, the government infiltrates student groups and unions. It invades the privacy of citizens using illegal means. What's good for the goose is good for the Gunther. There is, after all, a class war, and Gunther, unlike American journalists, makes no claim to be objective in these matters. Jack Newfield called this "advocacy journalism." The French call what Gunther's doing *"journalisme indesirable,"* unwanted by the power structure. In Germany they have a word: *Nörgler*. A bad-rapper. A troublemaker. Someone who refuses to shut up. Gunther is the cosmic *Nörgler*. Rehashing his books (six are now in print) and articles, one has to marvel at the guts and imagination of the guy. Here's a sampling of Gunther's greatest hits.

The Case of the Workers Defense Corps. That first

Frankfurt trial grew out of an investigation that established the existence of special antilabor vigilante groups
operating inside German factories. With the cooperation
of local police, the Ministry of Interior, and leading
industrialists, these quasi-military groups engaged in
surveillance and subversion of union activities. They
received armed training designed to blunt possible wildcat strikes. Playing the role of an official in the ministry,
Gunther was able to uncover the existence of the
antiunion conspiracy. Subsequently, he managed to secure secret files of the Association for the Protection of
German Industry to document his charges.

Where Are They Now? Posing as an insurance inves-
tigator, Gunther managed to track down and document
nineteen Nazi war criminals who had slipped back into
high positions of power and influence.

Down and Out. In stark prose reminiscent of the great
B. Traven's *Death Ship*, Gunther explored the world at
the bottom of the pile. He spent months living the life of
a derelict. Through him we enter a forbidden world of
fleabag hotels, mental hospitals, and lockups. Places
where men crowd eighty to a room, sleep on beds without
mattresses or linen, and eat food fit for dogs. As readers
we are compelled to experience nights in mental wards,
unable to sleep because of the coughing and the strong
smell of urine. Storehouses for people waiting for death
emerge in such vivid detail that fiction seems flat in
comparison.

Tattletales. Masquerading as a willing informer, Gunther earned the confidence of several police forces and
detailed the program for spying on leftist groups, coupled
with benign neglect of fascist groups.

On the Job. Two of his earliest books deal with
industrial reportage. Gunther working as a coal miner,
on an assembly line, as a steelworker, as a postal clerk in
an insurance company, and as a migrant worker in the
vineyards. Often he passed himself off as a foreigner by
dying his hair black and speaking with an accent. Far
from being one-night stands, he doggedly stayed at these
jobs for four years. His reports chronicle the exploita-

tion: unsafe working conditions, lack of job security, the totalitarian nature of the factories (loudspeakers everywhere, even in the john), cheating on paychecks, and the evils of piecework. Workers shared their experiences because he was one of them.

The Battle of the Bild. If ever there existed a Wallraff archvillain, it was Axel Caesar Springer, whose middle name aptly describes his position in the Deutschland social order of things. Springer has amassed a large hunk of the action in just about every phase of publishing. In newspapers alone, one out of every four bought in Germany is owned by Springer. His flagship is the giant *Bild*, with a daily press run close to five million, more than five times the circulation of the *New York Times* and, next to *Pravda*, the world's largest newspaper. Of course, none of the above newspapers remotely resembles the *Bild*. Sensational headlines, tits, soap opera, and sports are *Bild* mainstays, pushed even beyond Rupert Murdoch's wildest dreams. Yellow journalism in its most jaundiced form. Realizing Germans had little desire to think about anything after the war, Springer developed a form of journalism suited to the social amnesia. "The German People Are a Great People!" "Terrorists Plan to Kill Queen of England!" "German Women Beautiful, Sexy, Respected!" "Man Bitten by Pet Piranha!" "The Laziest Bum in Germany—Turkish Cleaning Woman." These are just a few samples of recent *Bild* headlines.

Viciously anti-working class, it seems to delight in featuring the misfortune of people. Strongly reactionary, it champions "tough-handed" Franz Josef Straus and scapegoats terrorists (all enemies on the Left) as responsible for all social problems.

Gunther had long been interested in the *Bild*. He once followed up a typical story: "Worker Says Bosses Have It Tough." For a day, one of the factory workers is given a chance to be the boss. To sit in the boss's chair, answer the phones, and dictate to a secretary (a photo shows her posed on his lap). After one day he could take no more and by evening concludes: "The life of a boss is no bed of roses." The article's filled with lines like: "His face grew

longer and longer as he had to decide difficult decisions."
The worker and the executive both began forty years ago
to the day as apprentices and switch on the anniversary.
The *Bild*, never one to let an opportunity pass without
reaching some moral lesson, concluded one worker
stayed behind because he was lazy and the other rose to
the top because of hard work.

Gunther discovered what many people had suspected
all along: that the *Bild* manufactured the news, then
passed it off as reality. The forty-year anniversary was a
hoax. The secretary was a model. The worker was asked
to pose for a photo. It all lasted ten minutes. The
"reporter" who by-lined the story had never even visited
the plant. Harmless? The worker became the buffoon of
the company and his neighborhood. He was held up to
ridicule and felt so ashamed he was planning to move.
Typical *Bild* stories profile loafers on the job or idlers
hanging around the street. One long article talked of how
a welfare recipient, "who is lazier than a sloth," rode
home from the welfare office in a taxi. In truth, the
person had walked home with his mother, a distance of
two miles.

Gunther made up his mind to tackle the *Bild*. He
shaved back his hairline, thinned his eyebrows, and
removed his mustache. An expert at phony résumés, he
had little trouble landing a reporter's job. What followed
was four months of madcap insanity as the monkey
wrench in the machine came alive. He started writing
some worker-oriented pieces and was told straight-faced,
"that's not the *Bild* style." In one story on the high rate
of accidents at a plant, Gunther concluded faulty equipment and unsafe conditions were to blame. When the
article appeared the headline read "Most Accidents
Caused by Mistakes and Alcohol." The book about life at
the *Bild* includes a stunning display of stories he wrote
and how they appeared in the paper. His point is
graphically made. After that, Hans Esser (Wallraff) was
shifted to covering stories about the woman who grew a
giant radish and the prime minister kicking out the first
soccer ball. In one feature, he climbed inside a suit of

armor ("a symbol of German past strength and future growth") and was singled out by the governor of Niedersachsen as an example of "men we need for the next battle."

In the office files he uncovered an explicit directive advising reporters "one of our objectives must be to launch a strong attack on any attempts to extend worker participation [in factory decision making]."

In one hilarious incident a landlord called the paper to ask how to prepare an eviction notice on a tenant. Gunther responded with sharp criticism. The landlord was flabbergasted. "But, *Bild* is supposed to be on the side of the landlords." After four months Gunther got a tip his identity might have been blown and he walked off the job. Adventures at the *Bild* and the exposé that resulted cemented Gunther's role as some sort of teutonic champion among present-day Germans. David versus Goliath. Springer blew the story with a typical blast-off. "Underground Communist Infiltrates *Bild*." Reporters for the paper returned the compliment by infiltrating Gunther's family, harassing relatives. His mother had to move because of neighbors' taunts. In Germany, especially in the language of *Bild*ese, *underground Communist* is synonymous with *terrorist*—a label as threatening today as was a yellow star forty years ago.

Tracking down Gunther was no easy matter. When aboveground he lives collectively with close friends in Cologne, just a few miles from where he was born the day Allied forces invaded North Africa, sealing the fate of the Third Reich. When he's working undercover these friends are the only people he contacts, and never through his home phone. Trusted intermediaries relayed the message that Gunther could be found in Paris in a week's time. He was to appear at the press conference of a young German student who was supposedly tortured (cigarette burns over her body) by the French police when suspected of associating with terrorists. Incidents like this are now commonplace throughout Europe, and hint of darker things going on inside Germany. Sitting in

Paris, listening to German students talk about things back in Deutschland, vaguely evokes images of the thirties. Not exactly but . . .

It began in 1971 when a set of laws called the *Berufsverbot* (job ban) were steamrolled through the legislature, calling for intense investigations and loyalty oaths for all current and potential civil servants. By now close to a million people have been subjected to scrutiny and something like five thousand people have actually been denied employment for no apparent reason other than at one time or another they expressed leftist views. Through all this, the *Verfassungsschutz* (security service to protect the constitution) had compiled some two million secret dossiers, built up a network of informers, and consolidated immense power. The terrorist scare has resulted in a stampede of revolutionary laws and unbridled police activity. Paris has a growing colony of German dissidents who tell of beatings, harassment, midnight searches, and book burnings. Book burnings? Currently it's illegal in Germany to write or publish anything supportive of violence against the government, and the definition of violence appears to be broadening. A host of antiterrorist laws now allow detention up to six weeks without access to a lawyer, warrantless searches of entire neighborhoods, increased use of wiretapping, prohibition of collective defenses, and denial of the right to choose counsel by suspected terrorists. Several lawyers have already been jailed under vague charges of supporting illegal organizations or helping to insure their survival. Others are in jail because their defense of terrorist clients was deemed too vigorous. Tom Wicker, in writing about the case of lawyer Kurt Groenwold, says he is being charged with "what in any other Western country is routine legal defense work." Sixty other attorneys have within the past two years been suspended from the bar for "slander against the state." A William Kunstler would have been in jail long ago, and the pressure extends well beyond the leftist lawyers. Hans Heidman, a successful corporation attorney, faces disciplinary charges for "disrespect to the courts" when he offered the opinion that aspects of the Baader-Meinhoff prosecutions were unconstitutional.

Things are the same at the universities. Police agents infiltrate student groups. Books "glorifying violence" have been banned. Anyone brave enough to attend a political demonstration is subjected to questioning and being photographed. Students have adopted the Iranian practice of wearing masks at rallies. Scores of leftist professors have been discharged and several are facing legal charges for "contributing to an atmosphere supportive of terrorism." In the spring of 1978 the courts rejected a law allowing conscientious objectors to choose alternate service to the military. An Ellsberg-like trial for publishing government memos authorizing illegal wiretapping is in progress. The Bertrand Russell Foundation, which in past years has held tribunals on Vietnam and Chile, has just concluded an extensive report on repression in Germany. Milton Mankoff, chairman of the Sociology Department at Queens College, told me Germany right now is going through its McCarthy era.

Under these stifling conditions, this chilling atmosphere, Gunther Wallraff works his trade. Even as his popularity grows, the probability of his landing in prison or being forced into exile increases.

The press conference takes place in an old library on Boulevard Saint Germain. It's standing room only as reporters from all over Europe flock to catch a glimpse of their hero-colleague. Everyone knows it's only a glimpse, as Gunther constantly changes his appearance. There are a collection of Wallraff photos taken over the past ten years that are worthy of Lon Chaney, Jr. Long hair, mustache, crew cut, beard. He'll put on or take off thirty pounds to better assume a role and think nothing of shaving his head bald. Without being introduced, it's possible Europe's most celebrated reporter could be in the room undetected. He's not the only one here incognito. German intelligence agents have left their black trench coats back at the office, as have the French Sûreté. Five years of fugitive living has made me a little camera shy and I'm wearing my best wig and dark glasses for the occasion. The mysterious Madame Ange, who accompanies me on such missions as bodyguard and translator (Gunther speaks no language other than German), has transformed herself into a blond model of Aryan respectability. There may be others in disguise, for press conferences dealing with any aspect of terrorism have taken on the appearance of masquerade parties anyway.

Gunther Wallraff, or at least the person introduced as him, walks quickly to the front of the room. Six feet tall, trim but muscular, with thin light-brown hair, cut short. His face is accented by high cheekbones and pale, narrow lips. A handsome thirty-six. He wears tinted glasses and the no-nonsense short-sleeve dress shirt, dark, cuffed trousers, and black shoes of a journalist whose sympathies rest with the working class. Chain-smoking Royales, he holds the cigarettes between the far tip of index and middle fingers in a distinctly rigid European style. His carriage and manner are a study of restrained discipline. However, a large shoulder bag, bulging with cassettes, newspapers, crumpled pads of notes, a change of underwear and a half-eaten sandwich, betray the born anarchist. In appearance and mannerisms he could easily pass himself off in the States as gonzo journalist Hunter Thompson. In fact the likeness is remarkable.

The press conference begins with Heide Kempe-Bottche describing in detail her interrogation by French police. What drew Gunther into the case was the fact that the *Bild* had published one of their fabricated hatchet jobs stating that the student, among other things, had been seriously wounded and had connections with ultra-Left groups. Both categorically untrue. Gunther announces that, with profits from his book, he has established a fund to help victims of *Bild* slander fight back. His own legal battle with Springer has cost him a small fortune but he is determined to see this through. His next book will catalogue scores of *Bild* case histories. Before, these victims had no champion and their pleas of mistreatment fell on deaf ears. Now things are different and people are coming out of the woodwork with stories.

Gunther then proceeds to detail his own problems. No

magazines or newspapers will hire him since he began his campaign against Springer. "I guess you could say I've backed myself into a career corner." Since the *Bild* book has appeared he's been ordered by the courts on several different occasions to delete parts. In exasperation the publisher is throwing in the towel. Germany's most popular book at the beginning of 1977 is now, six months later, no longer in print. The *Bild* has assigned reporters to track down the wildest rumors about Gunther. He has a habit of chewing grass; *Bild* writes as if it's marijuana. "No, no," insists Gunther, "I chew blades of grass like the cows." *Bild* quotes what Gunther has said about terrorist-slain industrialist Hans Schlyer, failing to mention he wrote it seven years ago. The words sound more cynical if said right after the kidnapping and murder. "They'll do anything to connect me to terrorists with which, incidentally, I have no sympathies. If one is caught in Cologne, they'd write, 'Terrorist Arrested Only Blocks from Wallraff.'" The courts, after pressure from Springer, have revived the old complaints about his methods and have laid out the tightest restrictions yet. Gunther's not even sure he'll appear at the next court hearing and talks openly of defiance. "I will not stop. I'll move to Sweden or go completely underground in Germany. My articles and books will be printed abroad." Obsessed? Fanatic? Someone willing to lock horns with the likes of Springer and Straus is a very dangerous man indeed. Gunther could be the most dangerous man in Germany.

Later during our interviews, I asked about his background. "My father was a worker. I never liked school much, it was too rigid." After a year of high school Gunther dropped out and got a job in a bookstore. Lacking formal education, he nonetheless was an avid reader. In the works of Kurt Tucholsky and Egon Kisch, he found examples of undercover journalism during the Weimar Republic that gave him ideas. When drafted in 1963, he claimed CO status but was refused. After making a speech in the induction center, he was sent to an army mental hospital. Following a month of tests he was released and classified "unfit for war or peacetime," which doesn't leave all that much room in German society for a Gunther Wallraff. "I am a product of sixty-eight," he explained. A veteran of sit-ins and antiwar demonstrations, he has been beaten and arrested several times. Sticking to his activist role, in 1974 he protested the military junta ruling Greece by chaining himself to a lamppost in Athens and leafleting with his free hand. He was sent to prison just before the dictatorship collapsed.

He began writing fiction in the early sixties but switched to reporting because it was more powerful than anything he could dream up. In 1968 he earned the German equivalent to a Pulitzer Prize for his industrial reportage. He donated the cash award to the Anti-Vietnam War Committee. As he became better known and trusted, disgruntled officials, employees in corporations, even neighbors and shopkeepers would pass him leads. He has amassed an army of anonymous collaborators, and has established himself as an effective opposition to the state.

Journalism as guerrilla theater. The reporter as life-actor. Through disguises and false papers you assume a role and enter society through the back door. In one of Gunther's short but interesting social plays he posed as a manufacturer of napalm bombs, who, tortured by guilt, sought absolution in the confessional. The word-for-word transcript of the priest's forgiveness rivals Bertolt Brecht. Once Gunther gets on stage we begin to see things in a different focus. The results make for the highest level of drama. Here's Gunther, disguised as an immigrant worker, wandering into the executive dining room of Germany's largest steel foundry. A dark-haired, poorly dressed worker sitting at the linen-covered tables of the corporate executives. The room goes silent. Finally a vice-president goes over to him. "Excuse me, my good man, but this food is not for you. It will make you very sick." Gunther in the factories is Charlie Chaplin in *Modern Times*. Once the play is over, the life-actor retires (without bruises we hope), becomes an author and writes the play by transcribing what occurred. In the final stages, the courts, the mass media, the government and the public all get involved. The deceivers have been deceived. Villains get their comeuppance and the victims gain hope at the same time having a good laugh.

Later that night I asked Gunther about the theatrics of his method. "I've gotten away with so much because I have the license of a court jester." "Are you having an effect?" "Definitely, *Bild* readership has actually been falling off since my book. Many victims have gotten the courage to talk about their treatment."

"What are your chances for surviving this latest trial?" "It's hard to say, each year brings more troubles. Not long ago, I was arrested on suspicion of supplying guns to Spanish anarchists, which was nonsense. Now the impersonation trials. The courts try to wear me down. The government watches my house, taps my phone, harasses friends if I disappear too long. With each new story it gets harder and harder."

"Is Germany becoming a fascist state?" "I won't say that. The owners of many of the big industries are ex-friends of Himmler. We always had that connection with the past. No one can deny there is a growing climate of intimidation. People are afraid to criticize. We're moving away from democracy, but forward not backward, to some computer-controlled state."

"But you still manage to get published?" "The German press is the tightest controlled of any in Western Europe. Informed people read the foreign press even to find out what happens in Germany. The cuts ordered in my last book. News laws prohibiting certain writings. My trial this summer. I know of many books not published because of pressure. Most reporters now censor themselves. Many subjects are now forbidden in the press. *Verboten!* No one can write about the Stuttgart prison suicides or anything about the terrorist trials that differs from the government."

"What do you think happened in that prison?" I asked. "No one knows, there's been no objective investigation, only the statements of government committees. One cannot say they were murdered or committed suicide.

There are many unaddressed questions."

"For instance?" "I heard on the radio they had committed suicide even before there was any investigation. They could have been driven to suicide. When Croissant, the lawyer, was jailed, he found a razor blade in his cell after it had supposedly been searched."

"Are you getting much support on your case?" "Unions and student groups have protested the court trials. The German Journalist's Union and PEN, the international writer's club, have made good statements. There is some solidarity."

Gunther's determined to fight. It's as if the past fifteen years of work have prepared him for this battle. "There's too much at stake," he said, "the past must not be repeated." There was no need to expand.

"What do you think all the good Germans will do?" I asked. Before the translation was completed he said it again for emphasis: "The past must not be repeated!"

February/March 1978

In Search of Philip Agee

A FEW YEARS back, I happened to find myself in Guatemala City trying to exchange a watch for a piece of jade that I hoped would let me coast a year in the event no job turned up when I hit the States. Still full of revolutionary piss and vinegar, I had come to Guatemala City hoping eventually to make my way south to Argentina, where I could join the guerrilla struggle. Fate, however, had other plans in store for me.

A week before, I was high atop Pyramid IV at Tikal, lost in mushroom/Mayan-induced time travel, when reality rudely interrupted. "Did you hear the news? Did you hear the news!" screamed a bunch of backpackers scampering up the slopes. "Nixon quit! He's through. All done. Finito! Kaput!" Roars of approval in seven languages could be heard piercing the jungle silence. I got so excited that I lost my footing, cascaded down the side of the pyramid and ended up tearing the ligaments in my ankle.

Recuperating in the capital, I realized this sudden change of events meant that the Feds would stop beating the bushes for me, and it might be safe to return to the land of milk and honey. Perhaps with Nixon gone the atmosphere would loosen up a little; maybe I could even stop schlepping around the globe and settle down in some nice, quiet place, like the South End of Boston.

The mail arrived before the jade swapper, and much to my surprise and delight it included a small package from England. I tore the wrapping off and spied a dull gray paperback of Malraux's *Man's Fate*. Inside what proved to be a false cover lay an advance copy of Philip Agee's *Inside the Company: CIA Diary*. It was, at the time, certainly the only copy in Guatemala and, Cuba excepted, probably the only copy in all Latin America. For the next two days I devoured the book. I read it first as an adventure story about this bright philosophy student from Notre Dame who gets recruited into the CIA and then gets sent to South America, where he dreams up and acts out political sabotage, eventually gets disillusioned and resigns. What follows is six years of dodging spooks, trying to research and recollect his experiences, and get someone to publish his diary. One lonely spy's attempt to come in from the cold, blasting away at his former employer. The CIA exists solely to protect the interests of American investments abroad. That is their chief responsibility and they carry out their work by subversion of governments and social movements through bribery, torture, assassination, frame-ups, and countless other illegal, covert techniques. Essentially, that was Agee's confession.

I then read the work as a textbook, noting in particular the detailed description of surveillance operations at airports and around embassies. No doubt comrades in Latin America would be interested in those who had been bribed and framed by the CIA, in the list of fronts, and, most importantly, in the names of agents and informers operating undercover in their countries. What a memory this Agee fella has! The book read like a computer on rewind. I found myself underlining more and taking more notes than any book since Carlos Marighela's *Mini-manual of the Urban Guerrilla*. I admired the book as an act of guerrilla theater, along with others such as the *Pentagon Papers* and, if I may, *Steal This Book*, all of which in their own way cut through the limits on free speech: Davids hurling flaming missiles at a Goliath whose power depended on secret information.

Yes, this Agee had really lobbed one. If he got away with spilling the beans, if he managed to survive as a former agent gone public, it would pave the way for more agents to come forth. From a strictly cynical, cash-and-carry point of view, how could the CIA match the rewards of being a best-selling hero? Reassignments to exotic locales? Pay hikes? Lectures on the code of honor? "You promised not to tell." "Yeah, but you promised we'd be a bunch of do-gooders out to save democracy. No one said anything about corrupting unions, framing politicians, and frying testicles." So the code of silence had been broken. Allen W. Dulles lay amolding in his grave. The Potomac guards choked on their Scotch-and-sodas. Paper shredders worked overtime. Psychoanalysts were put on alert. "Just one little bastard with a big mouth." "Sure, he's a commie."

I photocopied the lists, along with a hastily assembled summary of the book, and sent it to various contacts in Latin America. Of course, being in Guatemala, I could appreciate the book even more. Somehow, reading this in the United States just wouldn't have been the same experience. Back there, surrounded by multimillion-dollar movies, shopping centers, electronic toys, and those 27 billion Big Macs, the Third World and its problems seem so distant, like poison arrows and the moons of Jupiter.

Guatemala is about 96 percent U.S.-owned. It's been that way since 1954, when the CIA engineered the downfall of the last legitimate government and the assassination of its elected president, sort of a George McGovern type named Jacobo Arbenz Guzmán. Military coups came pretty cheap back in the fifties.

The CIA bought Guatemala, its banana plantations, its coffee and cattle ranches, for a measly six or seven million dollars. Just a few weeks before I arrived elections were to be held, and the current strong man, General Kjell Eugenio Laugerud García, was expected to return to power. Convinced his brutal suppression of the guerrillas and economic austerity programs had gained popular approval, García loosened up and ordered live television coverage of the returns. As soon as the polls closed, it became apparent that the liberal opposition was about to score a resounding surprise victory. All of a sudden, every TV set in Guatemala went blank until the next morning, when it was announced that García had been returned to power and his chief opponent had fled the country. (Of course, everyone knew he'd been threatened with murder if he stayed.) That was the end of elections for a while and for live television to boot. No one doubted the steady hand of the CIA was behind all this Latin instability. One just has to walk the downtown streets to recognize U.S. interests. Esso. Dairy Queen. IBM. The glare of neon imperialism hits you smack in the eyes. There are fashionable suburbs that are off limits to Guatemalans without a security pass. It's to these carefully guarded strongholds that the Americans retire at night, hot and sticky from the hard day's plunder.

That night I wrote Agee a long letter about how valuable his book was. I advised him that the CIA would continue to harass him, if not worse, and that in spite of any legal hassle it was his duty to return to the United States and give full publicity to his important story. I also sought out his advice about my own publishing problems. All the while, of course, I was being careful not to let on where I was but giving him a safe way of corresponding through the States. The letter was sent via Paris to his London publisher. As a rule, I'm particularly cautious with people I've never met, and I assumed his mail was being monitored. Besides, Agee was for twelve years a CIA agent, sabotaging movements and governments I felt close to. I never doubted his conversion was legitimate, but I found it impossible to enter his mind: Catholic, humorless, a machinelike killer instinct, which, thank God, had now pointed him in the right direction. I knew people like him on the Left but kept them at a distance. They were the type who most assiduously rejected countercultural life-styles, who might not take kindly to the ex-Yippie fugitive who zeroed out on a dope bust. Whatever the admiration, there were limits to long-distance trust.

A year passed. The book was now in the book racks. I could see its familiar cover, a photo of the CIA bugged and planted typewriter, in all the supermarkets of Dallas. CIA agents were being reassigned throughout South America. The government of Peru, inspired by the book, rounded up every agent they could net and sent them packing. There must have been a scramble to rename all those fronts, to bury (one way or another) informers, and to change communication techniques. Not since Kim Philby ditched the British Secret Service and scooted off to Moscow had a single individual caused so much disruption in a spy network. The CIA ranted and raved about lack of honor, deception, and traitorous behavior—but not once did it challenge the facts Agee bared. Moreover, congressional hearings were by then confirming many of the charges detailed in the book. Around the world, particularly in Washington and Europe, investigative groups were busily conducting their own research and going about the business of exposing agents. Their efforts were having a devastating effect on the agency's ability to conduct secret activity. In Athens two agents who had been identified were summarily executed as they left their office. Morale inside the company was at its lowest point in history. Rightly or wrongly, Agee was blamed for all of this. The agency tried to discredit him with rumors about excessive drinking, psychotic episodes and KGB connections, but journalists proved the stories false and instead told of an earnest, clearheaded crusader dedicated to ending CIA subversion.

Agee was by this time living in England and working on a second book, one that would document the history of the CIA. Occasionally he would travel to other countries to lecture. In September 1976 he was invited to speak before the Jamaican Council for Human Rights. Agee brought word of the CIA's current effort to subvert the government of Prime Minister Michael Manley. He pointed out the pattern of terrorism and economic sabotage. He told of the illegal flight of capital, and of the credit squeeze by international lending institutions and private banks, and how fresh capital was enriching the coffers of previously unheard-of right-wing newspapers. In other words, exactly the same program applied in Chile against Salvador Allende was now being applied in Jamaica. At the end of his tour Agee held a press conference at which he presented the names, addresses, phone numbers, and make and color of cars belonging to eight CIA agents working out of the American mission in Kingston, agents subsequently rounded up and deported.

Agee got a tremendous reception in Jamaica; some observers credit his revelations with helping to save the elections for Manley. Returning to England Agee was surprised to discover that he faced deportation. Friends in Washington passed the word that the plot he had unearthed in Jamaica was a joint American-British intelligence operation. In November the British government declared him a "national security risk" and began court proceedings aimed at expelling him from the country. Despite massive support by journalists, teachers, and several members of Parliament, the government succeeded in its effort: In July 1977, Agee, his wife, Angela, and his two children from a former marriage were forced out of England.

President Giscard d'Estaing, caught up with the fashionable human rights movement, had just that summer rededicated his government to ensuring that France remain a haven for political refugees and dissenters. After checking out Switzerland and Sweden, Agee moved to Paris. A month later the Giscard government declared that letting him stay would "jeopardize relations with friendly governments." In Boulogne-sur-Mer Agee waited for Angela to arrive from England. When they embraced on the dock, the border police, who had been waiting, placed them both under arrest. What followed was an anxious night. Papers were taken from Agee—to be photographed, analyzed, and presumably passed back to agencies of those "friendly governments" referred to in the deportation order. They were interrogated about all their contacts. After an hour they were separated. Agee was driven to the nearby police station and locked up. He knew nothing of Angela's fate. He was terror-stricken that she, traveling under a Brazilian passport, would be returned to Rio de Janeiro, where as a revolutionary she had been wounded, jailed, and tortured by the secret police. They would be delighted to receive her again. The next morning Agee learned Angela had been released. The French were concerned only with him. He was escorted by car and then by train to the Belgian border and warned not to return. *Au revoir* to the land famous for sheltering dissidents.

During the fight to stay in England Agee had traveled to Amsterdam. Friends urged him to stay. Lawyers made inquiries with government officials and found there was apparently no opposition. Amsterdam is the San Francisco of Europe. It's long been the citadel of free expression. The Netherlands since the seventeenth century has welcomed political refugees. Censorship seemed unheard of. You can purchase guerrilla manuals such as *The Anarchist Cookbook*, communist and fascist newspapers, pornography of every description, religious and antireligious tracts. It was the only foreign country besides Sweden that allowed the sale of *Steal This Book*. It has the oldest, most active gay movement in the world. It has decriminalized marijuana and started heroin-maintenance programs. Its social-welfare policies are the most progressive in Western Europe. When the hippie movement hit Europe, instead of offering resistance and repression, Amsterdam welcomed the long-haired wanderers: Parks were made available for sleeping, and city officials arranged rock concerts and other activities. As far as political freedom, the Netherlands at the time had no less than ninety political parties, of which some twenty-two were represented by legislators. It seemed like a good place for Agee to head, and the Belgians were more than happy to hurry him along. Belgium is, after all, home base of NATO.

The Dutch government indeed proved more hospitable than the French. Agee was issued a three-month residence permit. Angela, the kids, the refrigerator, and his files full of CIA secrets joined him in Amsterdam. He was free to continue his work, to come and go as he wished. The Agees, after a year (or six years, if you count the CIA harassment while Agee wrote *Inside the Company*), seemed safe at last—safe from deportation, anyway. There would always be disgruntled agents who in their wrath would hold him responsible for dishonoring the corps or contributing to some fellow agent's death. We are, after all, talking about people trained and licensed to assassinate enemies. What Agee did was not exactly akin to dropping out of his Friday-night poker game.

Our story now shifts back to the good ol' U.S. of A., where I had spent the intervening years evading capture, showing up in places like the FBI building, Los Alamos, and the Inaugural Ball. Doing live TV-show call-ins, holding press conferences in Canada, posing for photos crossing the Mexican border and hamming it up with Mickey Mouse at Walt Disney World.

I was now ready for bigger game. The most hunted dreamed of meeting the most watched. To walk up, doff the disguise and say, "Philip Agee, let me shake your fucking hand." This was not going to be all that simple. True, Agee had responded about a year ago by calling a friend and offering to do what he could. At least he didn't view me as some sort of Typhoid Abbie. But how was I to make contact? To crack the network of surveillance would be much more complicated than almost anything I had yet accomplished. I would need accomplices. We'd be working in a strange country. Besides, I had no idea where Agee was headed. All I knew was that the guy who had stuck his ass on the line to lay open the truth about who really controls foreign policy had just been booted out of two countries and was being hounded off the planet by the CIA—and no one was doing a damn thing about it. Obviously, a job for Superschmuck. I juggled the poetic symmetry. The Wandering Jew meets the Jumping Jesuit.

On some nameless highway I hit the phone booth. After a few calls, I put together Agee's stateside contacts and figured which end to plug into. Secret rendezvous.

Manhattan bar: "You don't understand A——. He's watched twenty-four hours a day. He sleeps in a different place each night." (Later, I found out Agee lives quite openly. His apartment has a two-inch plate with his name on the door. Practically anyone who calls his office is given his address and phone number.)

"Look, let him decide. Just deliver this letter to him. I'll call you in three weeks at this phone booth number."

I'm determined to get to Europe. I line up one other assignment, an interview with Charlie Chaplin. Three weeks roll by. Ring! Ring! Ring! "He wants to see you, but on one condition."

"What's that?"

"He doesn't want to see your face. Says some folks still think he's an agent and if you get caught they'll say he set you up."

So it was on. In the letter I outlined how I'd make future contact if he agreed. As per standard procedure, I let the courier believe it couldn't be arranged and I thanked the person; then I let Agee know, via another contact, that I agreed. Each step was going to be complicated. Agee's one condition was extremely interesting. We're such a visual culture: Living this lie, I had long ago come to realize that visual identification was one of the least of the difficulties. Anyone who doubts should examine the "Son of Sam" wanted poster and compare it to fat Mr. D. B. himself. Before he was caught, that famous drawing pointed to a face whose features included wide lips, high angular cheekbones and tightly drawn skin. In effect, a nonwhite. As anyone familiar with thematic apperception tests knows, witnesses pump all their prejudices into visual recollections. There were other security concerns, but no matter—Agee would meet the masked reporter. Each to his own hang-ups.

Another month passes and it's touchdown Schiphol airport. You'll have to forgive my paranoia about Europe. Twice before, in the sixties, I'd been whacked by French cops. I had been deported by Scotland Yard during a little consorting with the IRA eight years ago. And, of course, there was always the long gulp every time

you showed your passport and Immigration opened a big
book or punched a computer keyboard. Even if I had
none of this to worry about, there was still this lingering
anxiety. If you startled me in the night by shouting
"Europe!" I'd see Nazis all over the place. The nightmares of youth just never seem to die. On this day
security is particularly intense. Plainclothes police (many
of whom I later learned *were* Germans) appear everywhere. The RAF (Revolutionary Army Faction) had
threatened to blow up a few Lufthansa airplanes. A few
days previously, Dutch police had arrested two suspected
RAF members after a gunfight at a phone booth just two
miles from the airport. German BD intelligence agents
had spread out all over Europe. Tourists suspected of
being hijackers had been clubbed to the ground in
airports at Ibiza and Rome. Border officials were exceptionally jumpy.

The mysterious and beautiful Madame Ange arrived
from Paris with vital information. "Our first problem is
hotel registration. It's not like the States. Here you must
fill in your passport numbers, and they're filed with the
police. Amsterdam is small, and this RAF activity has
alerted everyone to suspicious behavior. I'll distract the
clerk; you fill in false information. We estimate a week,
though, before we have to change places and identities.
Agreed?"

She handed me a package containing notes and everything Agee had written. I sent it on ahead. I'll be up for
two nights cramming for the interview. Days we will
spend on strategy. Madame Ange will be the intermedi-
ary. She will use the elevator evasion ploy lifted from *The
French Connection*. (The Shell building seems to be the
only place in all Amsterdam that's high enough.) She'll
carry a change of clothes and a wig for Agee. Together
we carry out surveillance of his home. Once Agee and
Madame Ange are together and have "lost their tails,"
we'll make the initial rendezvous. I had worked that out
on the plane ride over. Anyone who engaged in symbol
warfare would pick the one place in Amsterdam that I
could meet Philip Agee: That was 263 Prinsengracht, in

the secret annex where Anne Frank hid out. If it was a setup, from here I could play a number of options, not the least of which was an appeal to Israel's Law of Return. Like all such laws, a hoax when applied to American fugitives, but what a way to expose it. If I had a Jesus, she was Anne Frank.*

After two days, we were ready when the news broke. Agee was being kicked out of Holland! The secretary of the Ministry of Justice had determined that Philip Agee's presence was "of such a nature as to endanger Dutch public order" and "disruptive to Dutch foreign policy."

There was a routine Lenny Bruce used to do about his legal hassles: "So I'd get busted in New York; then I'd get busted in Chicago. Everyplace it would make big news. So by the time I hit Podunk or Peaville, somebody'd say, 'We bettah bust him too. If we don't, how the hell will they know we have a police force?'" Agee was trapped in a Lenny Bruce monolog, and my chances of pulling off this assignment were fading fast. I had visions of following him to Denmark, to Sweden . . . and finally, in ten years, we'd rendezvous in some alleyway in Tripoli: "Mr. Agee, I presume."

We buried our blues under a twenty-course *rijstafel* dinner, one of the better by-products of Dutch colonialism in Indonesia. The next morning brought more bad news: Charlie Chaplin was dying in Switzerland. Madame Ange consoled me at breakfast: "Maybe they can use a short-order cook around here."

Determined to follow through on the meeting with Agee, we improvised on the original plan. Madame Ange would ring up, give the code words, and say we were in Paris and ready to proceed as scheduled (the following day was the agreed-upon date). Agee was nervous. Yes, he wanted to meet. Now was no good. Coming to Amsterdam was much too dangerous. Maybe in the future, but not now. Definitely not now.

---

*Readers interested in retracing events can find my signature in the visitor book.

"Not now? But, damn it, we're here!"

"You've got to see it from his point of view," insisted Madame Ange.

"But that's just it. He's worried about *my* safety and some bullshit New York grand jury when he should be concerned about *his* problems and the deportation. Besides, he should fight this from the U.S. They won't lift a finger to stop him. Not now, with Carter committed to human rights. With new revelations daily. That CIA code of silence was always an unenforceable law. Frank Snepp, a Saigon agent, just published a book without prior approval. There were lots of magazines running anti-CIA material. Naming names."

I came to Holland to convince him to go home. Frustration mounted. My isolation. His isolation. I brought him things to read. Ideas. Contacts. There was no doubt in my mind he was going about this ass backwards. The United States was the only place where the United States wasn't strong enough to disrupt his life and work.

The good Madame agreed to walk in on him and explain all this. She could be very persuasive. I stationed myself in a bar a few blocks from Anne Frank's house and waited for the call. Two hours later it came. Agee was adamant. Busto! Can't win 'em all. Agee was getting kicked out, Chaplin was tapping out, and I was about ready to flip out and go back to New York. We walked it off touring the museums. Vermeer's *The Milkmaid* cooled me out. Madame Ange enlightened me: "Vermeer went for absolutes, didn't he? Absolute truth."

The next few days we toured the city while I spent my nights composing long letters to Agee, then ripping them up. He held a press conference which Madame Ange attended. Not even Agee could have recognized her. She brought back his statement of events. I could easily have gone, but I was gradually cooling down, beginning to see his work as more important than our meeting. Later we read an article in *Vrij Nederland* denouncing the government decision. Agee was launching his counterattack. His case went up for appeal.

We spent time walking the quiet, narrow streets, exploring seventeenth-century neighborhoods, riding canal boats and waiting for Agee to change his mind or for some new approach to suggest itself. A thin patina of snow covered the cobblestones. A flock of swans, wings flapping, landed on a silent waterway. Charming Amsterdam rekindled love and hope. Automobiles had not conquered the city. Most people still traveled on bicycles or on the public trams. I remembered reading a piece by Frank Serpico (who is tucked away here) with nothing but praise for the Dutch police. The chief inspector of police in Rotterdam, a pacifist, publicly attacked West Germany for the Stuttgart prison murders of the urban guerrillas; very few here accept the "suicide" story being dished out by the Bonn government. Things are very loose. Gambling and prostitution are illegal, but there are slot machines in every bar and scantily clad women advertise their wares from windows along the street. Sex is, in fact, the big tourist attraction.

During the spring, marijuana plants are for sale in the flower market. We bought a piece of Afghanistan hashish just by walking into a shop off the street. The clerk behind the counter weighed it on a scale, just as you would tomatoes back in Texas. At a private club we noticed mirrors on the bar, for coke sniffers. "It makes sense," said the bartender. "They were tying up the toilets too long." Yes, Amsterdam seemed governed by the same enlightenment reflected in Rembrandt's portraits. Everyone agreed, "As long as you pay your taxes, nobody cares what you do." Why then were they booting out Agee, someone who hadn't violated any Dutch laws—or, for that matter, any other country's laws?

The answer came in recognizing a change in the Lowland wind. To put it mildly, the Dutch had weathered a stormy year. Half a dozen different embassies had been occupied: Iranian, Japanese, French, German. In Drenthe, South Moluccans took over a schoolhouse and a train for a siege that lasted weeks. In Utrecht, a German RAF member shot and killed a policeman. In Amsterdam, a millionaire industrialist had just been kidnapped. The open-clinic policy had attracted addicts from all over Europe, and muggings, previously unheard of, were becoming commonplace. Amsterdam had replaced Marseilles as the hub of the world's heroin-distribution network.

The Dutch were beginning to lose their patience with foreigners. Cries for law and order were being considered seriously. The coalition government, which had been paralyzed for eight months, was being regrouped under a center-right coalition. Andreas van Agt, of the Christian Democratic party, had just been instructed by the queen to form a new government. He was antiabortion, pro-big business, and he favored tougher criminal penalties. (The Netherlands has no death penalty, and the stiffest sentence for any crime is twenty years.) Van Agt was in charge of the ministry that decided Agee's case.

There were other reasons. Despite increasing nationalization and social-welfare benefits, large Dutch-based multinational corporations, such as Unilever, Philips (Norelco) and Shell Petroleum determine the foreign policy of the Netherlands. The BVD, which is the Dutch version of the CIA, depends on its U.S. intelligence ally for satellite reports and data gathered from worldwide electronic monitoring systems. The company has powerful friends among the tulips. It was only a matter of pressing the right button before Agee got the word. In Dutch, the word is *neen* as in "no way!"

Our last night in Amsterdam we found ourselves walking along the famed Zeedijk, a seafront melange of Chinese dope smugglers, African gunrunners and prostitutes, laughing and drinking. "Smack! Coke! Grass!" shouted the street vendors.

"How much for some grass?" I asked a guy, more as a reporter than as anything else. The price was outrageous.

"No, thanks," I replied.

"Give me money, man!" he roared. Before I realized what was happening, I was facing a screaming South Moluccan. White foam was pouring from his mouth, rage burned in his eyes, and a knife, clutched tightly in his right hand caught the reflection of the blinking sign.

"Don't look around. Nobody gonna help you here." He was right. In seconds I was surrounded. North, south, and west. Moluccans were popping out of the woodwork. Agee was right. Amsterdam was dangerous. Was this to be the end of little Caesar? Struck down by junkie madness? *Fuuuuck you!* I screamed at the top of my lungs. Madame Ange wrestled an uncooperative taxi to a halt and somehow we managed a getaway. "You know what it says in my guidebook about the Zeedijk—did you ever expect to find *this* in Amsterdam?"

So it was time to leave. Just blocks away was the man I came 5,000 miles to see, but we could not make it happen. The Blue Meanies had scored an unknowing victory. Agee and I passed in the night—two rolling stones with no place to go. Men without countries. I worked on the letter all night, scrambling my ideas, frustrations, and a bit of grab-ass philosophizing.

"Go home, Philip. You can win the fight. I'll always feel close to you because, for us, *la guerre, ce n'est pas fini.*"

Five days later, Dutch courts denied the appeal of Philip Agee to remain in the Netherlands. A week afterward, on Christmas Eve, Charlie Chaplin died peacefully in his sleep.

August 1978

Interview: R. D. Laing

IT'S BEEN more than eighty years since Sigmund Freud first outraged the scientific community with his theories on sexual repression and the unconscious. Today, the once-radical views of Freud and his disciples are not only accepted, they have become a rigid code. In recent years, a small but articulate group of antipsychiatry psychiatrists have voiced their opposition to the static views of their colleagues, accusing them of being reactionary and elitist and criticizing their methods as ineffective and often inhumane. R. D. Laing has been a powerful spokesman for this opposition. Not only have his unorthodox views revolutionized modern psychiatric theory, his books have reached an enormous lay audience as well. Laing's views had a vast effect on the consciousness revolution in the sixties, and they continue to shake things up today.

Over the past twenty years, R. D. Laing has written several easy-to-read books about hard-to-grasp subjects. He is a poet, as well as a doctor and scientist, who has used his gift for lucid expression to demystify psychiatry, a field long complicated with obscure symbolism and jargon. In his early books, *The Divided Self* and *Self and Others*, he argued that there is no therapeutic value in formal diagnostic labels (such as "paranoid" or "schizophrenic"), which psychiatrists use to keep a distance between "them" and "us," thereby justifying isolation, harsh treatment, and frequent exercise of total power over the patient.

Refusing to keep a safe, clinical distance, Laing explored the lives of the insane from a radically different perspective, trying to see the world as they see it. He carefully deciphered the language of "schizophrenics," humanizing them and revealing how they, like everyone else, are merely trying to cope with an often mad and hostile world. Delving into his own psyche, he spent a year in India and Ceylon studying meditation. He has often spoken of his experiences with hallucinogenic drugs.

In his most famous book, *The Politics of Experience*, Laing accused psychiatrists of caring little for patients and of using treatment more to enhance their own social status and power than to benefit others. His ringing manifesto condemned the typical therapeutic session as a factor contributing to the alienation at the core of the so-called schizophrenic personality.

As an alternative to existing therapeutic facilities, he and several colleagues founded the Philadelphia Association in 1964, pioneering a network of live-in households for those who are unable to cope with everyday pressures. At Kingsley Hall, the model for other households, patients were treated without drugs, electroshock, or other "violent" procedures. Instead, they were encouraged to "delve into their madness" in order to gain some understanding of its root causes.

Laing has become increasingly introspective in recent years. He has written several books of poetry and conversation, most notably *Knots* and *Do You Love Me?*, in which he has investigated his own experiences for clues to the emotional complexities of day-to-day human interactions.

R. D. Laing was born in 1927 in Glasgow, Scotland, to working-class parents who practiced the antithesis of healthy child rearing. His parents even denied his birth. "My mother and father still swear they do not know how I was conceived," he says. "According to them both, all sexual activity had ceased irrevocably before I was born."

Laing received his M.D. from Glasgow University in 1951 and spent two years as a psychiatrist in the British army. Later he worked in a variety of hospitals and clinics doing research and therapy. He still maintains a small private practice in addition to lecturing and writing.

When I called Dr. Laing from New York to set up the interview, the psychiatrist was startled. "Aren't you in trouble?" inquired the Scotsman. Then he quickly admonished, "Don't talk! My phone is tapped!" I replied that he shouldn't worry, only to expect me in London the following day.

The next day, as appointed, I knocked upon the door of a London flat and was greeted by a professorial gentleman who didn't seem the least bit alarmed. "Hi, Dr. Laing, I'm Abbie Hoffman." The gentleman nodded. "Glad to make your acquaintance, sir, but I'm not Dr. Laing. He lives down at the other end of the block."

I finally met with Dr. Laing in his spacious flat in the fashionable London suburb of Hampstead. I would expect any therapist to be particularly difficult to interview, and Laing, by his own definition, is an introvert.

We began by talking about old friends. Twenty years ago, I had come to this same suburb to visit someone my teacher, A. H. Maslow, felt was one of the world's best psychoanalysts. "Did you know Marian Milner?" he exclaimed in a Scottish brogue. "She was my supervisor in analysis. She's still alive and living here."

Laing had just returned from Rome, where he had spent time with the Living Theatre. "We had this huge argument about what you'd do if you were the conductor of an orchestra and one member insisted on playing another tune. They, being utopian anarchists, insisted that the whole concert either continue that way or they try to reason the chap out of his persistence." And Laing? "Well, I saw no choice but, if pushed to the limit, to call the police. Every situation has its limits." This seemed like a good starting point.

Hoffman: I have been spending time with Soviet dissidents lately and, as ᵀ think about what they say, I come to the conclusion that psychiatric diagnosis, be it in the Soviet Union or in Western countries, is a political decision. Could you comment?

Laing: American and other Western psychiatrists should be embarrassed to condemn those practices in the Soviet Union, since the treatment is the same here as there—imprisonment (involuntary hospitalization), violation of basic human rights by the same drugs, the same electric shocks. It's just a disagreement as to who to do it to. If electric shocks are so bad for dissidents, how come they are so good for mental patients? If these things are supposed to be destroying people there, what do they think is happening here? If behavior modification through past Pavlovian conditioning techniques is not the sort of thing that ought to be done to intellectuals and scientists, why should it be forced on anyone, except as punishment?

Obviously it's an ethics question and a political act. We have several eccentrics in Philadelphia Association houses in London—where people in so-called psychotic states can live it out—who have to be very careful when they go out in the street. If you walk about aimlessly or stand on a street corner too long, you're liable to be taken to a police station—in almost any city, I suppose, in the world. Eccentric (harmless, nonviolent) standing and walking are not defined as dissenting behavior, but as socially deviant behavior, and the political difference isn't great. At a seminar with eighteen student psychiatrists recently, I put a question to them: If you feel I need your help and I don't (I am no harm to others, not even a nuisance), what would you do? The majority were quite prepared to lock me up and treat me as they saw fit. Even if no one around me felt I needed treatment, they felt they had the right to decide—that it was their duty. I thought they were way out of line. They thought they were merely shouldering their medical responsibilities. I expressed my dismay and alarm that they were already so brainwashed that they sincerely believed they had a mission to prevent, serve, find, and destroy all states of mind that *they* thought were wrong, and which they *declared* to be due to some undiscovered medical pathology; they thereby invented for themselves the duty, the right, the responsibility, the obligation to do me in (as far as I was concerned) in the name of treatment (as far as they were concerned) and then finish me off and wipe me off completely, if need be, if I had the nerve not to be grateful, and to see my self-styled benefactors as my persecutors and destroyers. They thought I was paranoid. There you are, I said, exactly.

I can't picture any social group, from a country to a family to a couple, without rules of conduct. But what are we allowed to think, feel, remember, imagine? Are we even allowed to talk to ourselves, to have hallucinations, visions, trances? Psychiatrists (at least a lot of them) have come to regard it as their duty and function to put down all states of mind they think should not be allowed to go on in the interests of the person concerned. We have become a profession of mind police.

Hoffman: Then you see no need to isolate the mentally ill?

Laing: For whose sake? Their sake or our sake? As far as my neighbors are concerned, they can have any state of mind they desire. I don't care about their state of mind. If they throw a rock through my window, that's another story.

Hoffman: So madness implies a violent intrusion.

Laing: No. I'm saying I don't know whether he's [a neighbor] mad or not, and I don't care, it's none of my business. But it is my business if he throws a rock through my window. Let's live and let live. Violence has to be defended against. Those who intrude must be put back in their places. I think psychiatry is out of place, and so are those people who place bombs around. There have been two bombs exploded along the route my children take to school, and I condemn those acts. I was asked by a group in Paris to sign a petition to release a hijacker. I couldn't.

Hoffman: You've stated that you're not a political activist, especially after you appeared at the Dialectics of Liberation Conference in 1967 with people like Stokely Carmichael and Herbert Marcuse. But once the psychiatrist goes beyond the individual to examine and treat the family—networks of families—isn't the next logical progression communities and nations? Today the family, tomorrow the world?

Laing: Yes, indeed. There we go. It's not my ball game, though, if we are talking about activist intervention— more efficient, and more politically backed techniques of social engineering; that is, more ways and means of *controlling* people. The nature of *our* control system is complex, obscure, full of contradictions, conflicts, paradoxes, confusions, mystifications. My contribution to the commonwealth is an effort to elucidate the nature of this control system (comprising many interlocking subsystems). A bit more clarity seems comparatively harmless.

Hoffman: Doesn't your research in *Sanity, Madness and the Family* suggest that once we know the environmental factors we can predict schizophrenia?

Laing: No, it does not. That book attempts to show that experience and conduct generally regarded by psychiatrists as signs and symptoms of a hypothetical condition, called schizophrenia, are more intelligible, make more sense, than is taken to be the case by most psychiatrists. I do not myself adopt the hypothesis that there is such an entity as schizophrenia, so I am absolved from what to me is the pseudo-pseudo question of what "causes" schizophrenia: genes and/or environment and/or—in any mix. I do ask, however, under what social circumstances is this ascription (something is the matter with you and it is an illness) brought into play? What is the social function of this diagnosis?

Hoffman: And you see the social function of diagnosis, don't you, as a destructive "strategy for intervention," to use your terminology?

Laing: Yes. It's one of a whole set of interventions in my life, by the state, that I do not like. I don't even approve of the state having the right to insist that my children go to school. I don't like the state-backed medical monopoly of birth. Right now in England almost all women *must* go to the hospital to have their babies. Once you go to the hospital you *must* go through their whole routine, so often entailing depersonalization, regimentation, etcetera. In much of America it seems even worse. Babies are routinely taken away from their mothers and they're only allowed to be together for a very few minutes during the first ten hours. If you become helpless (there are crushing politics of helplessness), if you can't fend for yourself, if you can't take care of yourself, if your social power falls to zero, if you are at the mercy of others—God help you. If you're about to die, even your death may be taken away from you—for your own good. The general unofficial practice here (What's it like in the U.S.A.?) is not even to tell the person or the family that death is approaching. That's intolerable to me. By what right do doctors have to take over birth and death?

Hoffman: What are your feelings about the use of chemotherapy in treating mental illness?

Laing: It's way overused. Tranquilizers are awfully imprecise. I'd take any drug or recommend it if it made me feel better or more alert or more coherent. But tranquilizers will probably become more precise and therefore better. Once more the question is the *politics* of their distribution and use.

Hoffman: Getting back to therapy, it's hard to envision you, from your writings at least, in the classic fifty-minute psychoanalytic session.

Laing: I have a private practice and have seen people on that straight formal psychotherapy basis for years. It does provide an opportunity for two people to come together and consider the problems that arise. I find it a reasonably decent activity.

Hoffman: But in your households, which seem to allow for treatment on a larger scale than individual therapy, you don't say to the members, "You're sick—get better."

Laing: I don't think one is necessarily sick because one is crazy, but I don't recommend to people to go crazy or to go on being crazy. People who are crazy are usually not enjoying it. It's usually terrifying enough without further social intimidation. People who come our way are often crazy by their own definition, but they don't think the mental hospitals they have known have helped them out of it. If I were crazy, I wouldn't want to be near most psychiatric units I know. The people who come to us don't want to be treated against their will, because they can't defend themselves. They want a sanctuary, a refuge. Our treatment is in the way we treat one another. I suppose that's the big difference between our approach and others. We use the metaphor of "going through" the problem by trying to understand the problem.

Hoffman: Could you describe a household?

Laing: Several of us have just worked out a statement about what we are up to in London. Could I read it out? It puts it as succinctly as we have been able to get it.

Hoffman: Please do.

Laing: [Reads]

WHAT IS THE
PHILADELPHIA ASSOCIATION?

Suppose we, any of us, come to the end of our tether, can no longer cope, break down, go to pieces. To whom do we turn? Where do we go? A mental hospital is seldom a safe place to be, to live things through.

When a person's suffering becomes insupportable to himself, and to others, and yet persists, despite all, we may fairly say that such a person is in extreme distress.

The Philadelphia Association provides households, which, we hope, are places of refuge, sanctuaries, where people in distress can, if they choose, live through what they must, without jeopardy.

The Philadelphia Association is a network

of people, whose distinctive concern is both to cultivate skillful means of helping people whose relations with themselves and others have become an occasion of wretchedness, and to contribute to a theory of personal life that is adequate to experience. In the course of this enterprise we hope to come to a better understanding of how we occasion our suffering and joy, of the ways we may lose ourselves and each other, and find ourselves and each other again.

The treatment we offer is attention to each other, for *attentiveness is therapy.*

"Philadelphia" means brotherly or sisterly love. "Behold, I have set before thee an open door, and no man can shut it" (to the church at Philadelphia, Revelation 3:8).

Hoffman: How do they get cured?

Laing: Cured of what? But, okay, from the psychiatric point of view, some people get better no matter what you do, and some people don't seem to get better with treatment. In our system, where there is no *psychiatric* treatment—of any kind—more than 80 percent of people are psychiatrically better within a year.

Therapy, it seems to me, is the human community. The original term *therapist* comes from early Christian communities where the people called themselves *therapeuti*, meaning (it is thought, so I am told), an attendant, an ally. These were not monasteries but families living together. Everyone was to be a priest to each other, an attendant, an ally. We should all give *attention* to each other. Not just professionals. Of course, you can get better at practicing *attention* just as you can get better at playing the violin.

Hoffman: Is the 100,000-year grip of the family finally coming to an end in our modern age, or is that just the illusion of every generation?

Laing: Well, in the U.S.A., so a sociologist friend tells me, in divorce courts now, the judge often doesn't know who to *force* to take custody of the children. Neither party wants them. Each wants to unload them on the other. It's apparently a new, growing problem. It must be an index of total lack of bonding on the parents' part. Maybe I'm a sentimental fuddy-duddy but that seems very sad.

Hoffman: When I conceptualize the family it's a blur of names, births, deaths, new cars, old furniture. It's very hard picturing actual relationships. Even in the U.S. there was this incredible interest in the family inspired by *Roots*, with hordes of people swarming into libraries to map their genealogies, but it all seemed so mechanical, like charting horoscopes. No family ever sits down and asks itself how it relates.

Laing: There's no comparable social phenomenon here like *Roots*. Families here are probably closer than in the States. But it's increasingly becoming true that the father is absent. Until relatively recently children were never that interesting, so the history of child rearing is mostly supposed. There are surprisingly few facts recorded about how different periods in history managed family life. Personally, I like my own family and we have a circle of enjoyable friends who live in enjoyable families.

Hoffman: But in *Politics of the Family* and other writings, your description of the family as a maze of violent, angry, envious relations, where the wife is a slave and the children are hypnotized into submission, doesn't exactly seem a nice place to come home to.

Laing: If the wife doesn't have a skill she can escape with, she may be a slave. If she can't support herself, she, as Bernard Shaw pointed out, has got to become, in effect, a prostitute; a legal one but a prostitute nonetheless. She may have to make herself, or she may see no way out of making herself, available to a guy she can't stand. A miserable life. A trap. But if it's mutual desire, it's great. They can have children and love them and get off on it. There are still a few people who live that way. You know, when I go on tour in the U.S. and stay at a hotel, these hotels that seem all the same, and you go down to breakfast—all those middle-aged men, dressed much the same, all alone, eating their poached eggs, served by these waitresses with tinted grayish-blue hair piled up, wearing those same nurse's shoes—a frightening spectacle. Do all these guys *want* to be away from home?

Hoffman: Isn't there a new family story needed for this reality? I mean, if that's reality, why do we need the mummy-daddy-kiddie myth?

Laing: It's true the ideology hasn't caught up with this reality. I spend time each week with a group of women who live alone with their children. They have occasional lovers but no one permanent. I don't think guilt about not perpetuating the family myth bothers them, but they do become disheartened and sometimes bitter. They have to steel themselves not to feel too sorry for themselves. For a woman with young children, it's often an emotionally bleak life. What to do? There's so much wear and tear.

Hoffman: Even when you write of couples in *Knots* and *Do You Really Love Me?*, it seems like a bum deal. In fact, your use of Jack and Jill as prototypes seems to imply there's a lot of pain in a relationship. After all, Jack and Jill got pretty banged up falling down the hill.

Laing: Yes, there is that inevitable resonance, but I didn't select the names for that so much as they are verbally catchy. I didn't want to dignify bad relationships by making them archetypes for normality. I would have liked to have had more grist for picturing happier relations. The last book to come out in the States, *Conversations with Adam and Natasha*, is conversations with children and it's much more encouraging. A much brighter tone, to me anyway.

Hoffman: The human potential or growth movement during the past few decades talked of health as a superior state possibly only experienced by a few people. Are you less ambitious for people in this regard? Do you feel people are doing all right if they manage to break even?

Laing: Well, yes and no. They're doing all right but not perfect. Perfection is something we should all strive for. It's a duty and a joy to perfect one's nature. As long as one has any capacity to do so one should aim to be as perfect as possible in every respect.

Hoffman: Does that mean that everyone in the corporation should strive to be president?

Laing: Not in the least. In my scale of perfection there are no presidents or pay clerks. I don't have that type of ideology. That's not what life is about. Perfection of one's life is expressed in other ways. In spiritual perfection. The most difficult thing is love. A loveless, driving person that just competes in the rat race is far from perfection in my book.

Hoffman: Have you heard the term *workaholic*? It's a new term. Carter is the top workaholic in the U.S., Max Weber's complete capitalist nurtured on the Protestant ethic. Don't you think it's a strange term? I mean, on some level seeing devotion to work as an illness?

Laing: It certainly is strange and subtle. I'm sure you, like I, have had periods where you do an incredible amount of activity, what other people call work. And at other times just hang around. I can see work becoming an addiction and I often wish I became more addicted to it. It would make me feel more secure. There's a great feeling when you seem to hit your stride. Trouble is, it doesn't happen all the time. I find my ability not to work somewhat alarming at times.

Hoffman: Are you writing a lot?

Laing: I'm spending a lot of time (five to six hours a day) writing. The quantity of product is small. It will depend on the quality. This year I've been writing sonnets, of all things. It has been taking me about five hours to get one sonnet down in the first place. Most of the time I feel absolutely miserable. Not even satisfaction afterward, perhaps because it's not yet done. Writing doesn't get easier. *The Bird of Paradise*, for example, was absolute agony to write. It was because I was writing about unpleasant things. There were ecstatic moments, but the process of writing it was agony. I mean, here I am a very fortunate person, I'm not complaining about life. I've got a nice home, a lovely wife, I'm physically healthy, so the deal that other people have must be ten times worse. But no matter how difficult it is, it would be horribly difficult not to be able to express my feelings. I'd resent an unfulfilled life, a life where I couldn't share my experience with someone else—couldn't communicate.

Hoffman: What happens to people who can't express themselves?

Laing: Maybe they get into some work and keep on working. Mind work.

Hoffman: Are these men of resentment the ones that get to rule the world?

Laing: I don't know enough about these people. I proposed a television show where I could meet the rulers of the world. Wouldn't that make an interesting and highly commercial TV series? Meeting with people like Kissinger, Nixon, Carter, Castro, Sadat, General Giap. Of course, such people must have to play from quite far back. They must be used to playing it so far back, that whether we could actually meet in any real sense is possibly doubtful.

Hoffman: Could I ask some questions about sex? You don't seem to write about it that much.

Laing: I never felt I had anything original to say on the subject. It's important, all right. Everyone seems to have something to say. I might come up with something someday, you never can tell.

Hoffman: Well, what do you think of magazines like *Penthouse* and *Playboy*? I don't know how popular they are in England, but in the States magazines with nude photos are really popular. Do you see any harm or value in sexual fantasy being so public?

Laing: I feel that whole area should be unthrottled. So many people are guilty about the naked body. So put all these bodies together in any sort of combination. No need to get riled up. At the same time don't ram it down my throat. I don't like certain images, especially other people's. I wouldn't feel like going to Soho to see a sex movie or visit a sex shop, though I don't feel worked up about others doing it. I *like* the idea of censorship on television because I don't like my kids exposed to some sorts of sexuality that would be on if there wasn't censorship.

Hoffman: So you see harm in certain sorts of visual stimulation.

Laing: Yes. I believe in spiritual jeopardy. I regard the environment (visual, etcetera) I provide my children within the territory of my home as my responsibility. It's a bit late in the day, though, to start picking and choosing eroticism for them, when they see it in any bookstore in London anyway. I'm glad there's a double-X movie my kids can't see for a while. But viciousness seems to me much more potentially harmful, if excessively shown.

Hoffman: Do you see many people with violent fantasy worlds?

Laing: Many. Most are harmless people who are, however, absolutely tormented by the violent images in their fantasy worlds. Violence toward themselves and others. Constant images of bodies being torn apart like meat, and torture and slaughter. There are people who are terribly tormented by torture movies in their minds, which disgust and intimidate them and which they can't seem to stop, even though they don't feel they are about to put these fantasies into action. It must be horrible to live this nightmare. I can't see any value in having such fantasies fed by movies or television. I'm not saying they contribute to actual violence. I don't want other people's "want" nightmares crushing in on my living room. I'm glad somebody is screening out the extremes.

Hoffman: There's a new wave of French philosophers— Gluckmann, Dollé, Lardreau, among others. A cornerstone to their thinking, which I find disturbing, is that all recent social philosophies, in particular Marxism, have misled us; that these master thinkers promised us that progress would free us and, instead, that very belief in progress led to concentration camps and gulags. Do you share this view?

Laing: I feel very much in sympathy with this demotion of Marxism, both as a scientific dogma and as an ideology. I've never believed in history, you might say, as a myth of progress or its opposite. I never had the convinced feeling we were going upward or, for that matter, downward. I've never been imbued by these parameters and I have never believed in utilitarian socialism, this wedding of Marxism and social engineering. I've always been lacerated by the means-ends contradiction (to make an omelet you have to break a few eggs) because I've always been too much of an unformulated anarchist. I don't have that *systematic* a view of humanity. I'm aware we're living in a capitalist system, although I'm not sure what *capital* means. I'm aware of the existence of money, but I'm not sure what it is. From the glimpses I have of the noncapitalist world, there's very little of it I fancy for myself.

Hoffman: But we don't turn on the telly in the West and see interviews with happy workers in Russia.

Laing: Perhaps, but I have to confess I know so little of what's going on. We see the Russian gymnasts, these Chinese acrobats, so graceful and so beautiful—there must be something of value behind that. Friends of mine who study children in nurseries went to Russia and say the nurseries are very humanly warm and the staff and children share a lot of good feelings. But there are things that aren't in doubt. For example, my books are not allowed there and yet I was told that the Russian intellectuals know them and like the work. It's okay for the elite but not the general public. I couldn't tolerate living in a system like that. It wouldn't tolerate me.

Hoffman: Your concept of therapy doesn't entail a return to productivity.

Laing: Certainly not forced productivity. That would simply be slavery.

Hoffman: Don't all governments try to internalize fear to increase productivity, though? In our system don't we invent "scarcity" and then internalize it, as you suggest in *Reason and Violence*? Socialist countries have labor shortages, they don't have unemployment. They don't say there aren't enough jobs. Scarcity of work, of land, or energy seems to be a capitalist invention. The fear of ending up a bum on the sidewalk doesn't haunt the Russians.

Laing: Yes, this idea of expansion, of constant growth and development, is like being caught in a wave and timelessly suspended. I think the notion of perpetual growth is overplayed. We're a biological species. The body gives out. Decay sets in. We don't last forever and we can't be productive forever. The human race in due course will disappear. I've been programmed as a Protestant capitalist, but there is death and you can't take it with you. I sense the beginning, the middle, and the end of things. Ideas. Life. So "scarcity" doesn't seem to intimidate me, but hunger and thirst and cold and drudgery are daunting.

Hoffman: What do you see when you see old age or the approach of death?

Laing: I've got a happy and an unhappy image. The unhappy is the loss of faculties, mental and physical, before dying. Being at the mercy of other people. I don't want to be helpless or in pain. That's the negative image. The positive image is the healthy old man who's achieved enough to feel he's not wasted his time here. It must be very comforting to be honored in old age, to have one's fellows shower respect, awards, appeciation. But even then, I remember Paul Tillich at seventy-five. He still had a volume on his three-volume *Systematic Theology* to finish. He was weary with having to think and think it all through until he died. I don't desire that weariness. Maybe the feeling of incompletion keeps one going. But I'd hate to feel tormented in old age by feeling I had been deeply wrong all my life—to be caught in senile depression. Every age is difficult.

November 1979

In Search of Loch Ness Nellie:
A Fable

I FIRST SAW Lucky Nellie on August 25, 1954. This is how it happened. Me and Brenda, this girl from Revere Beach, were necking out on the Cape Cod Canal near Buzzards Bay. I was feeling her up and moaning real low, getting all excited, when all of a sudden I looked over her shoulder, through the foggy windshield, and I saw this absolutely gorgeous creature rise straight out of the water and smile at me with the prettiest smile I ever saw. Farther back, down the canal, I could see her huge, giant tail. Wow! She was all emerald green and scaly; she must have been at least sixty feet long and had to weigh at least eight tons, if a pound, or more. She was very, very pretty. She had a long, long neck and large gray eyes with eyelashes a good six inches long. She talked in a soft, sultry voice, not unlike that of Marilyn Monroe or Jackie Onassis. She called me by my first name and said if I would keep her secret, she would grant me a wish. I was really amazed that Brenda couldn't hear the voice. Luckily she had her eyes closed and was panting into my neck and shoulder. I nodded agreement. She said that her name was Nellie and that we could use telepathy to talk, and no one would hear but us. She said she was fifteen hundred years old and had three little children back home in Scotland in a lake. She was looking around for different places to live and have fun, and she liked to

178

live in private, but folks kept sneaking up on her. She told me that once, about a thousand years ago, some bloody miserable saint tried to transform her into the queen of Scotland. She had been really upset because she didn't want to be a superstar and go around giving people orders and signing autographs all her life. So she up and pulled out stakes with her kids and lived for five hundred years near the South Pole, even though it was mighty cold. After that, she got lonesome for Scotland and went home.

Everything went well for a while until about the thirties, when some really bad accidents happened to poor Lucky Nellie. First, some busybodies came out from London and saw her crawl across the road, heading for the North Sea. She was making secret raids on Nazi Germany at the time. They blabbed when they got home to London, and next year a scientist got a pretty good picture of her bobbing her head, so she bundled up the kiddies and headed for the Indian Ocean. Now she was looking around and asking different folks along the way for ideas and suggestions on where to live. Well, I said, if I was her, I'd talk to Greta Garbo or maybe go to these little islands I knew out in the Pacific. Oh, no, she said, Greta Garbo was a real bitch and those little islands I suggested were already being used for atomic-bomb testing. But she thanked me anyway and said someday she'd get back and see me again. Then she said that I could have my wish. So I thought real quick and I said I just figured maybe I could go all the way with Brenda. Lucky Nellie just smiled and winked and said she understood. And then she ducked out of sight. Just before she went, she said, "Oh, by the way, you don't think I'm a monster, do you?"

I smiled back and shook my head. "Oh, no, you're really pretty." And later that night Brenda and I really got it on something fierce.

Twenty years went by. I kept my promise and I never told anyone until now. By now, I was a fugitive on the run, roaming the globe myself, looking for a nice place to settle down. Sometimes I got lost, sometimes I got lonely. Once in a while I'd go up to a friendly face and I'd say, "Hi, my name is Abbie. Can you keep a secret?" I've had real good luck so far, no one's told and everyone's kept the secret.

One day, a few months ago, I was scuba diving off the Yucatan peninsula, out by the Isla de las Mujeres, looking for the place where the sharks go to sleep and get high. They do that down in some caves near there. I was going to check the caves out as a possible hideout, seeing how everyone's so afraid of sharks these days. When lo and behold, up swims Nellie.

Oh, Jesus, was she ever big! Underwater, everything gets magnified 25 percent. She looked bigger than the fucking *Titanic*. Immediately I knew something was up. She was sad and she was angry. She started talking, but it wasn't like Marilyn Monroe anymore. She talked very heavy street talk; she talked like a spade from Harlem. She was *angry*. "Hey, man, how you doin'? I got a real fat problem here. These goddamn scientists are on to my tricks. I had a neat deal worked out with the Scottish government, see. I mean, they kept pooh-poohin' the stories about me existin' for twenty or thirty years, you know? Kept a lot of the tourists and scientists and headhunters away, but then the depression came in, you know, recession and all that kind of shit. I guess it got to them and they got to make their money. I can't blame them, but Jesus, they sure put me uptight. You know what these folks are bringing in? Sonar beams and laser beams and TV cameras and wise punky college brats crawlin' all over my goddamn lake. I'm real uptight, man; they're going to stick me in a goddamn cage same as you, sure as shit. My kids are stashed near Canada with a baby-sitter. We're nomads; we're on the run; we're pissed. I talked to Bigfoot the other day, and I talked to the Snowman. You heard anything from Don Juan?"

Well, I thought, gee whiz, times are changing. "Oh, yeah, Don Juan, hey, it's a funny thing you should mention him. I met him, yeah, Mexico City. Uh huh, yeah, I didn't know him at first; I mean, he was wearing his suit and tie so I didn't recognize him right off. He said he's got the same goddamn problem: Ten thousand hippies crawling all over the Sonora desert looking for him and mushrooms. Goddamn, he even closed down his answering service. He told me he was headed to Las Vegas; he's up there now posing as a blackjack dealer. I got his secret number if you want it. I don't know, hon, what's your group have on this technological crap they're tracking you with?"

"Well, from what we heard, it's CIA, real advanced. They spotted Che with it in Bolivia, three thousand feet high in an airplane. They could measure the length of his beard. And that was ten years ago. Goddamn, it's open season on us creatures."

"What are we going to do?"

"I'll tell you, Abbie. I'm going to swallow the first fucking goddamn scientist I see. Dolphins are filling us in on all the goddamn boats; we're not even sure we trust Cousteau anymore, since he's gone commercial."

"Well, I met him once. I like him. Hey, take it easy, Nell. We've got folks working on your case. We've got two phone freaks fresh out of Leavenworth. They want to do freeze-ins in the Himalayas to stop them from looking for the Snowman. Yeah, they're together, they're really going to help. We've got folks all over the country who are going to call *National Geographic* magazine, saying that they just spotted you in South Dakota and Miami Beach and Las Vegas, things like that, sending all these bounty hunters on wild-goose chases."

"Hey, blood," Nell answered back, "you've got it; but dig it, we're just playin' games. I don't know what's gonna happen. This Bigfoot, Bigfoot's a mean motherfucker. He wants to sink the whole goddamn U.S.A., he's so pissed. You know what he did? He went and busted a fucking dam in Idaho the other day, and he says if that don't work, he's going to jump up and down on the San Andreas fault near Los Angeles next year, and my kids are going to join him. They like him. They think he's got the right approach; they're going to sink Los Angeles. Hey, tell them to leave us creatures alone."

Just before I left, she asked to borrow my knife. It was

my special underwater knife and there, underneath the Caribbean calm, we crossed blood. And just before she went her way and I went mine, I yelled out, "Hey, Nell, what's your code name?"

She shouted back, "Angel."

That's incredible, I thought. Every beautiful woman in the underground is called Angel. Maybe this *is* heaven.

December 1976

Hey, Vida!

~~~~~~

MARGE PIERCY'S *Vida* is a pretty good stab at depicting contemporary fugitive life in America. Vida is a member of the Network (read Weather Underground), a band of political activists who go underground after an undercover agent infiltrates their collective and blows the whistle on a bombing he investigated. The plot moves back and forth between the mass activities of the sixties and the more fragmented, isolated seventies. The latter period, a time of hand-to-mouth existence for the fugitives, is filled with all sorts of near captures.

Vida, first with one lover (I'm convinced only women writers use the words *lover* and *sensuous*) then another, races from Long Island to Cape Cod to Vermont, staying at safe houses, aiding battered housewives, holding the fragile underground coalition together and finally blowing up some equipment at a nuclear power plant site. The fugitive life seems an excellent vehicle to describe the sixties-turned-seventies mood alteration that followed the end of mass mobilizations around the Vietnam War. It's also an excellent vehicle for Piercy to put forth her decidedly left-wing politics and at the same time tell an exciting story.

She's on the safest ground when dealing with the collapse of the mass movement—an event which she experienced directly—and is on less sure ground when delving into the underground world. It may seem strange to those of us who grew up on such TV dramas as *The Fugitive* and *The FBI*, but the essence of underground life is more a mental struggle and has less to do with the FBI, phony IDs, roadblocks, and tapped phones. It's the agony that comes from being forced to pretend you're somebody you're not. Living daily in a state of controlled schizophrenia. It's a way of life only Kafka could do justice.

Piercy's book would have benefited from a crack-up scene; it would have added a touch of realism, a touch of the human dimension, because it's all too easy to cast fugitives as the perfect anti-Establishment hero. The characters in Vida's life that make up her support system ring a little truer than the fugitives themselves. Not forced to be obsessed with living underground, they can be shown enjoying and agonizing over the day-to-day existence that makes up the common aboveground life.

The problems I had with *Vida* were not literary. They had little to do with the politics (which I share). They had to do with the perpetuating of certain myths connected with fugitives, and especially political fugitives. Not surprisingly, these myths are shared by many of those of us on the run, as well as by the public at large. They involve an acceptance of the omnipotence of the state and tend to encourage a certain police state mentality among the citizenry.

First off, Vida is not Patty Hearst or Angela Davis. There is no all-out manhunt in her case. Yet throughout the book she acts as if there was. Project this tension over a six- or seven-year period and you can see the cerebrum getting a little frayed around the edges. There are about 300,000 fugitives running around the U.S. of A. That's about ten for each federal agent. But like nuns and tag-team wrestlers, FBI agents only move in pairs. So that's now a ratio of twenty to one. But agents are not just out there trying to net fugitives. There are bank robberies to contend with, kidnappings, hijackings, mail frauds, porno, espionage, Abscam programs and, of course, civil rights violations. They're much better at tracking down a car than a human. So you can see there is precious little time to look for fugitives.

In point of fact, in 95 percent of the cases the FBI does not "catch" fugitives. Fugitives catch themselves—that is, they turn to a life of crime in order to survive, and eventually get arrested. A check leads to apprehension. Oh, the Feds will go around making inquiries, but they do this less to gain a "lead" than to rattle the fugitive. Vida does not travel in circles where someone would sell you out for a few thousand dollars. In any event, the Feds just don't have the manpower to do things like stake out a corner known to be frequented by fugitives. Paranoid bullshit. Okay in fiction but not fact.

Turning to the subject of tapped phones, which permeates the book—again we're dealing with great police state mythology. First off, there's the live tap. Two agents (the court demands two) must sit with earphones in a basement of a nearby apartment acting as a recording extension phone. This is pretty costly and generally used on suspected Mafia figures involved in interstate gambling or prostitution. There are less than fifty live taps such as this in the United States. More common is a voice-activated recorder picked up weekly or monthly. Not exactly the type of a tap two sophisticated people can't talk around using code and vague language. Again, to tap Vida's support system would mean the FBI had to stop chasing a few bank robbers. Besides, anyone who wants to know if their phone is tapped simply has to purchase an inexpensive voltage regulator and measure the reduced output on the telephone. There is no way of drawing current off the line without it showing.

Let's talk about tracing a call, because that's really what a fugitive is afraid of. If it was a live tap with a setup such as a ransom-kidnapping demand, the call could be traced in seconds if originating in the same city. A minute or so more within the same state. That's if things go according to the book. Recently the Los Angeles Police Department set up a live tap with the best equipment available to trace a call from a potential murderer to reporter Bob Greene. It took two hours to trace the local caller. If the call is from out of state, all sorts of complications begin to crop up, because each state's phone system functions independently and permission to follow through the tap must occur at several levels of bureaucracy. After checking with both the phone officials and phone freaks, I estimate the quickest a call can be traced interstate is one half hour. *That's with a live tap.* When police arrive late at a scene with a call already in progress, it will take a minimum of one and a half hours and may not even be possible at all.

Perhaps the greatest mythology surrounds harboring, aiding, and abetting a fugitive. The FBI would like the general public to believe fugitives have legal plague and to even touch one of these shadowy figures or to offer a cup of coffee means you're subject to arrest. Wrong. Wrong. Wrong. To have a *legally* provable case of aiding and abetting a fugitive wanted for interstate flight to avoid prosecution, two FBI agents must have previously visited the suspect, shown them a photo, explained there was an outstanding warrant and warned the suspect that he or she could be guilty of a crime if they now helped. See, if you have never talked to an FBI agent, which no one compels you to do, you could never fulfill even that minimum criteria. It's not enough *legally* that a fugitive's been in all the papers and on TV. A citizen is just not expected to know the vicissitudes of the law in this case.

It's so hard to prove aiding and abetting that I know of only one person in the last ten or fifteen years held on the charge. This was in connection with the Susan Saxe –Katherine Powers bank robbing-guard killing case in New England. In the thousands of similar cases where people have helped fugitives absolutely zilch has happened. David Poindexter drove Angela Davis all over the country when she was the subject of the greatest FBI manhunt of her day. They were caught in bed together in a New York motel room. Poindexter was never even charged. Daniel Berrigan's short career as a fugitive ended when the FBI caught him in the backyard of William Stringfellow on Martha's Vineyard. Again, no charges against Stringfellow. Even in the most celebrated case in American history, it was pretty clear to everyone, including the Feds, that Micki and Jack Scott (among others) helped Patty Hearst. Again no aiding and abetting charges before or after she was apprehended.

A good chunk of *Vida*'s plot hinges on her sister, Natalie, being hauled before a grand jury for aiding her sister, and being slapped in jail. Every fugitive is in touch with his or her family. The Feds are big on public relations; they don't mess with families in a public way. Plus there's the complexity of the laws. It's not impossible to get arrested for helping a fugitive but in reality it rarely happens.

Vida and her comrades live in a world that's geared toward feeding on each other's paranoia. They persist by their dress in showing the rest of society they are different. They subsist on running small movement errands and panhandling from their support system. They can't handle a traffic ticket or figure out how to make an appointment with a doctor. One of their biggest problems seems to be making small (or big) talk with the outside world. In one telling scene, hiding out in Cape Cod, some neighbors approach the house while Vida and her running mate hide silently in the closet.

This is not the fugitive life as I've observed it for more than six years. The best cover is to make friends with your neighbors. You get busted for a traffic ticket—big deal. Millions do each year. The false ID problem so intriguing to nonfugitives is really one of the least hassles. An hour or two in the library studying microfilm of old newspapers will give you what you need—the obituary of a young kid who, if he or she had lived, would have been roughly your age. In the details you'll find particulars like birthdate and parents' names.

This info and three bucks sent to the Bureau of Vital Statistics will get you a birth certificate. From there you get a license, a passport, and whatever else you need. Following this method, your ID's as good as the next guy's. Maybe better, since you've got no bad credit rating and no accidents on your record. You need a doctor, ask your neighbor or look in the Yellow Pages. They're probably just as good as what your mother recommends anyway.

Piercy's fugitives believe in a Them and an Us. It was a stance not just of the underground on the run but one that characterized the entire left-wing movement of the early seventies. I can almost guess at the former fugitives Piercy used as source people. The kind of left-wing birds who are always making a point of "correcting" your vocabulary. People who worshipped at the Church of the Left. When the church moves underground, it inevitably ends up being guided by its most paranoid delusions. Removing oneself from the aboveground world, from friends and family severs the bridge with sanity. Perpetuating the myth that all roads back are guarded by an always present FBI is neither helpful nor is it true.

April 1980

The Fugitive Moonballer
Gets Off Return Volleys
at His Old Coach

THE MAIL comes late to my mountain hideout somewhere off the coast of Iowa, but not long ago I read a
copy of *Sports Illustrated* that contained a reminiscence
by my old tennis coach, Bud Collins (*Sports Illustrated,*
September 17, 1979). Bud wrote about those glory-filled
days of '59, when I captained Brandeis University's
netmen to the school's only unbeaten season. I knew
right off that Bud was going to say nice things about me,
because in the opening paragraph he promoted me from
the third spot on the roster to second. It took him twenty
years to move me up a notch. I appreciate Bud's gesture,
but for the sake of history I must break my fugitive
silence and correct this and a few of his other recollections.

There is the matter of our feud and who was in charge
of the team, he as coach or I as captain. It came about
because before Bud the captain *was* the coach. I mean,
before Bud our tennis team had zilch—just one beat-up
court. So we looked to Bud as our savior, a guy who
would approach Athletic Director Bennie Friedman and
try to get us new balls to practice with and maybe team
jackets.

Brandeis was only eleven years old at the time. Tennis
was a diddly sport back then, and the school, like most,
spent its alumni bankroll rounding up gridiron gladiators
so the school would look good on the sports pages. Of

course a football team at Brandeis was as out of sync as nuns at a cockfight. But the school wanted to prove it could break legs and dislocate shoulders with the best of Saturday's heroes. It didn't want the country's only Jewish-sponsored university to be known as a ghetto for brains, given stereotypes and all that. No one seemed to notice that except for the Goldfader boys, from my hometown of Worcester, Massachusetts, the whole team seemingly was made up of gentiles imported especially for that purpose.

So the athletic department gave practically all of its money to football, and the tennis team got new balls only for its matches, and no jackets. So we asked Bud, as our coach and leader, to change all this, and he passed the racquet back to me as captain.

I went to see Friedman, who ushered me into his office and pointed out the trophies he'd won, while I spelled out our complaints. Then he said, "Sonny, you know the two greatest things that ever happened in the history of the Jewish people?" I thought for a while and gave up. "Well, I'll tell you. The first was when the Jews got up an army and walloped the British, and the second was when I made all-American twice for Michigan."

Further into his article, Bud comments on my style of play: "Sadly, I must tell you there was nothing revolutionary about Abbie's style. He bordered on the reactionary, believing that every ball should be returned safely over the net." Way off, coach. The Big Serve *is* reactionary tennis. Pancho Segura knew as much about tennis as Pancho Villa knew about revolution. Just run the ball down and get it back. It doesn't matter if the court is tennis or judicial. I've always found it best to "keep the ball in play." After all, it was Che Guevara who wrote the famous guerrilla maxim: "Wait for the unforced errors."

I don't want to get picky. I really like Bud; he's the Walter Cronkite of tennis. He really has been a big factor in getting the game out of the country clubs and onto the streets. And he wasn't as bad a coach as he claims. Bud taught the game of outer tennis. Say your opponent likes to rush the net. Instead of giving him the satisfaction of slamming the ball down your throat, Bud taught us to hit it out of bounds, explaining that net rushers get frustrated quickly when prevented from testing their racquet strings.

Still, we all suspected Bud learned coaching from a how-to-teach-tennis pamphlet we once found next to his locker. We were never sure if he knew what he was talking about, because he always showed up for matches in his street clothes. He'd circle around the courts in his Florsheims, yelling instructions. "Hit their ankles!" "Go for the backhand."

Yeah, I remember those times, playing tennis in New England back when, like volleyball and Ping-Pong, it was considered less than a real sport. But I was hooked and I kept up my game even during the great riots of the sixties. Once I challenged then-Vice-President Agnew to a match. I told him I'd get a haircut if he beat me. I could have spotted Spiro five games plus Bobby Riggs and still have wiped his nose on the court.

I sometimes play on the run, so to speak, though underground courts do get a little damp. It was coincidental, Bud, but I read your article the day I got home from the doctor after getting shot with cortisone for my first tennis elbow. Time flies. You know, it's a funny thing: With age you are promised wisdom and instead you get tennis elbow. But don't worry about me being a fugitive and all, coach; it's just another road trip. I was sorry to miss the team reunion at the U.S. Open; maybe I'll show up next year. I enjoy your announcing shtick on all the big matches, though your colleague on another network, the Davis Cup coach with the lean-mean look, has gotta go. Tony Trabert still hasn't accepted the fact that tennis, like life, is just another ball game. I always brag when your face comes on the tube. "Hey, see that guy? He was my coach." So I was your most notorious pupil? You're a good guy, Bud, and you can call me anything you want—just don't call 911.

December 1979

Sixties Going on Eighties

~~~~~~

ABOUT THE BEST thing you can say of the seventies is that they didn't happen. Aside from two events—the forced resignation of Richard Nixon and the Arab oil boycott—it's hard to imagine historians of the next century getting worked up about this decade. Indeed, come New Year's Eve, when the TV commentators gather around tables to recapitulate, they'll begin by saying, "The seventies were not the sixties."

Now, there was a decade! People got out of their demanding bodies and neurotic heads long enough to effect historical change. Legal segregation fell, the mightiest war machine ever assembled was defeated, and our nation underwent a cultural civil war. Last year, when I spent time with the "new philosophers" in Paris, their seminal thinker, André Glucksmann, told me, "You people did something unprecedented. The Vietnam resistance was the first time in modern military history that a people successfully rose up against its own imperialist army. It was quite encouraging to those of us who believe in democracy."

In the shadow of such a period, it's no wonder the seventies appear as little more than one long, exhausted inhale. Major surgery followed by postoperative recuperation. Outward turned inward. Concern for others displaced by preoccupation with self. Politics superseded by sex and sports. If one question typified the seventies it had to be "What's in it for me?"

I've lived more than half the decade underground. Forced to be on the run, cut off from the past, I've had a unique opportunity to see America from different vantage points. I've been a cook, a teacher, and a writer. I've called several different regions of the country home. I've hung out in mansions and sucked the gum off food stamps in order to survive. In the past year I found myself returning to political activism, hurling once again into the crucible of change. I'm emerging as a local leader fighting one of the boondoggle nuclear plants that are sprouting up like huge concrete mushrooms in the countryside. Security prevents my giving too many details, but I can report a renaissance of grassroots protest building in the heartland of America.

If the historical pendulum swings every ten years (in part due to the media fashion makers) from active to passive to active, the eighties should be a decade that will again see the mobilization of huge numbers of people against rigid institutions and governments. Will the sixties repeat? Most definitely not. But there is the smoldering legacy of what happened. Back then we had to learn from scratch just how, in a democracy, you went about challenging your government from the street. We had to learn time-tested tactics of community organizing and experiment with newfangled ideas of communicating in an electronic jungle. With the rebellion against a repressive parent-society code still a bright memory, the eighties can move forward without our having to expend the energy needed to break through the eggshell. The spirit of resistance will be there; but the form, the faces, and the issues will be different.

America has never taken well to ideological movements. Maybe it's because ideology requires a good deal more reading than we picture viewers care to put up with. Perhaps it's due to our preference for action rather than thought. It could be due to the control of the ruling class and the education we receive. In any event, the sixties' break with ideology—the concept of participatory democracy—will carry into the eighties. Out of necessity there will be a politics suited to the situation.

Take our struggle here in the heartland. A nuclear plant and its waste threaten a beautiful valley. It involves a battle between the land and energy. If energy is a prerequisite to progress, what kind of energy, and progress to where? Won't nuclear energy concentrate power in the hands of a few technocrats who are directly under control of the conglomerate barons? Shouldn't science concentrate on harnessing the power of the sun, the wind, and other energy alternatives? What will the quality of our land and waters be, should we at last come to our senses and limit our human strife? Will future generations win the social revolution only to inherit a wasteland?

The eighties probably will not have its Vietnam. Let's face it: No nonwhite, volunteer army is going to fight in Africa or South America. Eurocommunism will become a dominant and unifying force in Europe. Increased trade with Russia will strengthen calls for disarmament. Here in the United States, through the ecology movement, tax revolters will find themselves on the same local committees as socialists. Pot-smoking backpackers will be breaking nutritious bread with beer-drinking fishermen and hunters. Rank-and-file union members will engage in wildcat strikes and challenge the old-guard leadership as the labor unions seek to exert stronger influence in Democratic politics. Police will increasingly come to see themselves as a part of the working class. Generational conflict, a hallmark of the sixties, will play a minimal role, as campuses revert to their "ivory tower" tradition. This new coalition of resistance will break through traditional thinking on both the Right and the Left. Americans will have to make the fundamental decision to stand isolated with the dying embers of imperialism or join the rest of the world in cooperative planning and sharing.

December 1979

Cold War Language:
An Editorial Reply

LANGUAGE SHAPES our environment. It is impossible to have thoughts without words. This well-established fact seems to be completely ignored by reporters and broadcasters who claim to be "objective" while using heavily loaded language. Smart guys like Edwin Newman and William Safire write books and columns about the misuse of English in everyday life but shy away from pointing out the politically biased vocabulary that daily molds our views of world events. Network executives pontificate at fancy dinners about fair treatment while media critics nod in agreement. It's almost as if no one actually reads or listens to the news, for if they did they would soon discover a naked emperor babbling advertisements for a free press not really all that free.

Recently I watched some reporters on one of those Sunday television round-tables discussing land reform in El Salvador. To be sure, there was gentlemanly disagreement on the effectiveness of the government's program (though the opposition's was never mentioned) but all seemed to have arrived at a consensus for how the various forces in that country should be identified, and curiously enough that language was exactly the same used by Secretary of State Haig in the day's press conference. No matter what "excesses" were caused by government troops they were still *security* forces, while the opposition of peasants (translate: "dumb farmers"), students (translate: "naive patsies") and union leaders (translate: "rabble-rousers") would be labeled the *ultra-left*. At times the *communist-inspired ultra-left,* which, although an exercise in redundancy, drives home the point that once again the bad guys in the mountains are disturbing cherished peace in the valley.

Once identified, who really has to examine the land reform program of an ultra-left? Indeed, what even is an ultra-left? We know "old left" and "new left," "left-of-center" and "far left." We even know "extreme left." Ultra-left rings of designer jeans, punk music, and Brian De Palma horror movies. A new-wave left. Something for the eighties, like Carlos the International Terrorist or the Red Brigades. But what exactly does this term have to do with the reality of El Salvador? What does it have to do with the tens of thousands murdered by the government and the tens of thousands offering resistance? How does it encompass the fact that Guillermo Ungo, titular leader of the opposition, was not so long ago the vice-president of El Salvador? Is it fair to confuse a people's liberation movement in Latin America with a small band of European urban guerrillas? They call themselves *democratic revolutionaries.* Is that term too hot to handle? How can an *ultra-left* speak to Americans who have been nurtured on the idea that truth, like the hole in the doughnut, rests firmly in the middle?

This is nothing compared to cold-war language on the grand scale. Does anyone know the difference between an *ally* and a *satellite?* What about a *government* or a *regime?* Or ,a *puppet government?* Certainly not the Philippines. Think fast: Which side has *policies,* which has *party lines?* They have *strong bosses.* We have *partners.* At times our Third World partners (only a First-Worlder could have come up with these rankings to begin with) practice *firm leadership,* which seems to be a broadcaster's term for the slaughter and jailing of thousands. Careful though. *Tough leaders* are not to be confused with the *iron-fisted rulers* on the bad guy's team. All the world's *dictators* are there also. So Cuba is destined to be *ruled* (not led) by *Dictator* Castro while South Korea's *President* Chun will get a warmer reception by the U.S. media. That he was brought to power by a Korean Intelligence Agency coup that murdered or imprisoned 25,000 political opponents matters not. He's our Chun so we love him. If he weren't how would we explain the 50,000 U.S. troops that *occupy*—excuse me— *assist* South Korea? Chun recently legitimatized his office through what the U.S. press termed a *free election*. Not entirely untrue since the Koreans had just one choice less than we get every four years.

Of course, things around Seoul are way better off than in *Communist* Korea. Nobody knows anything about Communist Korea but for some reason we all know they live in *slavery*—a term now synonymous with living *under* communism. As I understand it we all live "on top" of capitalism, never having to escape from under its *yoke*. The closest we ever hint of the "yoke of capitalism" is in April, when commentators talk about the nuisance of taxes.

Communist as a label is used by virtually every reporter in this country. Who's ever heard of *Fascist* Chile or *Capitalist* West Germany? It's impolite to use adjectives with friends. The only color in our vocabulary for a country is *red*.

And why be impolite? Our friends never commit *aggression* nor do they *intervene*. They *retaliate* or they *aid*. We help *rebels* in Afghanistan and Angola, they supply *guerrillas* in Latin America. Washington *advises* but Moscow *calls the shots*. The United States, always referred to as "the most powerful country in the world," never pulls strings, twists arms, or issues ultimatums to friends. In fact, it's a complete mystery as far as the press is concerned how exactly the United States uses all this accumulated power.

Then there has always been the baffling distinction between *commandos* and *terrorists*. *Commandos* are currently training with machine guns, mortars, helicopters, you name it, in southern Florida. Their aim is to recapture Nicaragua (a country with which we still maintain diplomatic relations). If those *commandos* were training in Libya they would obviously be *terrorists*. Of course, they would have to leave their helicopters behind, since *terrorists* would lose their classification if they bombed from the air. Our friends bomb from the air. The formula goes something like this: The forces of terror destroy from the ground, the forces of freedom destroy from the air. Freedom flyers, like God and Superman, can always count on rave reviews. And why not, they're our skies.

Last year, during the Iranian hostage crisis, Hodding Carter, spokesman for the State Department, became the nation's most influential English teacher. For the first month *students* held the hostages. By the second month, those same students were now *militants,* and by the third month they had become *terrorists*. As the months dragged on they went from *terrorists* to *extreme terrorists* to *cut-throat terrorists* to *fanatical cut-throat terrorists*. It's a good thing the hostages were finally released; the State Department was beginning to run out of bad words. What was of interest was the way the Washington press corps echoed each increment of slander even while mocking Iranian references to "Satan America" or "imperialism." In fact, *imperialism* is a nonword in U.S. semantics. It is always something they accuse us of doing, hence *propaganda,* hence a lie. Remember, nonwords mean nonexistence. No one has therefore ever heard a discussion of American imperialism in the mass media.

The terrorist-commando distinction is far from the only category the press uses to distinguish friends from foes. For example, our team has no *dissidents*. *Dissidents* are heroes, like the savage in *Brave New World*. What we have are *radicals, subversives, subversive radicals,* or *radical subversives*. I guess the thinking is how can you dissent when you have democracy? Democracy gets subverted, totalitarianism breeds dissidents.

We also, by the way, have no refugees. Since we and our allies live in the best of all possible worlds, why would anyone choose to escape? The correct term for our *refugees* is *expatriates*. And they are sure ungrateful. Not like a professional who's been educated at state expense in a socialist country and chooses to sell his services for ten times the price on our side. A typical refugee hero. Whereas expatriates are just writers not good enough to get published—mean, bitter little ingrates.

Last year 100,000 Cuban refugees swam to Miami Beach, escaping the crumbling economic chaos of Castro's communism (it's been crumbling for twenty years). They were reported down to the last detail. We know each by name, their pedigree, even dental charts. During the past four years of the Begin *regime,* excuse me, *government,* in Israel, 500,000 Israeli refugees, nearly 20 percent of the population, have fled to the United States as the Israeli inflation rate skyrocketed. Not only is this nonnews here, but under the rules of U.S. journalism there cannot even *be* an "Israeli refugee." But unless our government is sponsoring some massive taxi-driver educational exchange program, New York and Los Angeles are swarming with such unidentified Israeli refugees.

The *refugee* problem often arises in countries prone to *massacres,* another politically burdened term. We all know about the 87 billion Cambodians massacred by the godless Vietnamese. Not far away in Indonesia, a leftist government was overthrown by military-religious elements helped by the CIA. What followed was the bloodiest massacre in modern times, with estimates of nearly a million and a half victims. Not only was this bloodshed not given much coverage in the U.S. press when it happened but the just completed slaughter of 400,000 Timoreans by "our" Indonesian government has also gone unreported. The more recent carnage happened concurrently with the Cambodian atrocities, but alas, Indonesia is a valuable ally in the Far East. Think of it, the extermination of the snow leopard has received more press attention.

One way to tell our team from theirs is to watch how convoluted the terminology gets. For example, when Syria crosses into Lebanon it simply *invades,* but with Israel it's a *preemptive strike* or, better still, a *defensive preemptive strike.* In over thirty years of Mideast conflict

Israel has yet to invade a neighbor, an amazing record.

Another common practice is contrasting nationalism with ideology. Thus, in reporting the ball-score body-count each night during the war in Southeast Asia, broadcasters would say "Americans killed 175 Communists today." In the dozen years of conflict, no Vietnamese were killed in the media, and certainly no Capitalist ever killed a Communist. Kind of unfair, they didn't get a chance. This nationalism-ideology contrast makes it easier to understand just why we send troops all over the world—they defend "our way of life." Always a valid reason, media-wise, to eliminate millions of non-believers. After all, communism doesn't bleed.

By far my favorite cold-war term is *Free World,* as in "Free World spokesmen gathered in Vienna to discuss the latest economic crisis. . . ." Though I defy you to try to find the *Free World* on any map, it is a place as well known to all of us as the Panama Canal or Coney Island. Emotionally it's more important, for to leave the *Free World* means suffering the fate of ancient sailors who disappeared off the edge of a flat earth. All reporters use the term but TV broadcasters use it with such regularity that even the most skeptical viewers are susceptible to its devil lure. For Walter Cronkite the *Free World* was a place not unlike the Garden of Eden. To Chancellor, Brokaw, and Rather it's a more modern version—a vast productive enterprise in occasional need of minor repair but basically a reasonable, responsible vehicle. A corporation, if you will, not unlike those that had the good sense to recognize their talent. While to ABC's Frank Reynolds the *Free World* is the neighborhood he grew up in as a kid. Whatever the vision, the *Free World* is there, on the right side of the *Iron Curtain*—a huge mass of bountiful wealth and happy people, with its capital somewhere around Scarsdale, Illinois.

Tape tonight's news broadcast, play it back and list the value-ladened phrases. Take a news clipping about something like "arms build-up in the Soviet Union." Substitute "United States" for "Soviet Union" and read the article again. You'll quickly see a whole flood of adjectives and adverbs that are out of sync when describing our own stockpiling. Contrast the language used to describe economic problems in England and Poland. After all *union agitation* was about as healthy as bubonic plague until the *Wall Street Journal* discovered Lech Walesa. In fact, try and name another foreign labor leader and pretty soon you start to realize we're getting only one side of a one-sided coin. Has anyone ever heard of "management agitation"? There are a thousand ways to control the news. The Russians, clods that they are, have invented only one. The freedom of our system has forced us to come up with the other 999.

August 1981

Oh Boy, War with the Russians!

THE CURRENT war hysteria is reminiscent of the drum beating that went on during the early years of the Vietnam War. Rusk, McNamara, and the others were forever reminding us of how Southeast Asia was part of our vital interests. Lose this country, the next will follow. It was called the domino theory. If Vietnam and Cambodia went, Thailand, Burma, and India would follow. A good portion of the population held that the dominoes would topple the other way. Japan, Honolulu, Los Angeles.

In order to make war, such grassroots hysteria must be broadcast. American news media rarely question American foreign policy. In European countries there is real divergence of opinion in the media, but not so here in the land noted for freedom of the press. So just as in the early years of Vietnam another closing of the ranks behind a warlike policy seems to be occurring.

Afghanistan? All of a sudden this pile of rocks noted only for its black hashish has the United States in a confrontational state unseen since the Cuban missile crisis.

There is really no way to justify the Russians sending troops into Afghanistan, but it is important to understand some history and motive.

Afghanistan lies on the southern border of Russia. For the past few centuries it has more or less been ungovernable. Most of the country's terrain is mountainous and easily lends itself to the development of isolated warring tribes. The vast majority of these tribes are Muslim. Over the years some of the tribes have formed stable communities but the majority have remained nomadic. Intense warfare between the tribes has been persistent. Many of the tribes survive on smuggling and banditry. Often after a confrontation the victors will cut off an enemy's head and use it in a rousing game of polo. The traditional Koran system of law is practiced (despite Khomeini's pronouncement it is only paid lip-service in Iran), complete with hand-cuttings for stealing and stoning for adultery. The women help with the goats and have about the same rights.

For twenty years the government in Kabul has been pretty much neutral or pro-Moscow. In 1978 Russia backed an army coup and a Marxist government came into power. Then the process of making Afghanistan more a country and less a collection of feuding tribes began. Things proceeded brutally and pretty much unsuccessfully. The head of the Marxist government, Mohammad Taraki, was ousted and executed by Amin. Amin proved even more inept and barbaric. Either fearing that the fever of Muslim tribalism would spread back across the border into Russia or wishing to prop up the fledgling Marxist government, the Soviets made their move.

I, for one, accept the second motive. Since World War II the Russians have only sent occupation troops beyond their borders three times. Twelve years ago in Czechoslovakia and twelve years before that into Hungary. In all three cases the countries border Russia and in each case a Marxist, pro-Soviet government was under assault by internal elements.

The administration would like us to believe the Red Bear is on the march, headed for Iranian oil fields. History does not support such analysis even if it does produce campaign votes. If the Russians wanted Iran, they scarcely needed Afghanistan, since they already share a thousand-mile border, mostly plains ideally suited for tank warfare. Russia is self-sufficient in oil and all reports (except last year's by the CIA) insist the Soviets will not require petroleum imports at least until the next century.

I should note that some pretty heavy people think the Soviets went into Afghanistan reluctantly—such a move was voted down overwhelmingly by the Politburo last year—in part because they believe the United States and China are planning a war against the USSR. The Soviets, they argue, feared U.S. troops would go into Iran, seriously weakening that flank at a time when the vast bulk of Soviet might is being shifted to the Chinese border. People I know who study Soviet documents and press say that the Soviet leadership is absolutely obsessed with the Chinese and is convinced that China will provoke a nuclear war within the next ten years.

And then there's the view of French admiral Antoine Sanguinetti, who was forced to retire from the French high command two years ago for speaking out about European strategic policies. In a revealing interview in *In These Times,* the admiral pointed out that U.S. policy has changed toward Europe and that the United States now wants Europe to be able to fight an independent nuclear war with the Russians. To this end, the United States has forced the Europeans to accept two new nuclear missiles, the Pershing II and Cruise missile, despite the resistance of the Dutch and Belgian parliaments and many European political leaders. Although the U.S. press has barely reported this story, according to admiral Sanguinetti the Russians are crazed about the move and see it as a first step toward giving nuclear weapons to the West Germans. Sanguinetti argues that among the major considerations affecting the march into Afghanistan was the paranoia and fear of the U.S. missile step and a desire to secure a weak flank in the event of war.

The London *Observer,* which throughout this crisis has tried to maintain a level head, has scolded the U.S. press for exaggerating the number of Russian troops and the level of resistance by rebel tribesmen. The *Observer* points out that most of the reporting is done on rumors circulating in the rebel camps set up in Pakistan and Iran. The rebels will tell whatever story the market demands.

When White House foreign policy adviser Zbigniew

Brzezinski toured the border recently he was shown on television shooting a rifle back toward Afghanistan (the rifle jammed) and leading tribesmen in a football-style chant, "Back to Afghanistan." What we were not told was that the vast majority of the nomads who had crossed the border into Pakistan did not even know the Russians had invaded Afghanistan. They cross every year when winter comes.

Even George Kennan in a recent L.A. *Times* article and in an appearance on *60 Minutes* labeled the Soviet action defensive rather than offensive. Kennan is no peacenik apologist! For fifty years, he served as one of the chief formulators of U.S.-Soviet policy. In the fifties, as ambassador to the Soviet Union, he was a principal architect of the Cold War. Kennan is *more worried* about the U.S. response than he seems to be about the Russian occupation. By linking up with China, arming Pakistan, establishing new bases in the Persian Gulf and combining this with a NATO missile build-up—it's no wonder the Russians are paranoid. They are virtually encircled. The United States persisting in its present policy might be creating a situation where the Russians see no alternative but to fight.

Any fair reading of history will show Russia moving cautiously when it comes to warfare. Looking back over the past twenty or thirty years, it has been the United States and not the Russians who have repeatedly unleashed troops. We've sent troops off to Lebanon, the Dominican Republic, and military contingents to scores of other places, not to mention the bloody business of Korea and later Indo-China. We helped launch and gave support to an invasion of Cuba. We helped overthrow the governments of Chile, Guatemala, and Iran. We assassinated Africa's greatest leader, Patrice Lumumba.

Throughout all this the Russians kept their troops muzzled. They have condemned us in the UN, but nothing they ever said compares to what Clark Clifford, the president's envoy to India, had to say in New Delhi. Leaning right into the bank of microphones, the old Vietnam warhorse literally bellowed a warning to Moscow: "One more step and this means WAR!"

I have a theory no one really gives a damn about Afghanistan. I really have two theories, the first being we used Afghanistan as an excuse for pulling out of the Olympics, the CIA having convinced Carter the United States would win only a few medals. No, the real reason Carter and Brzezinski responded so fiercely to the Russians is to cover and conceal their true purpose: to establish a strong military presence in the Persian Gulf. Actually, they began planning this a few years ago, as several political figures, among them Barry Commoner, have pointed out. They painted the tanks desert camouflage, started negotiating for Persian Gulf bases, and Carter even began talking about the draft, though no one paid any attention to him. All this to keep the oil fields safe for the oil companies.

Right after the Iranian revolution, the intelligence community was assigned the task of compiling information on the stability of all Persian Gulf states. Throughout the area they found two new and growing trends, especially among the young. Since Iran, more and more young men can be seen sporting the beards bearing witness to the Islamic revival. Also growing in popularity are the politics of Colonel Qaddafi of Libya. A combination of the two would prove deadly to any pro-American regime. There are strong indications that the next Iran will be Saudi Arabia. For all its gold and oil, the Saudis have done little to benefit those outside the royal family. The recent takeover of the holy mosques at Mecca was just the tip of a boiling anger waiting to gush forth.

The United States is aware that without its military forces the days of its royal friends are numbered. Our young people will not be donning army fatigues to withstand Soviet aggression. Carter and Brzezinski do not fear so much another Afghanistan as they do another Iran. The troops will be used the way we have used troops since World War II: to prop up corrupt regimes. For the Russians we'll have to use the Big Bomb.

Don't be down about all this. Just consider it another Olympic event.

February 1980

An Open Letter
to Congressman Zeferetti

DEAR CONGRESSMAN:

Let me introduce myself. My name is Abbie Hoffman and I am currently a prisoner in the Downstate Penitentiary in Upstate New York doing one to three years on a coke rap. For sixteen years, while posing as a civil-rights and antiwar subversive, I was in reality one of the biggest coke dealers selling to Hollywood celebrities. Through the years I kept very careful account of each and every user, assembling a list of 150 satisfied customers, many of whom themselves became dealers (called in the trade "subdealers"). I stashed this list in a bank vault in Beverly Hills thinking someday it might come in handy. Now is the time. Like all convicts, I hate prison. There're no broads and the food sucks, so I'm ready to turn state's or nation's evidence. But for a price, of course. I'll get to that later. First, as my patriotic duty and as evidence that I'd be a good witness and that I know the coke scene, I'll sweeten the pot with some advice and hot tips.

You need me. I have believability. Who's gonna believe Richard Pryor, a guy who tries to kill himself by holding a lighter to a bottle of rum? No way! You believe that, you'll believe Chrysler's working on a car you'd like to buy. Then that Cathy Lee Crosby. Ha! A bit player who couldn't act her way out of a blind date. I mean, would you go to a hearing with Cathy Lee Crosby? Forget it. You need me 'cause I know what from what.

Okay, for starters, where does all this cocaine come from? I was asked that by the prosecutor in my case and I refused to tell, but prison oils the tongue. Congressman, cocaine comes from South America. Now, if you could make the Panama Canal the Great Panama Wall, it'd be finito on la old cocaina. *Savez!* But I don't think it's possible with spending cuts—and if I recall, we gave that canal away. So the answer to how that cocaine gets from South to North America lies in the Cuban connection. J. Edgar Hoover guessed this to be true. I *know* it's true. However, *this* testimony I am offering to Senator Jeremiah Denton and his committee on subversives, terrorists, and young Democrats. Sorry.

Now, why do they use so much cocaine in Hollywood? Another good question. They use cocaine because Hollywood is such a laid-back (sleepy) place they need a way to wake up real fast. No-Doz just doesn't make it. Coke lets you be asleep but entertain the illusion that you are wide awake; since Hollywood is an entertaining illusion anyway, it's the perfect drug.

By the way, since coke is white, I suggest your committee call what you're doing *white-listing*. This will have the advantage of not confusing your important work with what happened in the fifties. The list contains no less than twenty-six Academy Award winners, twelve Grammy winners, two Golden Globe winners, nine leading men, five following ladies, four sex symbols, eight baby moguls (two Jewish), sixteen has-beens, three deal makers and four TV actors who play policemen. Two of these are subdealers who, ironically, deal to eight other TV actors who play crooks. That should get the Moral Majority wet!

I mean, the names on my list are not just regular Americans, mind you. They tend toward your subversive-chic type. And most of this is a secret. They're the type of people who at coke parties talk about how Charlton Heston caps his teeth and how Frankie has never forgotten the time he walked in on Ava Gardner (his wife at the time) and Lana Turner making love. You know, the folks who refuse to appear on the Jerry Lewis

Telethon: bad types. They make Vanessa Redgrave look like a Girl Scout.

Here's a clue to spotting stars on coke. See, everyone thinks coke has to do with the nose. Sure, it goes in there, but that's like saying New York's about the Lincoln Tunnel. It ain't the nose, it's the eyes, Zef. Now go to some movies. Sit up real close and watch the faces of the actors. Look at the eyes. See that little dark circle in the middle? If it's bigger than the outer circle, that's coke! Also watch to see how wide open the eyes are. Your average eye is open maybe a half inch (a quarter inch on downers). Coke eyes are open a full inch sometimes—even as much as two inches, depending on quantity, quality, body weight, and religious background. For some reason only very skinny people seem to use cocaine. So right away you know Orson Welles, Marlon Brando, and Carol Burnett are not on the list.

There are other ways to spot cocaine users. Watch for people walking into restrooms with mirrors. Why do they need mirrors? Restrooms *have* mirrors. Well, they put the coke on the mirror, see, and chop it up. The mirror makes it look like twice as much. I can't explain it better, but it's an important part of the drug ritual. They always, by the way, chop it up with Gillette razor blades, so if you are into paraphernalia busting you can make this an issue. The Schick people (big Falwell-Reagan backers) will love you. There's also spoons. Say you're at a dinner in the Hills and you hear someone say, "Pass the spoon." *Subpoena the fucker right on the spot.* Those people are rich enough for separate soup spoons; *only* coke spoons are passed. They carry their tiny spoons chained to tiny brown bottles in which is kept the evening's supply. The dealers have all agreed to use these tinted bottles so the junkies can't see if the coke is all used up or not. This way they throw the bottle away with some cocaine still in it, or they get so mad when they can't get that spoon inside the shrinking bottle that they spill a lot. And that means moola from pasadola. This stuff costs six times as much as gold! Besides, in Beverly Hills they don't want to hear from gold: That you can't get up your nose.

Also, while you're at the movies, look for code lines. For instance, in nature movies, if someone says, "When will it snow?" that's coke! Snow is coke, see, in drug lingo. Or like a gangster movie they say, "Blow that guy away" (as opposed to "Blow that guy"). Again, "blow" is coke. The writers and producers are signaling the dealers that their supply is dangerously low (confirming reference: *TV Guide*).

I knew, of course, several other coke dealers. Many dealers. They come from all walks of life. For example, probably most of the dealers in Hollywood are dentists. They buy the stuff legal for $18.75 an oz. (as in Wizard of) and sell it for $2,500 sealed (that means factory wrapped). If your committee reads a little-known study by Merck and Mallinckott of the University of Southern California School for Dental Hygiene, they will find that people in Hollywood go to the dentist five times the national average. Root canals? Wrong. Snow-blow. The dentist rubs it on the patient's gums and they get almost as high as the bill. So if you hear Hollywood types say "Have you seen your dentist lately?" write down their names.

This, of course, only scratches the surface of what I know. Another guy on the block here in prison was the chief dealer for the New York Knicks. That's a basketball team—sort of, anyway. This guy said he cut the shit so bad with powdered Tylenol that they couldn't slam-dunk for beans. He says the Celtics' dealer was more honest, hence they get higher—and higher counts in basketball. Same in the National Football League. I mean loaded. I'll just drop two tidbits well known in the coke trade (or coke zone, as it's properly called). Pete Rozelle has a piece of everything going down or up, if you catch my drift, in pro football. Fidel Castro is a personal friend of Rozelle's and he vacations in Colombia. Check his passport if you have any doubts. The second tidbit revolves around Pittsburgh Steeler lineman Mean Joe Greene. You just go up to Mean Joe and confront him. Say, "Mean Joe Greene, you're nothing but a low-down coke junkie." I guarantee he'll drop on his knees, confess his sins, and spit out names faster than he sacked quarterbacks last year. Then give him some coke. He'll give you the shirt off his back. You know what the ads say: Coke adds life! (In New York it adds fifteen to life!)

Well, it's lock-in time and pencils in the cells are contraband. By now you can see I know coke from talcum powder, so let's do some business. But as we've all learned in the eighties, everything has its price. I'm sacrificing just about all my friends rich enough to lend me money. I could end up the Elia Kazan of this generation. People will say "Abbie Hoffman sneezed" ("squealed," in the coke zone).

Now you think I want my freedom. Nah, that's in the cards anyway with the Denton deal. Maybe you think I want a new identity like in that James Caan movie. Wrong again, I've had loads of new identities. You got to get the list. Without it you're washed up. I mean, drive-in schlock—send it to Hong Kong on the has-been express. You need me *more* than I need you to get ratings. Ask Barbara Walters and I could wear the black-and-white-striped prison suit and shave my head. So what I want after you've cleaned out Hollywood and done your job and become real famous—you know what I want? Universal Studios. Why? Because I want to make movies that will entertain people. All my life I've wanted to entertain people and I never really got the chance. There were always these left-wing collectives holding me back. You know: people with messages. So that's it, Congressman, the list for Universal. Even-Steven. Trust me, baby, it's a good deal.

Abbie Hoffman
81A-1671
Downstate Correctional Facility
Fishkill, New York
May 1981

The Crime of Punishment

AMERICAN PRISONS are exactly halfway between Sweden and Argentina. For Jack Henry Abbott, prison was a lot closer to Argentina than most Americans would choose to believe. At thirty-seven, with the exception of a nine-and-a-half-month respite, he has spent his entire life since the age of twelve behind bars. It was during that respite that he took part in a bank robbery—his only serious outside crime. Inside, he stabbed another prisoner. Through the long twenty-five years, he endured strip cells, blackout cells, mind-jelly drugs, beatings, starvation diets, and swing stretching. He was abused, humiliated and tortured in a variety of other ways. But he survived. He endured the pain, the isolation, and that special insanity that comes from dropping any sensitive soul down a bottomless well of irrationality. His is a timely voice. A voice written in blood. A voice meant to shatter complacent glass. A voice that takes you inside your closest prison. (Do you know where your closest prison is tonight?)

Abbott lets you experience the sensations, "the atmospheric pressure, you might say, of what it is to be seriously a long-term prisoner in an American prison." You will not get this experience reading Solzhenitsyn or Jacobo Timerman. Nor will you from any reporter, because no reporter is going to witness a gang rape or a murder or go bugs locked in a small, dark box, or know the fear of being stalked by an enemy with a blade.

You can get a very intelligent view of the problem by reading Charles Silberman's *Criminal Violence, Criminal Justice*. However, that is the laboratory of sociology, and Abbott is writing about life as it is lived. It is the best anyone has done since *Soul On Ice*.

What a damn find! Hearing that Norman Mailer was doing a book on Gary Gilmore, Abbott, having been in many of the same prisons, offered his services. They met via letters and those letters, extremely well edited by Erroll McDonald, form the book. But do not turn away if you are not a fan of "letter books," they are sutured together with the skill of a fine plastic surgeon. No scars. A continuous flow of tough, tight writing.

I can appreciate exceptional prison writing. On several occasions I have spent time in jail. Short bids, in the end, they would total less than twenty months, nothing compared to the likes of Abbott but enough to never forget. This man can write like the devil, and in committing his story to print so well he manages to tell everyone's story.

He has faults; his rage, though certainly justified, sometimes distracts. He has not managed to capture the enormous boredom that is prison. The numbness of playing the same card game ten thousand times with the same players. Of staring at walls. Of counting time. Though, maybe after twenty-five years boredom becomes something else. At time, he goes beyond what is there, but I think that is part of Abbott's excruciating ordeal. Like being in the hole, shut off from all light, human contact, on a starvation diet, loaded with tranquilizers and then all of a sudden yanked out and told to write. They do the same with fighting bulls, and as a result they hook blindly until they fix their target. But fix it he does, and consistently there remains good, honest light, a clarity of vision and a righteous disturbing message. Through all the sorrow and the pain Abbott remains the bull who has somehow not fallen. The stubborn survivor. There is also something here that stuns to the point of jealousy, namely, an esthetic continuum called poetry.

Prison writing often has its politics; it rarely has its poetry. *In the Belly of the Beast* is a song of prison.

These are things that Abbott claims. "In San Quentin, as well as many other prisons, if a guard on a gun-rail sees you touch another prisoner he will shoot you down with his rifle" and later "if a guard searches your cell and you make a move toward the toilet you will be shot down." There are more examples like this. Obviously these things have happened in American prisons but not every time. No one could deny that penitentiaries are an experience in abusive authority. Brutality is an institutionalized way of life. Abbott's book is a catalog of homegrown atrocities. He was shot up with heavy doses of tranquilizers against his will. He has seen electric shock treatment used to punish. He has been deliberately starved to the point where he ate insects. Inmates have been ordered to get him. He has often been beaten unconscious and has incurred permanent internal injuries. Let me add some I have witnessed over the years. A prisoner who "acted up" in his cell was battered unconscious with a high-powered hose sprayed through the bars. A prisoner "sheeted," that is, suicided on his bars. A gang urged by guards to attack a troublemaker. They ripped an eye out of his head. A prisoner stripped, laid on the concrete floor, handcuffed and legcuffed to the bars and left to defecate and urinate on himself for eight days. Abbott has seen more. Much more. He shows us just how inventive cruelty can be. But the thing about brutality, be it physical, psychological, or institutional that has always made an impression was that it was, like all punishment, so arbitrary, so random. Remember what Hemingway said about teaching you the rules, then when they caught you off second base they killed you. In prison they don't bother teaching you the rules. There is a famous prison in New York, Dannamora (the very name shivers the spine), and legend has it that the first three prisoners arriving off the bus are clubbed to let everyone know who's who and what's what. But I doubt if it works that way, because the real smart-asses would know this and stand in the rear. No, I'm sure they go on the beat up at the gateway to Dannamora, but it's always more random than legend or song can have it.

So, all this randomness, this Catch-23 absurdity; first the carrot, then the stick, then the carrot *and* the stick reduces prisoners to sniveling idiots. Every prison book begins with "I," everyone, even Timerman, is a complaining sniveler. "Then they stuck those electrodes on *my* balls. Ouch! It hurt!" A mass of snivelers, that's guard reality. Who cares, no guard has ever written a prison song.

Mailer complains some that Abbott's guards have no character. Norman is a good man but he has been in prison a total of five days. It does not matter if a guard is okay. So what. They have to conform to a system that if it operated with humanity would not operate at all. The good guards quit. Everyone has met guards who are relatively good guys and more often than not they'll be teamed with a sadist. There is an old yippie proverb: "If you shit in a pitcher of cream, the turds will rise to the top." In other words, evil wins out over good if the container is small and tight. Prison is a very small, tight container.

So that institutional violence, which incidentally pervades all our polite society, gets transferred to the inmates, who are trained to act like gladiators or bulls ready for the arena. Higher-ups in prison relate to violence much the same as National Hockey League officials do—it's part of the game. There is so much killing in prison. It is, after all, a death of numbers. "Six hundred forty weapons uncovered in a quick search of Attica." "Who bought it?" "Nobody in Two H." "What's your number?" "He stuck him *three* times." "What's your fuckin' number, man." It's all numbers and all death. In fact, when you do die, you're "off the count." The count being the most serious moment in any prison. To move or talk means a ticket. The guards rush about counting you. It happens maybe nine times a day. Weighing the meat, chillin' out the jailhouse.

Abbott understands all about numbers dying violent deaths—the cat and mouse survival game behind the walls. He writes one of the most gripping descriptions of murder you will ever read. It is his murder. The one he did as executioner, but also the haunting murder he fears as possible victim. Then he takes us into solitary confinement with him to share the punishment. Abbott has spent fourteen years in solitary. He calls it "the hole." In the East it's called "the box." Both sexist expressions for the vagina. Dry vaginas with concrete teeth.

There is not a lot of remorse in Abbott. Society is very weird about remorse. Prisoners are supposed to feel bad about their crimes, and although there is a long line of repentant sinners outside a thousand parole board meetings, there is not a true ounce of remorse in any American prison. Everyone sees themselves as a victim. Everyone got fucked. And if you listen carefully to the prison jokes you'll see that the protagonist usually ends up the victim. Ironic, since society insists here are the captured predators, the guilty ones. Freud would have had a field day in prison.

So if there's no remorse happening why exactly do these prisons remain? Well, take my case. The judge said I did not have to be segregated from society, and obviously didn't need to be rehabilitated, but there was some good to be gained by making an example. The deterrent theory of punishment. It was first applied in thirteenth-century Holland when a dog who bit a *Bürgermeister* was hanged as a lesson to other dogs. Then followed those wonderfully successful public hangings of pickpockets in London. Occasions that proved easy grabbings for fellow pickpockets who worked the excited crowds. Deterrence is an assumption. The 525,000 inmates in America plus triple that on probation and parole are proof that assumption is questionable. Rehabilitation? There are extremely few prison officials who still cling to the idea that such alchemy occurs. This pretense went out with notions like the "New Frontier" and the "Great Society." The statistics are extremely tragic. Out of every ten inmates released, seven quickly return to prison. This gloomy reality maintains itself in all systems, regardless of region. It has become an American constant. Furthermore, what that statistic hides is that the other three were probably innocent and that two of the seven who returned do so because they "learned" their next crime in their last prison. In other words, in addition to tough economic conditions, conservative trends, and so on, the prison system actually grows its own population. It will be hard to control this phenomenon. More difficult, perhaps than cancer. It is common for officials to explain this as older inmates teaching younger inmates new tricks. Abbott says that is so much jive-ass. Inmates don't talk about how you saw up a stolen car and sell it piecemeal to a Bolivian parts dealer. No one talks about outfoxing border patrols in smuggling operations. You can learn more about that watching television. Criminals don't crack safes anymore, they stick a gun under your nose and steal your money. Unskilled labor. But what you do learn is *capability.* "What is forced down your throat . . . is the *will* to commit crime . . . no one has ever come out of prison a better man." A very true, blunt statement, and it will not be very popular outside because society wants desperately to believe something positive happens behind those walls. That men become men. That sin becomes virtue. That when it's over, ex-convicts get jobs, go to church, and buy a house. Right!

So in the end there is just segregation as a reason. If you lock a "criminal" up, that's one less animal preying on society. Well, eliminating the obvious fact that there is lots of crime inside prison, doesn't this assume a finite number of criminals? Doesn't it stand to reason then that stuffing the prisons will lower the crime rate? That's not reality though. Economic conditions, not morality, determine crime rate, as they have since time immemorial. We're in tough times, so people steal. Jean Valjean was only a criminal in the eyes of the Moral Majority, themselves murderers of ideas. Hypocritical sneak thieves.

Our middle-class education about justice for all is rudely jarred by reality. Like holding onto the fairytale about every poor blah-blah being entitled to a fair trial. To our suburban grammar school mind that is truth. In reality, 85 percent (90 percent in NYC) of all defendants are forced to plea-bargain away their freedom. Expedience, not justice, is the rule of contemporary American law. Abbott will explode most of your mythology about crime and punishment. He is not reviewing movies, remember, he is talking about what *is,* not what was promised.

Abbott knows why inmates are locked up. "The purpose of prison is to ruin me, ruin me completely. The purpose is to mark me, to stamp across my face the track of this beast they call prison."

In short, to bust balls. The guards are there "to bust your balls." To jam you and save the institution. Their main objective is to "cover their ass."

To make it look like they are not responsible. *Cover Your Ass,* is the guard's prison song. People go out worse than they come in. Sixteen-year-old kids get raped, serious medical problems go untreated, people get stabbed, thousands go crazy, and while all this is happening everyone with any authority thinks only one thought: Cover your ass. Isn't that what Warren Burger is doing— pontificating about prisons being our national disgrace and yet legalizing bad conditions at Manhattan's Metropolitan Lockup and more than one inmate to a cell? Overcrowding is the main cause of riots and much violence. Warren Burger, our Chief Injustice, the man probably most responsible for making things bad, publicly deplores the situation. He is simply covering his ass before God.

Finally Abbott deals with inmates. And here there is much overglorification. He rebukes Mailer's attempts to cast him as hero but he turns around and makes all other inmates exactly that. But inmates are not like James Cagney or Paul Newman. They are not even George Jackson. They are no one you've seen in movies or on talk shows or read about. Here are a few shameful statistics: 85 percent of U.S. prisoners are nonwhite, 65 percent black, 20 percent mostly Spanish-speaking. The rest are your Paul Newmans, your Tommy Trantinos (a very good writer caged in New Jersey), and your

G. Gordon Liddys, although most are poor, scared farm boys. Why a society that is 85 percent white locks up a society that is 85 percent nonwhite is the kind of question not permitted in decent circles. One either needs a Doctor Shockley-type to explain how blacks are inherently evil, that their long arms encourage them to theft, or one has to accept that we are a racist society.

The other statistic is a sad legacy of that racist neglect: Half the inmates in prison cannot read or write. The world is so restricted. There is no interest in news, in a typical group a third cannot name the president, none the vice-president. A fellow inmate once asked if I had something for him to eat from my commissary. "Salmon," I replied. "Does it have pork in it?" he questioned back. I don't tell this to be funny, I tell it because it's sad. Sad, the way prisoners will plot a year to escape successfully and then be caught in a few days hanging out at their neighborhood poolhall. Abbott and I would have had some good conversations about Afghanistan, movies, Cuba, abortion, revolution; the chances of us having met are exactly 525,000 to 1. More likely than not we'd be talking about jammin' bitches, or snivelin' about our bids, or braggin' about facin' down some dumb-ass hack. Very few people talk in prison, it is the ultimate face-saving event, more rituals than a Japanese tea ceremony. For when prisoners relate to prisoners, they too must "cover their ass."

Where Abbott sees revolution pounding in every prisoner's breast, I see a craving to watch more television cartoons. When Abbott explains he came in looking for individual justice but should have expected social justice (he says this to excuse black "oppression" of whites in prison), he forgets the absence of communal justice. For every prisoner that will cover a brother's back, there are ten who will not. Whoever said there is honor among thieves had to have been a thief. Maybe years ago, the sixties were very much a phenomenon inside the prison walls. But the Me generation has replaced that and there is very little revolutionary consciousness left. There are few insurrections, many riots. There are not even that

many Muslims left, for that movement seems to be dying
also. A typical prison conversation is not about revolution. Here is a typical conversation:

> A: What do you want, S?
> S: I want money, lots of money.
> A: What for?
> S: I will buy a city.
> A: Why?
> S: So everyone will work for me.

Today, for the most part, the authorities seem to have
broken any collective will. Everybody hates the system all
right but hardly anyone carries the vision of the united
proletariat. S. doesn't want any fuckin' revolution, he
just wants to be king, like the other asshole kings out
there.

Abbott is very good on understanding the "reverse
racism" in prison. To his credit, he doesn't get distracted
by the nuisances of being dominated by a different
culture. He gets along with blacks. They don't beat up on
him. In fact, most prison violence is not interracial. Black
on black, white on white, or brown on brown. Just like
outside. However, also like outside, when it does become
interracial, an incident can lead to tribal warfare. Warfare enclosed by forty-foot-high walls. The authorities use
this reverse racism as an excuse. "We don't have good
prisons like the Scandinavians do because of the blacks."
You will hear that every time from experts. What a cop-
out. There is always conflict in prison. Age conflict.
Religion. City-country. Politics. Straight-gay. To say
nothing of the bug cases. We don't have prisons like the
Scandinavians do because on all the basic issues of life
they encourage collectivity and we do not. They try to
institute community. They don't push men to rat on each
other, to ass-kiss in competition for favors, to eat their
self-esteem like a hamburger. They don't divide in order
to conquer. If they do, then their prisons stink too.

The whites, of course, reinforce racism. They want you
in their "culture" and that culture is racist. So white
guards will instruct you about the behavior of "jungle

bunnies" and the excuses you have to make for "spics" who, after all, still have one foot on the banana boat. White inmates pull "integrationists" back into their camp "for your own good." There are some caucasians like Abbott, but this is still the rule. The turds rising to the top of the cream pitcher, again. It is hard to emerge from prison not a racist. Just as it is almost impossible to emerge with no burning thoughts of revenge. This is what Abbott means about prisons teaching you the capability for murder.

So I start out reviewing Jack Abbott's prison experience and end up telling my own thoughts. Every American prisoner does that. We are conditioned to make prison an individual experience. Compare. Why did he get two milks and I only one? Are you medium or max? How come I got ten years and he only five *for the same thing*? Is he a squealer? Can I take him? Prison is a sniveler's supermarket. A place you learn jealousy, suspicion, and hatred. It originates with how people get to be prisoners in the first place. With the arbitrary definition of crime and the *not* so arbitrary selection of who gets to define that definition. One class is, after all, judging another. There are not "all kinds" here as the tour guide claims. Sure, one of one kind, a thousand of the other. It is here that Abbott's courage ventures the furthest. He declares himself in the end to be a Communist. He risks thousands of well-meaning people closing ranks with him. Of being judged before his day in the arena of ideas.

A Communist!? At one moment of poetic provocation, he declares only Communists help prisoners. Which is sad because given our "democracy" we are free to choose everything but that! For all intents and purposes there are *no* American Communists. Hence no one helping. Perhaps Abbott means that. This declaration, this fixation with "American injustice" as opposed to "human nature" as cause of crime, turns the passive reader into an active prison guard. Abbott waves the red flag, his turn at matador. He corners you against the wall, you must think and act too quickly to survive. With his description of

prison life, he shoves in the sword, with his blunt politics
he yanks it straight up to your skull.

This song sayer is not filled with self-pity. He is not
crying for mercy. He is toughing it out, laying all his cards
on the table, the way Gary Gilmore did at the end. They
are very close in spirit. . . . When a fighting bull kills the
matador, usually another toreador will finish him off, but
if he has fought exceptionally well, as say the bull who
put an end to the great Manolete, they will turn him loose
to pasture. Jack Henry Abbott is out among you now. Do
not welcome him back. He has not been there before.
Yet hear this man's song. You will know nothing of
prison until you do.

June 1981

Following Jack Henry Abbott's involvement in a despicable and heinous murder last summer, he jumped parole
and fled to Mexico, then to the oil fields of Louisiana,
where he was apprehended after two months as a
fugitive. He has since been returned to Manhattan and
faces a murder trial as well as a serious parole violation.
Even if acquitted on the murder charge, he is certain to
be returned to prison to finish out his life sentence. No
event in memory has so jolted the New York literary
community. When *In the Belly of the Beast* was first
published in June, it earned universal praise from critics,
and Abbott was hailed as a brilliant literary discovery. He
was dubbed Norman Mailer's protégé, for it was mainly
through Mailer's efforts that the convict's writings came
to print. A circle of admirers, centered around the *New
York Review of Books,* joined Mailer in petitioning for
Abbott's early release on parole.

After the brutal murder and flight from justice, the
literary community did a complete double take. The
book was shown to have several misstatements of fact, it
was immediately removed from the "Editor's Choice"
section of the *New York Times Book Review,* and at least
a dozen investigative reporters sifted through Abbott's
prison career and his brief one-month tour of the literary
jet set. Almost universal scorn was heaped on Mailer and

friends, culminating in a vicious swipe on the first *Saturday Night Live* show of the season.

Many of the reports point to the complete disorientation of Abbott in moving from twenty-five years of incarceration to the glamour world of big-city life in the fast lane. He did not know how to open a bank account, where one bought toothpaste, or how to order from a menu. From two telephone conversations I had with him, it was obvious he has talked just a few times on the phone. In trying to arrange a meeting, he insisted I meet him at a restaurant on Third Street. "Third Street and what?" I inquired. He did not understand the question. His interview on *Good Morning America* was extremely disassociative, with several of his answers drifting off into space. An interview with *Rolling Stone* was so disjointed it could not be published. No critics blamed the prison system for failing to equip released inmates with even the barest coping mechanisms to make it on the outside. In fact, the prison system remained remarkably outside the scope of criticism as angry fingers were pointed at Mailer and friends as naive do-gooders, if not willing accomplices to murder.

In all, a complete lack of understanding of how the prison system works has been evidenced. Abbott was due for parole just two months after his release from prison. Prison authorities—and no one else—hold and decide who can use the keys of freedom. What was apparent from subsequent disclosures of Abbott's records was that outside support for his literary talent was of little consideration to the parole board. Of far greater concern was Abbott's apparent willingness to serve as an informer inside the prison during his last year of confinement. His record shows he gave authorities information they wanted on several prison organizers. In addition, supporters of Abbott received letters from convicts who claimed he had also squealed on a group of young lawyers falsely accusing them of smuggling drugs into the prison. Prison officials consider informers prime candidates for early parole, not just for the services performed, but for their safety as well.

Whether one blames the prison system, Abbott, or a combination thereof, it's difficult to see how scorn can be laid on those who recognized and spoke up for talent. The United States has a per capita prison population topped only by South Africa. The only social program pictured favorably by the Reagan administration is a call for $2 billion more in prison construction funds. Reagan himself chides theorists for blaming crime on factors like poverty and racism. Across the land, politicians scream for stiffer penalties and longer sentences. Little attention is paid to the lack of rehabilitation and resocialization programs. The demand is for increasing the *quantity* of life behind bars, not the *quality.*

The tragedy of the Abbott affair is not just that one victim lay dead on a New York sidewalk, though that, of course, is tragic. The greater tragedy is that too many prisoners who deserve a break will be denied, and too many people who care about reform will turn their backs. Hope has received a shattering blow.

Postscript
October 1981
Edgecombe Correctional Facility, Manhattan
(minimum security–work-release program)

The Great St. Lawrence River War

~~~~~~

I WAS introduced to the St. Lawrence River in the summer of '76, approaching via the Thousand Island Bridge from the Canadian mainland twenty miles north of Kingston, Ontario. It is the best approach, for rising to the crest of the bridge a passenger's vision is completely filled by hundreds of pine-covered islands. Scattered as nature's stepping stones across the northward rush of the river's swirling waters. Here and there you can pick out a summer camp hidden among the trees. Its location betrayed by a jutting dock and shiny boat. A few islands even boast "Rhineland" castles and mansions, rising in testimony to an opulence that existed a century ago. But for the most part the islands remain wild, inhabited only by rabbits, foxes, badgers, skunks, and deer who had crossed the frozen river some winter before. In the wetlands feed ducks, geese, loons, and the great blue heron. While nesting on land are scores of whippoorwills, woodpeckers, bluejays, martins, swallows, robins, cardinals, orioles, hawks, and hummingbirds. Virtually every northern bird pictured in a guide book can be found here. The waters, considered among the choicest fishing spots in the world, host varieties of bass, perch, carp, and northern pike as well as salmon and occasional sturgeon. Highest on the list: the prized muskelunge or "muskie," fished on long trolling expeditions in the fall. The world-

225

record size for freshwater fish is a 69½-pound muskie boated here just down river from Chippewa Bay near the American mainland. In winter migrating bald eagles, wolves and coyotes can be found feeding at the water pools.

A wonderland of beauty, indeed, it's something of a mystery that such a scenic region, not part of any national park, has endured the ravages of development and pollution.

The river has seen eons of history. It began with the scraping of ice glaciers for millions of years. About twelve thousand years ago a huge gorge 1,200 miles long, in places 10 miles wide and 500 feet deep was created. At first the waters rushed in from the North Atlantic, forming a vast ocean inlet where hordes of whales came to migrate. Gradually the slope of the riverbed shifted and the ocean water rushed out leaving the river as the drain flow for all the Great Lakes. Making it, by volume, the largest river in North America. Indians were, of course, the first inhabitants of the region and attributed great spiritual powers to the river and islands. The Great Spirit, after having given the Indians everything, gave them paradise on the shores of Lake Ontario near the river's source. Upset with constant tribal warfare he gathered up paradise, rose into the sky, but just as the Sky Curtain parted, his blanket opened and paradise tumbled back into the river. This created the "pieces of paradise" known as the Thousand Islands. In Iroquois legend Hiawatha paddled his canoe up this river on his last sojourn to heaven.

The river had always been a great transportation route, although only specially built barges and steamers could make it downriver to Montreal. The chief obstacles being two long stretches of rapids considered among the most beautiful on the continent. One, the LaChine, so named because the early trappers thought it pointed the way to China, supposedly created the illusion of a bubbling wall of water rising straight up into the air for twenty feet. One can only rely on past descriptions because the great rapids along with other "obstacles," including many river towns and islands, are now gone forever.

Our story really begins in the 1950s. At the apex of the American empire, when politicians and engineers allied to steamroll through any public works project that was thought to contribute to the country's imperial power and glory. Corporate need was equated with people need. "What's good for General Motors is good for America," and "Here at General Electric progress is our most important product" were two of the decade's most famous slogans. Flags waved when we bulldozed a swamp. Progress was the bitch goddess of the fifties and to stand in the doorway left one open to charges of heresy or, worse, of giving in to the Russians. The Army Corps of Engineers, by swapping one boondoggle for another stockpiled more than enough congressional votes to firmly stamp its imprint on the landscape.

No project excited the corps more than the idea of connecting the Great Lakes to the Atlantic Ocean. The political machinations both here and in Canada took years and years. Eastern states felt their economies would be ruined; railroad and trucking industries joined them. In all these battles no one mentioned obvious damage to the river, the complete destruction of the unmatchable LaChine Rapids, or the threat to fish and wildlife. Such a thing as an environmental impact statement was not even known. The argument was geographical and as the corps and the Midwest industrialists vote-traded with western mining and lumber interests, a formidable coalition built up. The time-tested argument that finally swayed Congress was the claim of "national security." The corps argued that with the St. Lawrence Seaway in place, ocean-going vessels could be built on Great Lakes ports and utilized in the cold war with the Russians. (Needless to say twenty-five years after the fact no such industry ever developed.)

The seaway was no small feat. Herbert Hoover, himself an engineer, watched over the project as would a patron saint. "Without doubt," he once exclaimed, "this project is the greatest engineering accomplishment in the history of man." It was called upon completion "the Eighth Wonder of the World."

The figures are staggering. Twenty-five thousand workers employing specifically designed giant earth loaders moved 250 million cubic yards of earth and rock. That's enough to cover all of Manhattan with about twelve feet of dirt. Twenty miles of earth dikes, some fifty feet high, were constructed. Water basins, the largest of which covered 44,000 acres, were dug out. The Eisenhower Locks at Massena were built as were two giant dam-power plant complexes. One, the Moses-Saunders Dam, being the third largest in the world. In addition there were bridges, highways, and completely new communities.

Of course, a price was paid. Towns were destroyed. Whole islands demolished. In all ten thousand people were forced off their land. Indians fought land agents. Bulldozers caved in kitchen walls, while families, believing it would never happen, were eating at the table. A fisherman, seeing that a favorite fishing hole had been destroyed, threw himself into the river to die. Disappointments were many.

The seaway was sold to New York under false pretenses. River towns of just a few thousand were assured aid that never materialized. Economic growth was expected to occur from the increase in ship traffic. There were predictions that some towns would increase one-hundred-fold. Of course, the contrary took place. But almost the entire work force was from out of state. When the project was completed, the workers returned home. Ocean vessels or "salties" proved capable of traversing the full length of the seaway without pulling in for repairs or fuel. The project single-handedly bankrupted the rail industry in northern New York. The population of the towns decreased as unemployment rose and became chronic. Massena, which was touted as a future "Pittsburgh of the north," today has but a few thousand people.

Yet New York wasn't the only loser. The American taxpayer also took a loss. The plan was to charge shippers tolls that would pay the complete bill. Department of Transportation officials repeatedly assured Congress the seaway would pay for itself within ten years, thereafter showing a continuous profit. But there were no profits. Midwest shippers still seemed to prefer the cheaper Mississippi-Gulf route while Canada made it attractive for the grain industry to use its nationalized railroad system.

In twenty-one years of operation the seaway has appeared in the black only once. In the past five years the overall tonnage increase has been a dismal .05 percent. Last year a 10 percent decline occurred. Recently Canadian Parliament canceled an $841 million debt and a similar bill sits in the U.S. House to defray $122 million in unpaid loans. Last year a staunch supporter of the seaway in the fifties, the Chicago *Tribune*, was reluctantly forced to conclude, in an editorial titled "The Seaway's Unmet Promise," that things had not gone according to plan, and Chicago had been one of the ports expected to reap the greatest benefits. Of course, the Army Corps of Engineers is not an organization prone to admitting mistakes. Prodded on chiefly by U.S. Steel, which does benefit by the waterway, the corps reasoned that the seaway did not turn a profit because it closed down for four months a year due to ice conditions. This interruption of service caused huge stockpiling, making seaway transportation undesirable. The answer lay in a program called winter navigation, breaking up the ice by means of a variety of as yet untested mechanical means. This would be no mean accomplishment. The St. Lawrence-Great Lakes transportation system is some 2,400 miles long. The winters are bitter cold. Today, as I write this, the ice in front of our house is frozen two feet solid, the temperature is below zero. At Tibbets Point, where the river begins, the ice during spring breakup can get thirty feet thick.

Of course, the corps *really* had another project even closer to its heart than winter navigation. Once year-round traffic could be guaranteed, the Eisenhower locks, already antiquated, could be replaced with larger chambers and twinned to allow two-way traffic. Then when the river was channeled even deeper, the whole system could handle supertankers. The corps thinks not small potatoes. They are unquestionably the most gung-ho, can-do organization in the entire federal bureaucracy. If the money was there, the corps would move mountains from Colorado to Iowa. Theirs is not to reason why, theirs is to submit the bill and try. The bill for winter navigation—a cool $2.5 billion. For the supertanker project about $20 billion. In other words, about $500 per American, with Canadians kicking in even more. Then the first fifty years of maintenance would equal this initial outlay, making this easily the most expensive engineering project in history—fifty times the cost for the entire original sea-way. The corps moves like a Supreme Being. It doesn't build, it creates. Its 45,000 public relations experts, lawyers, and contractors directed by a few hundred army brass at the top are almost unbeatable in the field. Almost.

Of course, back then in '76 I knew nothing of all this. Being a city boy *river* was just a word in a banjo song. Thousand Islands was a salad dressing. And the Army Corps of Engineers just went around rescuing flood victims. Johanna, my running mate since almost the beginning of my underground odyssey, had brought me here from Montreal. Her family had, as the DAR certificate on the wall attested to, lived in the region for seven generations. Their cottage, right on the riverbank, had been built by her great-grandmother. Wellesley Island, about the size of Manhattan, has but three thousand residents, only seven hundred in coldest winter. Fineview, our town, boasts all of eighty-seven people, with only thirty of those toughing out the coldest four months. We live in downtown Fineview, diagonally across from the post office. The place where townfolk gather each morning to talk about the weather. An important activity because forecasts from the distant TV and radio stations rarely applied to the islands. Island weather is unique and often troublesome. Windstorms with gales up to sixty mph. Torrential rains. Waves up to six feet. Fog so dense it's impossible to navigate a boat. In winter there are white-on-white snowstorms where you cannot see your extended hand. Snow piles fifteen feet high and helicopter airlifts of food are sometimes needed. Weather is accepted here even more than death and taxes. The islands have made the people individualists. The weather has made them rugged. For eight months each year the air is filled with the sound of rebuilding. They say nothing lasts forever; up here they say nothing lasts ten years. So you learn how to use a hammer and saw, to lay in a foundation, or recrib a dock. It is part and parcel of river life. The people are hard-working and extremely conservative. Democrats are practically an endangered species.

It fit my purpose to busy myself on badly needed house repairs. The work kept me away from a great deal of socializing. I needed so much help in my carpentry apprenticeship, I asked far more questions than I answered. Slowly I was becoming absorbed into a world unto its own. Of course, I never forgot the great secret of my life when each morning I'd walk past the town's Hall of Justice. Here, rowdies who had disturbed the peace over at the state park or would-be smugglers bringing who knows what in from Canada were brought for booking. Judge Kleinhans would be summoned to hold court and set bail. Serious offenders were packed off to Watertown in state trooper cars affectionately dubbed "Tijuana Taxis" because of the gaudy blue and yellow colors. I always felt someday I would be handcuffed and dragged across the road, dogs barking; kids, including my own, screaming; Mrs. Jerome, our next-door neighbor, having a heart attack on the steps we share. That image burned in my mind a thousand times. The law was literally across the street, so I never forgot what it would mean to make a mistake.

We were not actually "natives" of Fineview, since we fled the cold to hunt up jobs, but on the other hand we were not summer residents either. As soon as the ice broke we returned to the house, staying at times well into December, huddled around the fireplace in our long johns, rigging up heat lamps and insulation so we could still pump water from the river. The first two years I built new steps, reshingled the roof, installed a new water heater, and built a counter in the old-fashioned kitchen. The most ambitious project was a mammoth floating dock, which the river took all of fifteen minutes to sweep from its mooring. Determination and neighborly help combined in the construction of an even more permanent dock. Dick-Dock II. Massive rock cribs were sunk in the river and every inch of Johanna's forty feet of shoreline used to create an L-shaped dock and harbor. Hardly an ornamental plaything, a good dock is essential to island life. We traveled by boat more often than car—to do laundry, shopping, and to party with our fellow river rats at the local bars and dance halls. Returning in the summer of '78, I began work to correct for winter ice shifting and to finish off the staving and decking. The residents of Fineview, prizing hard work, began to accept me, but still after more than two years I had yet to even volunteer a last name. I was just Johanna's friend Barry. I worked in the movies as a scriptwriter or something equally exotic. After four years of being a fugitive I had learned how to make friends without having to explain much.

In July, just as I was nailing down the last of the decking, Steve Taylor boated by and called out that I could forget about the dock, everything was going to be destroyed—the islands, the shoals, the boathouses. "Read this," he said, tossing a little-known government report my way.

I retired inside and plunged into the study. Local scientists of the New York Department of Environmental Conservation had drawn up an estimate of the environmental impact rising out of a demonstration test being proposed for the coming winter. Through a combination of ice breakers and log booms, an ice-free corridor fifteen miles long would be maintained. This test would demonstrate the feasibility of winter navigation. Plowing through the data it was easy to determine that something sounding so simple and harmless on the surface was, in fact, spelling out a second and final step of the river's destruction (the first being the seaway itself). Watering pools for the endangered bald eagle would be destroyed. Aquatic life chains and wetlands would be ruined. The waves of the test ship passing under ice would magnify, ripping apart the shorelines, causing great erosion. The river's fast current would be deliberately slowed to maintain a stable ice cover. This would cause great flooding all the way back and into Lake Ontario. Increasingly the lake has become a chemical dumpsite for PCB, mirex, mercury, and other toxic wastes. Mechanical intervention on a scale the test proposed would release great quantities of imbedded chemical wastes into the water. Most river towns drew drinking water from the river. A 15 percent loss of hydropower was predicted. One didn't have to be a genius to project these findings to a winter navigation program up and down the entire river. Corps figures showed 94 million cubic yards of river bed were to be drained or dynamited from the U.S. side alone. The river would end up little more than a year round barge canal. A disaster!

I called Johanna upstairs. "Unless *we* act, the river is doomed," I said. "The Army Corps of Engineers will bully their way in here. The people are not ready to fight the system." I told her what it was like taking on segregation in the South, organizing against the Vietnam War. The enemies one made attacking the power structure. I was convinced joining this battle would mean I would be caught. Yet the arguments against the project seemed so strong. How could I stand on the shore and watch corps engineers wire up the small islands across the way for demolition? I had listened to old-timers in the bars talk of how they had heard the explosions and watched whole islands float downriver during the fifties. They had watched and cried; now they were alcoholics. "A six-thousand-year-old river," I thought, "and the last twenty-five years have been its worst." My fate was fixed. The rest of the night we spent shaping our identity. Of the twenty or so names I had used as aliases not a one had significance—wallpaper names I called them, easily forgotten. No stories. Mr. and Mrs. Barry Freed sounded respectable. At first I missed the significance of the name.

In August the corps would come to nearby Alexandria Bay for a public hearing; we would use the occasion to announce the organization to the community. We began with small meetings on the front lawn. I remember it well. "Bring back the sixties," someone exclaimed. "Gee, it would be great if we had Rennie Davis here," said another. Inside, way inside, I nodded agreement. We named the group Save the River! Names are very important. Best verb first. *What* you want people to do. "Shouldn't we have the word *committee*?" *Committee* is a bore. People want excitement, charisma. "What about St. Lawrence?" No, keep it simple. Everyone knows the river. Better for a name to raise a question than give an answer. Questions encourage involvement and involvement is what makes a citizens action group. I wrote an ad for the local paper, *The Thousand Island Sun*. In time I would be writing weekly articles for them. People made sails announcing: No To Winter Navigation, and boats toured the islands. We formed telephone trees. When someone complained about how high our first phone bill was, I lectured how our allies as well as enemies were "out there." When the bill got ten times as big we would be on the road to winning. Skepticism ran high. Either "it wasn't going to happen here" or "it was inevitable" were the prevailing attitudes. Oddly, there are people who can entertain both positions simultaneously. The committee pushed ahead.

That first public hearing was quite historic for our community. Usually these hearings draw thirty to forty people who have nothing better to do that day. The corps, which legally is supposed to be gathering facts and sentiment, instead uses the occasions to propagandize for its projects. We packed an overflow crowd of six hundred into the school auditorium. There were signs saying "Ice Is Nice" and "Army Go Home" but in general the tone was polite.

After the army slide presentation showing winter navigation in a positive light and the ease with which it was being introduced on the upper Great Lakes, the audience had their turn. The corps was quick to learn it was trying to sell iceboxes to Eskimos. People were extremely articulate, as farmers, marina owners, bartenders, school teachers, teenagers, folks out of work rose to the challenge. Economic-environmental battles are usually lost in a maze of complicated data and terminology. To successfully oppose winter navigation we eventually had to become proficient in subjects like water-resource economics, cost-benefit analysis, water level prediction, aquatic life cycles. It would take twenty minutes alone to describe just how the corps intended winter navigation to work. Within a few months we would have work-study sessions in which we searched for corps errors in a stack of literature at least three feet high. But in this our first confrontation the arguments came from the heart. The people of Grindstone Island, certainly one of the most rugged communities in the United States, wanted to know how they were to drive their pickup trucks across the river with an open channel. The corps' answer just about said their community was finished. Someone had taken the trouble to study the corps' predictions of water level changes over the past one hundred years and found they had been wrong 85 percent of the time. One of the slides showed a man standing next to a ship traversing a channel in the ice. "See how calm that man is," said the army PR guy. Much to his surprise the man was in the audience. "Calm? I was never so scared in my life. It was like an earthquake." He went on to detail the tons of vegetation, dead fish, and debris the ship's wake had hurled on the riverbanks.

Probably our biggest concern was oil spills. U.S. Coast Guard Marine Safety Office statistics count fifty-six oil spills in our waters since 1973. The worst happened in the summer of '76, when 300,000 gallons of crude oil poured out of a broken NEPCO tanker. Damage ran to the millions. Piles of dead fish and birds were everywhere. Ugly scars can still be seen along the river. The corps was now trying to assure us this would never occur in the winter but there were no believers. No technology to clean up an oil spill locked under ice exists, and none is likely to be developed.

After that hearing, Save the River was on the map. People meeting in the street would say just that: "Save the River!" like you'd say "Right on!" or "How's it goin'?" Barrooms carried donation jugs. Snack shops put up posters. Everybody sold the popular blue heron T-shirt Johanna designed. In all we relate to thirty-two river communities spread out along a fifty-mile course. Ten percent of our membership is Canadian. Early opponents who saw us as radicals or obstructionists were blown away by our overwhelming support. Renegade scientists long suspicious of the project let us know they would help. At Syracuse University, Steve Long, an economist, explained how the corps used and misused figures to prove feasibility. In the end predicted economic losses would help us win valuable allies. We constantly fought the label "an environmental group" in an effort to gain more legitimacy. We published an eight-page booklet breaking down the material into layman's terms. The booklet was discussed in classrooms, at Bible study groups, in bars and pharmacies, everywhere.

The first office was right in our back room. I was venturing into the domain of the northern Wasp. A soft-spoken conservative bird appreciative of good manners and highly respectful of institutions. We had to convince people it wasn't rude to protest. The harshest curse to cross my public lips was "Chrimis!"

I gave speeches at fishermen's banquets, church suppers, high schools, universities, just about anywhere I'd get invited. I was a guest of several radio shows and even a few television spots venturing as far as Syracuse to stage a press conference. Once there was a scare as one of the scientists told a close friend Barry might be Abbie Hoffman. Within an hour, I was out on Route 81, hitchhiking out of the area. A later telephone conversation convinced me it was a lucky hunch and I returned. But still a lucky hunch by a former marine captain in Vietnam.

Probably the most awkward speech I gave that year was to the Jefferson County Board of Supervisors. I was slotted in between the American Legion Post and the

Boy Scouts. We failed in getting their support, but several local Chamber of Commerce people heard the speech on radio and drew up endorsements for Save the River. Support also came from the St. Lawrence County Board and several town councils. Our group was quickly gaining a broad-based respectability. We sent delegations to monitor Winter Navigation Board meetings in Baltimore and were quick to point out that not a single decision maker lived closer than within five hundred miles of the river. We lobbied the railroad and trucking industries and established contacts with conservation groups along the Great Lakes.

With all this local support, it was time to pressure Albany. By playing one department against another we were able to break through the bureaucratic crust, and within a few days of contact our material was on the governor's desk. A telegram of support followed, which I read to a panel of startled corps officials at a meeting in Ogdensburg. Hugh Carey's endorsement had given our group some real clout. He was to watch over our development during the next few years. You can imagine my surprise when later I received a personal letter from him saying, "I want to thank you for your leadership in this important issue, and for your sense of public spirit." I never showed the letter to anyone, but I didn't throw it away.

The only time I used Abbie's contacts was in the search for the ideal lawyer. Environmental law is a relatively new course of study and it's still far easier to find lawyers willing to alibi chemical dumping or other industrial atrocities than to find advocates for citizens' groups. The search for competent counsel narrowed to the East, finally settling on Irv Like from Babylon, New York. He had successfully fought attempts to build a road through Fire Island, had represented Suffolk County in an offshore oil drilling suit, and had authored New York State's Environmental Bill of Rights. Suffolk County was almost as conservative as our neck of the woods. It had the same tensions between summer and winter people. It had high unemployment. After several meetings and phone calls, I realized we had lucked out by snaring a brilliant strategist.

Late that year a delegation of us went to Albany and got a $25,000 commitment from the Department of Transportation to hire John Carroll of Penn State, one of the four experts on water resource economics willing to bite the hand that feeds them.

Carroll's colleague Robert Braverman, at the University of Wisconsin, had just uncovered a $1.5 billion error as well as fictitious reporting in developing the cost/benefit ratio of the Tennessee-Tombigbee Canal project. He fed us the valuable information that the same Chicago accounting firm, A. T. Kierney Corp., had worked up the figures for winter navigation. *Sports Illustrated*'s staff ecologist, Bob Boyle, wrote an exposé regarding the promise of $50 million in award grants for U.S. Fish and Wildlife to monitor the project if they would drop their major arguments. If you're battling a boondoggle, you are safe in assuming a scandal lurks in the weeds. We raised such a holler.

The winter tests were postponed but work still intensified on the upper Great Lakes. Steering committee members went to Washington to testify before Congress. Rick Spencer carried most of the weight, parrying the thrusts of Representative James Oberstar, U.S. Steel's pointman. Congressman Robert McEwen introduced me and I added to the testimony. Later there was the ritual picture-taking by the congressman's photographer.

That spring and summer '79, a Clayton activist, Karen Nader-Lago, became our office manager as we moved to Alexandria Bay, then to Clayton. Housewives; carpenters; Fran Purcell, then teacher at one of the few one-room schoolhouses left in the country; Rick Spencer, a merchant seaman; small businessmen; farmers; landowners; boat builders were the type of people most active. Our first River Day was a big success, with marathons, hot-air balloon races, and some 3,500 people lighting candles in a night vigil celebrating the river.

Carroll's report was completed and after boiling down the essence winter navigation warranted no tax money from New York and would end up costing the state $100 million to $150 million in lost revenues annually. We now had the ammunition we needed, and we lobbied for Senator Patrick Moynihan, who held the pivotal seat on the Senate Environment and Public Works Committee, to hold field hearings in our area.

Up to this point we had been extremely successful. The postponement of demonstration tests resulted after a record number of Save-the-River inspired letters had been received at the corps district office. Publicity in the *New York Times* and on ABC's *20/20* had gained national attention for a project difficult to justify to a national tax paying audience. Moynihan could prove to be our greatest ally.

We chose from a flotilla of antique boats to guide visitors around the islands. We spent hours deciding the boat to fit each personality. Moynihan was outfitted to a turn-of-the-century paddle boat. That night I worked on my speech. It would take about twenty minutes and be aimed at the people who attended, as much as at Moynihan. His staff predicted about one hundred would attend but we knew the community by now. We had established the river as a deeply personal cause for everyone who used it. We were not surprised when close to nine hundred people showed up. After a string of local politicians had their say, it was my turn. I was sweating right through my shirt and jacket. There was polite applause and TV cameras up from Syracuse whirled away. I was sure the police would charge up the aisle and drag me away. But that was not to be the day. The speech went well. The crowd rose to its feet and applauded. Moynihan, sitting directly opposite, not more than twenty feet away, looked at me and said, "Now I know where the sixties have gone." Way, way inside where Abbie lived I fainted. Then he said, "Everyone in New York State owes Barry Freed a debt of gratitude for his organizing ability," and complimented other committee workers as well.

We stayed on good terms with Moynihan's office. By now we felt pretty secure along the river; what troubled us was the work being done on the upper Great Lakes. "Someday we'll be surrounded," we reasoned. Congress has already spent $30 million on winter navigation. That fall and the next year we tried to expand the scope of the committee. Nuclear wastes were being transported from Canada across the bridge. We protested. The shippers chose a bridge farther downstream with less resistance.

In the spring of 1980 the corps, at the insistence of Congress, deleted all requests for authorization and funds for work on the St. Lawrence River.

Environmental groups from all over the country called to congratulate us. They said the corps had never before been beaten without a long court battle. River Day was succeeding in resurrecting a love for the river not seen since the twenties. We uncovered chemical dumping sites leaking into nearby tributaries. We joined the Akwesasne Native Americans living on Cornwall Island in their protest over excessive fluoride dumping by the aluminum companies that use the river as a sewer. We sponsored a congressional debate on river-related issues and the statements made it apparent we had become a serious political force. We began to fight local power brokers insistent on building an amusement park at the river's gateway. On the last issue, we were a house divided. When we finally decided to fight, the horse had already left the barn.

After a speech against the amusement park to the town zoning board last summer we adjourned to the sidewalk. Chairman Vincent Dee of the Bridge Authority, Ralph Timmerman, our town supervisor, board members like Buggy Davis, who lent me his roller for the lawn, were there. So was the sheriff's patrol. About thirty people milling about. John Quinn, a customs agent on the border was telling me how much he agreed with the speech. . . . "Okay, Barry, so we lose this battle, tell me one thing, what the hell are we gonna do when everybody finds out you're *Abbie Hoffman*." "Oh, John, you really got a sense of humor," I said making light of what he had just said. Inside I keep thinking how loud it sounded. I was convinced everyone had heard. Maybe they didn't.

Maybe I heard wrong. Maybe they don't know Abbie Hoffman. Maybe. Maybe. Fugitives can "maybe" themselves into the nuthatch.

I decided that night to return and face the charges. The kid was packed off early. We rushed to complete the ongoing house repairs. I would have rather kept the story quiet but as soon as I hit New York City my face would have been recognized and broadcasted to the world. Better to tell it to as many people as possible up front. The choice was between *20/20* and *60 Minutes,* and for a variety of reasons ABC seemed the best choice. A team of about twenty-five local friends and five city friends worked with me. Telling Barry's friends was quite an experience. One guy cried. Karen, the office manager, just kept saying, "Nope, nope, nope." She had once quoted Abbie Hoffman to me. Karen's husband, Greg, kept saying, "Is that you? I've been wondering where you were for years." Dege, the young businessman who was inches from swinging the deal to have Woodstock II up here, was stunned. Of course, to some people I had to explain who Abbie was. It didn't matter, to them I'd always be Barry.

Well, Barbara Walters came and went. As did the hundreds of newspersons who followed in her wake. One of our neighbors counted thirty-seven interviews. The tour boats now point out the house and tell the story on loudspeakers. Tourists take photos and like to sit on the bench where Barbara Walters rubbed her tushy.

Nothing quite like this has happened in Fineview since the glaciers hit town. I've been back five times since. Frankly, I don't like being anyplace or anybody else. The committee's membership has grown to 2,200 members. The New York *Post* sent a reporter to find locals willing to bad-mouth me. After two days he came up empty-handed and went home. The local newspapers still call me Barry Freed, though I fear that may change.

In July we're sponsoring a national conference for all river lovers, with workshops, singers, speeches. We hope to have the St. Lawrence River included in Phillip Burton's (D. Calif.) protective legislation for scenic rivers. Of the fifteen largest rivers in the entire world, the St. Lawrence is the cleanest, and one glimpse of its beauty will convince even the most cynical of urban dwellers that here is a treasure not to be surrendered without a fight.

The Army Corps of Engineers has halted working on the lakes for a year of tests and study. They've invested a lot in this program and procorporation cabinet appointments like James Watt are bound to encourage them. Look at any map and you'll see we're the bottleneck in some engineer's grand fantasy. The corps is not an agency that rolls over and dies. For sure, they'll be back. When they do, they'll find us alive and well. Twice as strong. Twice as smart. And twice as many. For me the war has just begun. I can't wait to return home.

March 1981

People wishing to become members and receive our monthly newsletter can send $10.00 or more to:
SAVE THE RIVER,
Thousand Islands, New York 13624.